MW01716403

The Experiences of Queer Students of Color at Historically White Institutions

This significant text employs an intersectional analysis and considers the role of queer frameworks to understand the experiences of Queer People of Color at historically white institutions of higher education in the U.S.

By presenting data from student interviews and reflection journals, the book explores what it means to hold multiple minoritized identities, and asks how such intersections are navigated, contested, and experienced on college campuses. Exploring both micro- and macro-level mappings of marginalization and power, the text reveals issues including institutional erasure, pervasive whiteness in college and LGBTQ+ communities, institutionalized racism and heterosexism, and offers in-depth insights into the material, psychological, emotional, and social impacts on queer students of color. Ultimately, the analysis highlights the necessity of employing intersectional frameworks for addressing interlocking systems of oppression and offers recommendations for the integration and support of queer students of color at historically white institutions (HWIs).

This monograph will offer invaluable insights for scholars, researchers, and graduate students working in the fields of gender and sexuality, higher education, and issues of educational equity, who wish to realize the potential of intersectionality as an analytic framework for the study of identity and development of affirming educational environments.

Antonio Duran is Assistant Professor of Administration of Higher Education, Auburn University, USA.

Routledge Critical Studies in Gender and Sexuality in Education

Series Editors Wayne Martino, Emma Renold, Goli Rezai-Rashti, Jessica Ringrose and Nelson Rodriguez

17 **Gender and Care in Teaching Young Children**
A Material Feminist Approach to Early Childhood Education
Denise Hodgins

18 **Gender, Definitional Politics and 'Live' Knowledge Production**
Contesting Concepts at Conferences
Emily F. Henderson

19 **Girls, Single-sex Schools, and Postfeminist Fantasies**
Stephanie D. McCall

20 **Latina Students' Experiences in Public Schools**
Educational Equity and Gender
Susan McCullough

21 **Lad Culture in Higher Education**
Sexism, Sexual Harassment and Violence
Carolyn Jackson and Vanita Sundaram

22 **Queer, Trans, and Intersectional Theory in Educational Practice**
Student, Teacher, and Community Experiences
Cris Mayo and Mollie V. Blackburn

23 **Young British African and Caribbean Men Achieving Educational Success**
Disrupting Deficit Discourses about Black Male Achievement
Cecile Wright, Uvanney Maylor, and Thomas Pickup

24 **The Experiences of Queer Students of Color at Historically White Institutions**
Navigating Intersectional Identities on Campus
Antonio Duran

For more information about this series, please visit: www.routledge.com

The Experiences of Queer Students of Color at Historically White Institutions

Navigating Intersectional Identities on Campus

Antonio Duran

Routledge
Taylor & Francis Group
NEW YORK AND LONDON

First published 2021
by Routledge
52 Vanderbilt Avenue, New York, NY 10017

and by Routledge
2 Park Square, Milton Park, Abingdon, Oxon, OX14 4RN

Routledge is an imprint of the Taylor & Francis Group, an informa business

© 2021 Taylor & Francis

The right of Antonio Duran to be identified as author of this work has been asserted by him in accordance with sections 77 and 78 of the Copyright, Designs and Patents Act 1988.

All rights reserved. No part of this book may be reprinted or reproduced or utilised in any form or by any electronic, mechanical, or other means, now known or hereafter invented, including photocopying and recording, or in any information storage or retrieval system, without permission in writing from the publishers.

Trademark notice: Product or corporate names may be trademarks or registered trademarks, and are used only for identification and explanation without intent to infringe.

Library of Congress Cataloging-in-Publication Data
A catalog record for this book has been requested

ISBN: 978-0-367-89432-0 (hbk)
ISBN: 978-1-003-01913-8 (ebk)

Typeset in Sabon
by Apex CoVantage, LLC

Contents

List of Figures and Tables vii
Acknowledgments viii

Introduction 1

PART 1
Introducing the Intersections 11

1 Complicating the Study of College Student Identity Using Intersectionality 13

2 Centering Queer Students of Color: Setting the Stage for the Study 29

PART 2
Exploring the Intersections 43

3 Intersectional Influences: Manifestations of Overlapping Systems of Power 45

4 Navigating Historically White Institutions and Beyond: The Role of Salient Experiences During College 60

5 Race, Sexuality, and More: The Intersecting Identities of Queer Students of Color 74

6 Who Am I?: (Un)Learning and Identity Exploration 85

7 Moving Forward: Hopes Shared by Queer Students of Color 104

PART 3
Embracing the Intersections 115

8 Implications for Intersectional Theorizing in Higher Education 117

9 Implications for Historically White Institutions 125

10 Implications for Professionals 134

Epilogue 144

Methodological Appendix 147

References 159
Index 175

Figures and Tables

Table 2.1 Participant Information (Disclosed on Demographic Form) 38
Figure 2.1 The Intersectional Model of Identity Exploration for Queer Students of Color 40

Acknowledgments

This book was only possible with the love, support, and care of so many people who comprise my community. To begin, it is important to acknowledge the people that are the reason where I am today: my family. In particular, my mom, sisters, as well as nephews and niece are a constant motivation in my professional and personal life. From the very start of my educational career, they supported my curiosity and the fervor I had for learning. As I wrote the dissertation that led to this book, they called to check in on me and perhaps without knowing it, gave me the energy that I needed to complete the product. Specifically, my mom, Marina Duran, has always been the hardest-working person I know. She gives so much of herself and is my role model. She has instilled in me a fire to always do what is right and to advocate for minoritized communities. My sisters keep me humble and tell me to achieve what initially appears to be impossible. My nephews and niece inspire me to continue to fight for equitable environments in education, as they will eventually access and move through these spaces. So to Marina, Brenda, Priscilla, Damian, Aaron, and Sofia – thank you.

Beyond my family, I want to take the opportunity to name another person who was vital to me completing this project. My partner, Adam Leftin, has consistently been my number one cheerleader as I have undergone my scholarly journey. He holds me when I feel overwhelmed, encourages my interests, and knows how to make me smile. He brought joy to me while I wrote this book and I am so lucky to be able to spend my life with him. Without him, this would not have been possible.

Another group of people whom I would be remiss not to thank are the faculty at The Ohio State University who assisted me as I conducted this research. First, Susan Robb Jones served as my dissertation chair, doctoral program advisor, and consummate mentor. Her guidance, probing questions, and motivating words were integral to the development of this project. I am so grateful that our paths crossed and will forever benefit from her presence in my life. Additionally, Marc Johnston Guerrero and Wendy Smooth served as the other two members of my dissertation committee. Their enthusiasm for the research and the points of inquiry they provided during my dissertation defense helped me reflect on how I wanted to frame the purpose of this text. I was fortunate to have the opportunity to interact with their humility and brilliance. Finally, Anne-Marie Núñez was an instrumental part for the genesis of this project, having taught a class on intersectionality that led me to fall in love with this framework. She has long given me wise counsel that makes me a better scholar. In addition to this faculty who worked closely with me in the dissertation, I want to send appreciation to the rest of The Ohio State University Higher Education and Student Affairs community (both faculty and students) for their constant advice and assistance. I was truly blessed with amazing cohort members, peers, and professors who taught me that anything is possible.

Additionally, there are countless members of my chosen family that constantly asked me how the book writing was going, helped refined my ideas, and served as possibility models throughout this process. People like Alex C. Lange, David Pérez II, Romeo Jackson, Z Nicolazzo, and many others are the reason why I have found a place in the academy to do this work that unequivocally centers the lives of Queer and Trans People of Color. Each and every one of you have been incredible thought partners and friends who push my thinking. You challenge me to be more critical of systems in postsecondary education, all while doing so in a way that puts love at the forefront. One of my main hopes is that I can continue to make you and my other mentors proud. Also, thank you to the friends who have been alongside me for years (including people like RJ, Matt, and Victor) and who have shown me what it means to create queer worlds.

And finally, to the 20 participants who shared their stories with me – Alejandro (Alejo), Avery Demán, Carmen, Dash, E, Ezekiel, gentle-breeze, John Doe, Levix, Max Aguirre, Mirella Blackwell, Ness, Oliver, Parker, Richard, Rosa, Rose E., Sarah Ray, TJ, and Wren – I will never have the words to sufficiently thank you. During each of our conversations, I stated that I was committed to having your narratives recognized in order to positively impact the conditions of other Queer People of Color at HWIs. This book represents one of the steps that I will take in order to honor the time and energy that you contributed to this project. I will forever treasure and cherish the moments that we spent together, imagining better futures for Queer Students of Color that will follow us.

Introduction

Questions of identity have intrigued researchers and practitioners in the field of higher education and student affairs since the profession's beginning (Jones & Abes, 2013; Patton, Renn, Guido, & Quaye, 2016; Torres, Jones, & Renn, 2019). Namely, both scholars and professionals alike are fascinated by today's college students and how they develop nuanced views on their identities as a result of attending postsecondary institutions. This academic interest is then mirrored in the belief adopted by many in U.S. society that college is a time to explore who a person is and what values they hold. With both this scholarly and societal discourse around the influence that collegiate environments have on students' development, it is no surprise that the literature on college student identity development continues to increase, building upon decades of research attempting to answer the central question of how people view themselves in relationship to the social world around them.

It was this body of scholarship that intrigued me as a student affairs educator, especially as I came to learn that college students in the United States are progressively becoming more diverse as it relates to a number of social identities (e.g., race, sexuality, gender) (Quaye, Harper, & Pendakur, 2019; Renn & Reason, 2012). But as I dove deeper into this research, I found myself upset about whom I saw represented in these theories, theories that were used to guide practice for those who work on college campuses. More simply, I was disappointed about who was *not* represented in the literature given my own positionality and experiences. As a queer Latino man, I have long contended with feeling both invisible and hypervisible in spaces, especially in a society that operates from white and heterosexist norms. As I have moved through and navigated numerous higher education institutions, I have experienced marginalization tied to racist and heterosexist structures. However, these realities are not oftentimes foregrounded in conversations about sexuality or race on college campuses, as people regularly overlook the presence of Queer People of Color in postsecondary settings.

I came to learn that this erasure was then replicated in the very theories that professionals in higher education use to explain how people explore their sexuality (Dillon, Worthington, & Moradi, 2011) or their race (e.g., Cross & Fhagen-Smith, 2001; Gallegos & Ferdman, 2012; Horse, 2012; Kim, 2012; Renn, 2003, 2004). Though these scholarly perspectives on matters of sexuality and race offer important insight into the processes that queer individuals or People of Color undergo in their development, they failed to attend to those who hold both social identities and who are thus exposed to intersecting forms of oppression. An intervention was needed, and I made it my commitment to build upon the limited but rising literature centering the experiences of Queer People of Color on U.S. college campuses.

In particular, I wondered how Queer Students of Color explored their intersecting identities at higher education institutions given the belief that college could be "the first place in which deep questions of identity may be broached" (Stewart, 2009, p. 253). I was especially interested in the experiences of Queer College Students of Color who attended historically white institutions (HWIs), recognizing the literature that underscored these individuals may feel a heightened sense of minoritization given the historical and contemporary legacies of oppression permeating these campuses (Blockett, 2017; Duran, 2019b, 2019c; Goode-Cross, 2009; Goode-Cross & Tager, 2011; Harris, 2003; Holloman & Strayhorn, 2010; Mitchell & Means, 2014; Strayhorn, 2012a). Since scholarship about college student development needs perspectives that implicate systems of power, an approach characterized by Jones and Stewart (2016) as the "third wave" of student development theory (p. 21), I observed the potential for research about identity for Queer Students of Color that acknowledged the role that oppressive systems play. These points of intrigue inevitably led me to construct a study in which I interviewed the experiences of 20 Queer Students of Color enrolled at HWIs across the country, attempting to understand how they explored and navigated their intersectional identities on and off campus. To frame the research, I mobilized the framework of intersectionality, an analytical tool that attends to how overlapping structures of oppression shape the realities of those with multiple minoritized identities (Crenshaw, 1989, 1991).

This book is the product of the interviews that I had with these individuals, representing the time, energy, and labor they contributed in the hopes of making a positive impact on higher education institutions moving forward. In their stories, the 20 Queer Students of Color shared the ways that their HWI allowed them to ask vital questions about their identities through coursework, extracurricular activities, and the relationships they cultivated on campus. Yet, throughout this period of exploration, these individuals also faced constant interpersonal and systemic manifestations of racism, heterosexism, and other forms of oppression. Their process of exploring was thus characterized by a continuous cycle of (un)learning, in which they attempted to unlearn the negative messages they had internalized about their identities while at the same time, learning how to embrace their whole selves. Their complex and vulnerable narratives are centered throughout this text, serving as lessons for those reading this book.

In this introductory chapter, I lay a foundation for the stories to come. I begin by situating myself in this work, echoing Jones and Abes (2013) who argued the importance of making explicit one's positionality when writing about identity. Following this autobiographical entry, I provide further reasoning of my selection of HWIs as the context of interest for this investigation. I additionally elaborate on the necessity of studying matters of college student identity and development using a critical and intersectional lens. I then conclude with an overview of the book's structure and my reflections on what I desire that readers will take from this text.

My Journey Toward This Research

My earliest memories as a child are of my neighborhood. I lived in a vibrant community of Black and Brown people where afternoons after school consisted of walking to the *tienda* [store] to buy Slurpees and Hot Cheetos. Family gatherings were always loud with Spanish music blaring out of speakers. My school environment was no different, composed of people from all different races and ethnicities. Though labeled one of the most at-risk schools in the Phoenix, Arizona area, I remember my days at Wilson fondly. It was here that I found a love for education, supported by teachers with a genuine desire to assist students already disadvantaged by the system. However, everything soon changed when I received a scholarship to attend a prestigious high school: Brophy College Preparatory.

Even though Brophy was only a 15-minute drive away from my neighborhood, it felt like a world apart. An all-boy school located in the heart of central Phoenix, Brophy catered to the city's brightest students with a hefty price tag serving as a barrier for those who would otherwise be eligible to attend. As a student who received a full-ride scholarship as long as I completed my work-study hours, I soon experienced sentiments of isolation and difference surrounded by my affluent white peers. A once hyper-involved student at Wilson, I retreated into a small group of friends that I developed who largely were from similar racial and class backgrounds at me. We started a coffee and tea club, which unknowingly became our place of solace. At the same time, I started to develop an attraction to men, which was anything but normalized in this all-boys Jesuit Catholic school. With these experiences happening concurrently, my general affect changed with people viewing me as a strange, angry child who rarely spoke to others. When the time to apply to college approached, I knew I wanted to get out, to escape to a place where no one knew me. Though I did not have the language necessarily to describe why at the time, I was searching for a location where I could explore my identities more thoroughly – different from the environment at Brophy that thrived on classism, hegemonic masculinities, heteronormativity, whiteness, and so many other oppressive structures.

This journey led me to New York University, a school I could attend thanks to the financial support of a first-generation college student scholarship program known as the AnBryce Scholars. Gone was the sea of white that I had been accustomed to, and in its place- was the presence of diversity in every sense of the word on the streets of New York City (NYC). Though there was an undercurrent of class privilege concerning who could attend New York University, I found myself leaning into my Latino identity, as well as my queer identity, on campus. Fostered by leadership retreats that asked me to reflect on areas where I was oppressed, as well as those where I held privilege, I searched for opportunities where I could make meaning of my identities. Eventually, this desire inspired me to find the LGBTQ Center and to become a participant on a service-learning trip to the Dominican Republic, which was one of the first times I thought concertedly about what it meant to be a queer Latino man. Experiences such as these allowed me to shake off the embarrassment and hate that I once held relative to my identities, even if I did not recognize these feelings as such while I was at Brophy. Instead, I developed a sense of empowerment and a passion for helping other minoritized people engage in similar developmental paths, which was the catalyst for me to pursue a career in higher education and student affairs.

With this new goal in mind, I traveled to Oxford, Ohio to enroll in the Student Affairs in Higher Education master's program at Miami University. At this point, I was thrust back into a similar environment to the one that had once made me shut down. Oxford is nothing like NYC, with only one main street of restaurants and shops compared to the countless neighborhoods where I had once walked in NYC to find myself. Similarly, I learned that people referred to Miami as "J Crew-U," an apt nickname for a predominantly white and affluent student body. And yet, my experiences in New York City prepared me for this new destination. I no longer felt like the kid at Brophy College Preparatory that thought that being Brown and queer was a point of shame. Instead, I was able to manage the effects produced by this white and heteronormative environment.

However, these personal reflections caused me to wonder: what would it have been like if I went to Miami for my undergraduate years? How would I have found communities that affirmed who I am as a Queer Person of Color? Why is it that the theories I read in class leave me without potential answers to these questions? With this curiosity serving as motivation, I pursued my doctoral degree at The Ohio State University (OSU) where I developed the skills necessary to seek out responses to the questions noted previously. I learned from scholars who dedicated their academic careers to answering similar inquiries. From my time growing up in Phoenix to the years I spent obtaining my doctorate degree from OSU, these experiences collectively are the reason why I conducted my dissertation research on Queer Students of Color. Thus, I held these memories close as I underwent this study, interacted with participants, and composed the stories that are present in this book.

Historically White Institutions as Sites of Investigation

In the short story I just related, I reflected on the institutional environments I had navigated as an undergraduate and graduate student. In particular, living in a small college town in the Midwest and Miami's long history as an institution that catered toward a homogenous student body challenged me to think about the role that institutional environments play in the process of identity exploration for Queer Students of Color. How do colleges and universities like Miami, for instance, shape how Queer People of Color come to understand matters of identity? Surely, institutional types would substantially influence this process.

When it came time for me to hone in on my areas of interest for the dissertation, I did more digging into the uniqueness of predominantly white institutions (PWIs). In this search, I happened across the distinction between PWIs and HWIs. Whereas predominantly white institutions point to a student demographic that is majority white in nature, HWIs more accurately captured how I thought about how systemic inequities are ingrained in the fabric of many colleges and universities. Smith, Allen, and Danley (2007) defined HWIs as encapsulating the "historical and contemporary racialized infrastructure that is in place, the current racial campus culture and ecology, and how these modern-day institutions still benefit Whites at the expense of Blacks and other groups of culture" (p. 574). More than simply demographics, the term HWIs and how it is operationalized better described the ways in which structures of whiteness are present on campuses even if the majority of students are not white. Therefore, many campuses could be described as historically white if they were not founded with an explicit mission to serve Communities of Color (i.e., Historically Black Colleges and Universities, as well as Tribal Colleges and Universities).

Paired with this understanding of HWIs, I did more reading into their histories. From their inception, HWIs perpetuated systems of racism, anti-Blackness, and settler colonialism (Lee & Ahtone, 2020; Wilder, 2013). Furthermore, HWIs have also been sites of heterosexism, in which queer people have been systematically excluded and targeted because of their sexuality (Graves, 2009, 2018; Nash & Silverman, 2015). It is thus unsurprising that these historical legacies manifest themselves in contemporary times with Queer Students of Color reporting experiences of racism, heterosexism, and other forms of oppression (Blockett, 2017; Duran, 2019b, 2019c; Goode-Cross, 2009; Goode-Cross & Tager, 2011; Harris, 2003; Holloman & Strayhorn, 2010; Mitchell & Means, 2014;

Strayhorn, 2012a). Though more empirical research is still undeniably needed on other institutional types like Historically Black Colleges and Universities (HBCUs) and Tribal Colleges and Universities (TCUs), it was HWIs that I set as my contexts of interest. Specifically, because I was interested in understanding how institutional environments shape matters of exploration for Queer Students of Color, these colleges and universities are unique because of their historical and contemporary expressions of racism and heterosexism, among additional structures of domination.

An Intersectional Lens to Understand Identity

The decision to interview Queer Students of Color at HWIs was intricately connected with my desire to use a critical intersectional lens to make meaning of the participants' experiences. In doing so, I sought to contribute to the growing body of literature situated in what Jones and Stewart (2016) would refer to as the third wave of college student development. Specifically, the third wave uses critical and poststructural frameworks in order to reimagine the study of student development and identity. This wave thus builds upon earlier theories that investigated social identities, but that lacked an attention to how structural oppression informed critical developmental processes.

Hoping to engage the third wave's "explicit acknowledgment and foregrounding of hegemonic norms . . . through analyses of the impacts of structural and systemic oppression and privilege on individuals and their learning and development" (Jones & Stewart, 2016, p. 21), I employed intersectionality as a guiding framework in my research. Elaborated on in Chapter Two, many scholarly debates exist about the relationship that intersectionality as an analytical tool has with matters of identity. For instance, intersectional higher education scholars have cautioned against the use of the framework to interrogate issues of identity without also examining the overlapping structures of power and oppression that shape the lives of people (Duran & Jones, 2019b; Harris & Patton, 2019; Jones & Abes, 2013; Nuñez, 2014a, 2014b; Tillapaugh & Nicolazzo, 2014). Therefore, when I use the phrase *intersectional identities* in this book, I do not do so in order to assert that *intersectional* is a proxy for *intersecting* identities; instead, I use the phrase in order to call attention to the interlocking structures of power that constitute how Queer Students of Color explore their identities on college campuses. In other words, it is impossible for me to think about understanding students' identities in the third wave without a clear centering of a structural analysis that implicates systemic oppression.

Moreover, in my mobilization of intersectionality as a framework to comprehend the experiences of queer individuals, I push back against post-intersectional scholars who contend that intersectionality was not meant to capture the realities of those who are sexual minorities

(Hutchinson, 1997, 2001; Kwan, 1997, 2000; Valdes, 1995, 1997). In Chapter Two of this text, I explore the connections to queer theorizing, politics, and identities by arguing that queerness has been integral to intersectional theorizing, drawing upon the contributions of those such as the Combahee River Collective (1977/1983). By asserting this argument, I put my work in relationship with other scholars who argue that queer studies and intersectional theorizing can be put in conversation with one another to more deeply engage how power operates in society (Bilge, 2012; Christensen, 2018; Collins & Bilge, 2016; Duong, 2012; Olive, 2015; Rahman, 2010). Through these power-based lenses, for instance, I argue that I was more attuned to the nuances that existed in Queer Students of Color' identity exploration, nuances that are significant for readers hoping to enact change at HWIs.

Organization of the Book

The book is divided into three different parts. The first part, "Introducing the Intersections," offers a foundation for the stories shared by the Queer Students of Color. Chapter One elaborates on the scholarly debates that exist concerning the central constructs relevant to the study. In particular, this chapter explores what it means to use the framework of intersectionality (Crenshaw, 1989, 1991) to understand issues of college student identity, especially given intersectional theorizing's focus on overlapping systems of power. Moreover, the chapter will discuss intersectionality's relationship to queer communities and politics. Chapter Two then sets the stage for the study by overviewing the existing literature relevant to Queer College Students of Color. Namely, scholars acknowledged that research on Queer Students of Color continues to increase in the field of higher education and student affairs (Duran, 2019d; Duran, Blockett, & Nicolazzo, 2020; Lange, Duran, & Jackson, 2019; Rankin, Garvey, & Duran, 2019). However, I also articulate what future directions exist for the study of Queer People of Color in postsecondary settings. Both chapters thus provide conceptual clarity for readers to view the participant narratives.

The second part, "Exploring the Intersections," covers the findings from the constructivist grounded theory (Charmaz, 2014) research project about the experiences of 20 Queer Students of Color at HWIs from across the country. Each chapter has a preceding vignette providing an in-depth look at one participant's story, providing readers the chance to intimately get to know the individuals and how their stories connect to the study results. For example, Chapter Three begins with a vignette focused on Wren, an African American (Black American/Creole) queer non-binary boi who was studying at a small Midwestern HWI. In our conversations together, Wren spoke about how systems like anti-Black racism, heterosexism, and trans oppression intersected to create the conditions that they navigated daily. Wren's excerpts exemplified how various sites in which overlapping structures of power manifested (i.e., HWIs, local contexts, sociopolitical climates, cultural dynamics/norms, and interpersonal interactions) shaped how participants viewed their identities. Chapter Four introduces the readers to Ness, an Asian American pansexual non-binary individual enrolled at a large public HWI in the Southeast. A fierce advocate for Asian American communities on and off campus, Ness' vignette leads into the several experiences that participants encountered during college that allowed them to ask and answer questions related to identity – including their academic interactions, extracurricular involvement, social/romantic relationships, as well as their off-campus and study abroad connections.

In Chapter Five, I begin with Carmen's vignette. A Mestiza queer non-binary individual at a large public HWI in the Mountain West, Carmen spoke at length about how their non-binary identity and undocumented status shaped their understanding of race and sexuality. With Carmen's story at the heart of it, Chapter Five discusses the other social identities that informed participants' exploration of race and sexuality (e.g., gender, ability, socioeconomic status, undocumented status). Chapter Six then covers a significant finding from the study: participants explored their identities by engaging in a cycle of (un)learning. Beginning with a look into the life of Richard, an Asian queer man attending a large Southeastern public HWI, his vignette will show how Queer Students of Color needed to unlearn negative messages relevant to their identities, in addition to highlighting how they learned positive views about them. The second part of the book concludes with Chapter Seven, shining a light on the hopes that the Queer College Students of Color expressed about the relationships they had with their identities. Max's story serves as an apt way to start off this chapter as they had multiple instances in which they detailed their dreams for life beyond college. As someone who is especially motivated by the potential of the third wave of student development (Abes, Jones, & Stewart, 2019; Jones & Stewart, 2016), I conclude each of the chapters in Part Two of this text with "Reflections on Identity," communicating how the participants' stories teaches the field of higher education and student affairs something new about student development.

Part Three, "Embracing the Intersections," invites readers to consider how they can better construct environments for Queer People of Color to explore their identities and thrive while doing so. Chapter Eight includes reflections about the use of intersectionality in the present research, generating recommendations for those hoping to mobilize the framework in their practice and research. The following two chapters then interweave comments from the participants themselves as they articulated what they would want to see change at the HWIs they attended. The 20 individuals who engaged in this research were hopeful that their stories would not only be read, but that those who learned about their experiences would be motivated to positively impact the lives of Queer People of Color on their own campuses. Chapter Nine describes shifts that need to happen structurally at HWIs (e.g., policy, funding) in order to better support those who identify as Queer College Students of Color. Specifically, the participants in the study often named these structural barriers as negatively shaping their perceptions of identities such as sexuality and race. Chapter Ten will then offer concrete recommendations for faculty and staff pertinent to affirming and advocating for Queer People of Color. Of note, participants described how it was everyone's responsibility to contribute to validating environments on college campuses that help students embrace their intersecting identities.

I conclude the book with an epilogue in which I offer my own reflections on this project, while further centering the lessons that I learned from the participants who spent time with me and shared their knowledge. Their words served as a personal reminder for me to better attend to those with multiple minoritized identities in postsecondary settings, and I hope they will do the same for readers. Finally, I offer readers a more detailed outline of my research process in the appendix. For those interested in this line of inquiry, it is my desire that the methodological appendix peaks their curiosity and allows them to dream about the studies that they can conduct to build upon this project. The stories of Queer Students of Color deserve to be centered as postsecondary educators place value on creating equitable practices, policies, and environments at colleges and universities.

Conclusion

Having the opportunity to speak and be in community with the 20 Queer Students of Color represented in this book inspired and invigorated me. Their narratives touched upon topics of resilience, love, and care and expanded my ideas about what it means for Queer People of Color to explore their identities at HWIs. This text is my attempt to capture their passion, light, and wisdom so that others may learn from their experiences. The purpose of this book is thus to show how Queer Students of Color navigated their intersectional identities at HWIs. In doing so, their stories serve as a call to higher education scholars and practitioners to address the racism, heterosexism, and other forms of oppression that exist at HWIs. By attending to these structures of domination, institutional agents shape and influence how Queer People of Color explore their identities.

Part 1

Introducing the Intersections

1 Complicating the Study of College Student Identity Using Intersectionality

Before introducing the scholarship on Queer Students of Color in higher education, I see it important to provide an overview of the central constructs that I interrogated in my research. Highlighted in the introduction to this book, the study that I engaged in sought to intervene in the scholarship on college student identity by using intersectionality (Crenshaw, 1989, 1991) as a theoretical framework. Yet, with intersectionality's rising popularity in education (Barnett & Felten, 2016; Bhopal & Preston, 2012; Byrd, Brunn-Bevel, & Ovink, 2019; Davis, Brunn-Bevel, & Olive, 2015; Mitchell, Simmons, & Greyerbiehl, 2014; Mitchell, Marie, & Steele, 2019), scholars have warned against its misuse and misapplication (Duran & Jones, 2019b; Harris & Patton, 2019; Jones & Abes, 2013; Nuñez, 2014a, 2014b; Tillapaugh & Nicolazzo, 2014). Hence, this chapter examines what it means to leverage intersectional theorizing in the study of college student identity.

I begin by outlining the relevant research in the area of college student development and identity that served as sensitizing concepts (Charmaz, 2014) in the study. Specifically, I survey how college student development theorists think of identity, the self, and meaning making. Following this section, I dig deeply into the landscape of intersectional scholarship. I do so by first offering an historical rendering of intersectional-like thought, following the words of Hancock (2016) who asserted that being a good steward of intersectionality involves paying credence to the genealogy of activists who laid the groundwork for the framework. Then, I describe how intersectionality performed key theoretical interventions in the academy, guided by the work of Dill and Zambrana (2009). Importantly, these theoretical interventions guided how I approached the research covered in this text. I conclude with ruminations on the scholarly debates circulating around intersectional scholarship and echo the work of Nash (2019) who believes that there is still untapped potential for this framework. In particular, I investigate intersectionality's relationship to identity and queer studies as a couple of ways that I move intersectional theorizing forward.

Relevant Concepts From College Student Development and Identity Research

Research on college student identity is located under the larger umbrella of student development theory, a body of literature that attempts to understand "the ways that a student grows, progresses, or increases his or her [or their] developmental capacities as a result of enrollment in an institution of higher education" (p. 153). A hallmark of the student affairs profession, practitioners use student development theories to inform their practice including their interpersonal interactions, programmatic initiatives, and educational trainings (Reason & Kimball, 2012; Patton et al., 2016). However, as emphasized throughout this text, these theories have fallen short of their potential to expose how systems of power and oppression inform the development of students (Abes, 2016; Abes et al., 2019; Jones & Stewart, 2016).

Additionally, because many theories in fact originated from other disciplines (e.g., psychology, social psychology, sociology; Torres, Jones, & Renn, 2009), professionals lack an in-depth comprehension of how colleges themselves contribute to student development (Patton et al., 2016). Therefore, though Knefelkamp, Widick, and Parker (1978) argued long ago that one of the pressing questions surrounding student development theory involves understanding how colleges themselves "encourage or inhibit growth" (p. x), this line of inquiry is still rich for investigation. In the next subsections, I elaborate on the relevant concepts pertaining to this particular study while bringing to light how this book functions as an intervention into this research.

Perspectives on Identity, Identity Exploration, and the Self

As someone interested in matters of identity, I had to trace how scholars have understood the concept over time. This investigation brought me to the work on psychosocial development by Erik Erikson (1963, 1964, 1968, 1994), considered to be one of the formative theorists about identity. Of note, Erikson argued that people moved through eight stages of psychosocial development, of which "identity versus role confusion" was the fifth stage. In his scholarship, Erikson (1963) spoke about ego identity, which he defined as "the ability to experience one's self as something that has continuity and sameness, and to act accordingly" (p. 42). Moreover, Erikson believed that the ego identity involved how people viewed themselves in relationship to others, meaning that identity was formed through people's social interactions. Though Erikson situated this examination of identity in the fifth stage, others argue that ego identity formation transcended each stage in the psychosocial development process (Côté & Levine, 1987).

Moving forward, theorists started to expand on Erikson's (1963, 1964, 1968, 1994) perspectives on identity, including James Marcia. Marcia-(1966, 1994) is largely known for his research on ego identity statuses, arguing that people can experience four statuses within the ego identity (i.e., achievement, moratorium, foreclosure, and diffusion). In following the trail on identity research, Marcia's (1966, 1994) scholarship stuck out to me for a variety of reasons. Namely, Marcia (1966, 1994) believed that people's identity status depended on their degree of *exploration* (originally termed crisis) and *commitment*. The notion of identity exploration, which involved "re-thinking, sorting through, and trying out various roles and life plans" (Kroger & Marcia, 2011, p. 33), caught my interest. Though not necessary for every person's development, Marcia's work showed that many undergo the process of identity exploration, which included a cognitive (exploring meaningful alternatives) and behavioral (actively seeking out chances to learn these alternatives) dimension. As someone fascinated by college students' development, this period of exploration was especially intriguing because Marcia asserted that this process occurred largely in late adolescence (Kroger & Marcia, 2011). Though college students span all ages, I wondered how postsecondary settings influenced exploration for those in this particular point of their life. How do college students cognitively and behaviorally explore who they are at higher education institutions and relatedly, how do systems of power and oppression play a role in this process? These questions inevitably set me on the path to engage the concept of identity exploration as it pertains to Queer Students of Color.

However, in researching identity, I also came across the idea of a "sense of self," a construct that Queer Students of Color would go on to reference in their interviews (see Chapter Seven). On their surface, sense of self and identity seem to be synonyms, a reality that Côté and Levine (2002) echoed when they wrote about the definitional slippage that exists between the self and Erikson's notion of the ego identity: "the 'self' has not been clearly differentiated from the 'ego' " (p. 24). In attempting to distinguish the two, Côté and Levine (2002) argued that the self is akin to "cognitive content" and the ego identity applies to a "cognitive process" (p. 88). Put more simply, they stated the self more accurately gets at "a person's internalized behavioral repertoires" while the ego identity articulates the "inter-relationships between the self and the other" (p. 88). Therefore, a person's identity encapsulates both one's sense of self *and* how it is constituted by their engagements with others. As mentioned, this differentiation becomes increasingly relevant when the Queer Students of Color described their hopes that resulted from navigating their identities at HWIs . . . so stay tuned. Adding further complexity to my operationalizing of identity, I then examined the scholarship on social identity exploration and development.

Emerging Focus on Social Identity Exploration and Development

Different from the research on ego identity, researchers later investigated the notion of social identities. For instance, the work on social identity theory by Henri Tajfel (1978, 1982) argued that people construct a positive personal identity by being in relationship with particular groups – showing the interconnection between personal and social identities. Moreover, Tajfel and Turner (1979) asserted that a person's sense of self was connected to their membership in social groups, which contextualizes others' interest in understanding salient socially constructed identities (e.g., race, sexuality, and gender). With this in mind, I decided to examine the literature on social identities, and in particular, the scholarship relevant to queer individuals and Communities of Color.

Departing from James Marcia's initial work on identity exploration, scholars later applied this concept to social identities, including the study of ethnicity as well as sexuality (e.g., Dillon et al., 2011; Phinney, 1993; Syed et al., 2013; Umaña-Taylor, Kornienko, Bayless, & Updegraff, 2018; Whitehead, Ainsworth, Wittig, & Gadino, 2009; Worthington, Navarro, Savoy, & Hampton, 2008). For instance, Jean Phinney's (1993) scholarship on ethnic identity development showed that identity exploration was a vital part of the developmental process. Of note, Phinney extended Marcia's (1966, 1994) research when she argued that people explored their ethnicity through cognitive, behavioral, *and* affective dimensions. By introducing an affective domain, Phinney asserted that exploration also involved the sentiments and feelings that people encounter in this formative period. When it comes to sexual identity development, researchers like Dillon et al. (2011) and Worthington et al. (2008) also maintained that queer people participate in this period of exploration. Specifically, Dillon et al. (2011) described sexual identity exploration as consisting of "purposeful exploration, evaluation, or experimentation of one's sexual needs, values, orientation, and/or preferences for activities, partner characteristics, or modes of sexual expression" (p. 660). However, these theorists made limited mention of how exploration of these identities (i.e., ethnicity and sexuality) is influenced by other salient social identities. Consequently, they helped me to think through my research while also showing the necessity for more complex perspectives illustrative of Queer People of Color.

An important distinction here is that *identity exploration* is different than *identity development*. The former is a developmental task that many undergo in order to develop (Kroger & Marcia, 2011), thus suggesting that the latter is a lifelong process. In fact, a much broader scholarship on identity development exists specific to sexuality (Dillon et al., 2011) and race (e.g., Cross & Fhagen-Smith, 2001; Gallegos & Ferdman, 2012; Horse, 2012; Kim, 2012; Renn, 2003, 2004). In the research I conducted,

I was more interested in matters of exploration rather than development. Nevertheless, I acknowledged that theories focused more expansively on development suffer from the same inattention to intersecting identities. Consequently, another sensitizing body of research for this study involved the literature on intersecting identities.

Investigations on Intersecting Identities

To more accurately depict the diverse communities that are present on college campuses in contemporary times, higher education scholars have developed models that represent how individuals view their intersecting identities (Abes, Jones, & McEwen, 2007; Jones & Abes, 2013; Jones & McEwen, 2000; Reynolds & Pope, 1991; Wijeyesinghe, 2012). Given my own interests in intersecting social identities, this subset of literature was particularly relevant to this present study. For instance, two models that have shaped the field of higher education and student affairs' understanding of intersecting identities include the Model of Multiple Dimensions of Identity (MMDI, Jones & McEwen, 2000) and the Reconceptualized Model of Multiple Dimensions of Identity (RMMDI, Abes et al., 2007).

Using a grounded theory approach, Susan Robb Jones (1997) conducted a study that investigated how women college students perceived the relationships between their social and personal identities. From this project, Jones and McEwen (2000) developed the MMDI, a model that shows how these students' social and personal identities intersected with one another, relationships that were in flux depending on the contexts that individuals were in at the time. Based on these contextual variables (e.g. family, college environments, and sociocultural factors), specific social identities may be more salient and closer to a core self. Later, Abes et al. (2007) built upon the MMDI by incorporating attention to the construct of meaning making. Specifically, Abes et al. (2007) used data from a narrative study on lesbian college students (see Abes & Jones, 2004) to show how a person's meaning-making capacities play a central role in the relationship between the contextual variables and their intersecting identities. Further elaborated on in the subsequent sections, meaning-meaning structures involve the "sets of assumptions that determine how an individual perceives and organizes her life experiences" (Abes & Jones, 2004, p. 613). Because of the connections that these structures have with social identities, the final area of scholarship I surveyed was that of meaning making.

Meaning Making and Its Connection to Identities

Scholars attribute the work on meaning making to a constructivist-developmental psychologist, Robert Kegan (1982, 1994). Kegan's (1994) research revealed five different orders of consciousness that most people move through in their life. In order to have a shift in consciousness, people develop in three different domains: cognitive, interpersonal, and intrapersonal. Furthermore, as individuals progress through these orders, their meaning-making structures become more complex. These meaning-making structures capture how people organize and process their experiences, moving from a reliance on external influences to a position where they have the ability to construct meaning for themselves. According to Kegan (1994), complexity in meaning making transpires when we "liberat[e] ourselves from that in which we were embedded, making what was subject into object so that we can 'have it' rather than 'be had' by it" (p. 34). Interested in the assertions put forth by Kegan, Marcia Baxter Magolda (1999a, 1999b, 2001, 2009) interrogated how these orders of consciousness applied to college students through a longitudinal study. Specifically, Baxter Magolda (1999b, 2001) found that most students are situated within the third order of consciousness, a position where their meaning-making structures still rely on the influence of external factors and where they are incapable of using an internal voice (which is termed self-authorship).

Baxter Magolda's scholarship set the stage for higher education researchers who sought to understand how meaning making applied to minoritized students (e.g., Abes, 2012; Abes & Jones, 2004; Abes & Kasch, 2007; Hernández, 2012; Torres, 2009; Torres & Hernandez, 2007). What these scholars began to show was the connection that exist between meaning-making structures and the presence of systemic oppression (Perez, 2019), making this literature particularly relevant to the questions that I was interested in concerning Queer Students of Color. This scholarship ultimately showcased how oppressive structures influence meaning making and vice-versa. For instance, Abes (2012) used intersectionality to interrogate how a lesbian college student viewed her intersecting social identities. In this investigation, she discovered that understanding how oppressive systems influence one's view of their intersecting identities necessitates a more complex form of meaning making, but that "interlocking inequitable social structures make complex development challenging to achieve" (Abes, 2012, p. 204). The work of Abes (2012) and other scholars were formative to how I designed the present research on Queer Students of Color. Namely, scholarship produced by Elisa Abes and Susan Jones allowed me to think through how I could leverage frameworks like intersectionality in the study of developmental concepts like identity and meaning making.

The Landscape of Intersectionality Scholarship

In surveying the literature on college student development, I recognized the potential that is unlocked when scholars apply critical and poststructural frameworks to this research. As I sought to reveal how overlapping axes of oppression shaped how Queer Students of Color explored their intersecting identities at HWIs, for instance, intersectionality emerged as a framework that could provide me the conceptual underpinning to engage in this examination. Notably, intersectionality has expanded into a field of study in itself (Cho, Crenshaw, & McCall, 2013), representing an analytical tool that has traveled across academic disciplines (Lewis, 2013). Though this traveling has caused worry for some intersectional theorists who assert that people have misused the framework (Bilge, 2013; Collins, 2015; Davis, 2008), scholars like Jennifer Nash (2019) believe that individuals need to resist a one-dimensional application of intersectionality in order to reveal its true power. In my own work, I leaned into the knowns and unknowns of intersectional theorizing, a journey I expand on in the following sections. To show intersectionality's reach and its application to the current investigation, I initially situate my reading of intersectionality as connected to Kimberlé Crenshaw before then acknowledging its larger history in Women of Color activism. I then detail how intersectionality performed several theoretical interventions in the academy, which led to my use of the framework in this research. This foundation setting then allowed me to employ a unique reading of intersectionality to center the lives of Queer Students of Color.

Crenshaw's Contributions to Intersectional Theorizing

Many both in and outside of the academy now associate intersectionality with the scholarship of Kimberlé Crenshaw (1989, 1991), a Black feminist legal scholar. Frequently referred to as the person who coined intersectionality as a term, Crenshaw (1989) initially used the language of intersectionality in order to describe the ways that legal systems failed Black women and Women of Color by conceptualizing oppression through a single-axis lens. In the courts' eyes, Black women could make a claim of discrimination based on their race or their sex but not both simultaneously. However, as Crenshaw (1991) contended, "The intersection of racism and sexism factors into Black women's lives in ways that cannot be captured wholly by looking at the race or gender dimensions of those experiences separately" (p. 1244). Crenshaw (1989) used the image of a four-way traffic intersection to depict how Black women experienced the effects of racism and sexism at the same time, each constituting the other. She also employed the analogy of a basement to show how overlapping structures of oppression contribute to social stratification with those who are most minoritized present at the bottom, whereas those who hold higher degrees of power are at the top and have more of an ability to leave the basement. Despite its effectiveness in revealing how minoritization affects people differently based on their social location, this metaphor is often forgotten in favor of the four-way traffic stop analogy (Carastathis, 2013).

In her 1991 text, Crenshaw further elaborated on her framing by showing how intersectional oppression functions in structural, representational, and political categories. Each of these three illustrate how oppression manifests in numerous and insidious ways. For instance, structural intersectionality describes how social institutions and the policies they employ disenfranchise those who hold multiple minoritized identities. Political intersectionality elucidates the limitations of social movements when they understand social categories in a monolithic fashion. For example, Women of Color were oftentimes overlooked in movements focused on women or People of Color because each group repeatedly centered the needs of the majority (e.g., men in antiracist groups or white women in women's activist communities). Lastly, representational intersectionality sheds a light on how cultural discourses and imagery around Women of Color positions them as other using racist and sexist tropes. What is surprising is that many theorists who presuppose to engage intersectional theorizing fail to take up these three levels of analyses in favor of simply thinking about the framework as one that gets at intersecting identities (Cho et al., 2013). Furthermore, others have critiqued those who obscure the larger histories that led Crenshaw to generate this framework.

Histories of Intersectional Theorizing

Of note, intersectionality has a rich history in Black feminist mobilizing and the activism of Women of Color (Collins & Bilge, 2016; Hancock, 2016). In fact, in her own work, Crenshaw (1989) credited her intersectional theorizing to figures such as Sojourner Truth and Anna Julia Cooper who long pushed back against the violence that Black women experienced in chattel slavery. However, in tracing the history behind intersectionality, Hancock (2015, 2016) asserted that intersectional thought went as far back as 1831, citing the advocacy of Maria Stewart. In particular, Stewart wrote a pamphlet in which she detailed the unique forms of marginalization that Black women faced during this time. Either way, both Crenshaw (1989, 1991) and Hancock (2015, 2016) acknowledged that intersectionality thrived far before it found its way to the academy.

Moreover, in the genealogy of intersectionality are the other academics and advocates during the 1960s to the 1980s who communicated ideas similar to Crenshaw's (1989, 1991). For instance, Collins (2015) demonstrated that Women of Color feminists across different racial backgrounds had articulated ideas similar to intersectionality (e.g., Beal, 1969/1970; Combahee River Collective, 1977/1983; García, 1997; Lorde, 1982; Min-Ha, 1989; Moraga & Anzaldúa, 1983). Though not named explicitly as intersectionality, these Women of Color had detailed the ways in which Women of Color encountered the compounding effects of racism, sexism, and other forms of oppression. In being a good steward of intersectionality (Hancock, 2016; Moradi & Grzanka, 2017) in my own work, I saw it necessary to honor the framework's genealogy, seeking to understand how its history contributed to the theoretical interventions that it made when it was introduced into the academy.

Intersectionality's Main Theoretical Interventions

With intersectionality's popularity across academic disciplines, scholars have mentioned that there are inconsistencies in the ways that people mobilize the framework (Collins, 2015; Nash, 2008). However, Collins (2015) contended that there are several defining contours that are frequently present across intersectional theorizing. For the purposes of my own research, I often refer back to the work of Dill and Zambrana (2009) to identify these contours. Namely, Dill and Zambrana (2009) believed that intersectionality performed four theoretical interventions when it was introduced into the academy:

> (1) Placing the lived experiences and struggles of people of color and other marginalized groups as a starting point for the development of theory; (2) Exploring the complexities not only of individual identities but also group identity, recognizing that variations within groups are often ignored and essentialized; (3) Unveiling the ways interconnected domains of power organize and structure inequality and oppression; and (4) Promoting social justice and social change by linking research and practice to create a holistic approach to the eradication of disparities and to changing social and higher education institutions.
>
> (p. 5)

In designing the study that led to this book, I carefully considered each of these interventions.

For instance, one of the first interventions that intersectionality made involved the centering of People of Color and other minoritized groups to develop theory. Of note, critical theorists believe that when moving the needle toward equity, it is imperative that society centers the needs and perspectives of those most disenfranchised (Harris, 1989; Matsuda, 1987, 1992). The reason being is that "marginalized subjects have an epistemic advantage, a particular perspective that scholars should consider, if not adopt, when crafting a normative vision of a just society" (Nash, 2008, p. 3). Because minoritized individuals are the targeted subjects of social inequities, they are the most knowledgeable about crafting structures that are just. For example, because Queer People of Color have experienced legacies of racism, heterosexism, and others, they are the most qualified in society to reimagine a world where these systems are eradicated. As a result, if HWIs were to combat their histories of oppression, learning more about the lives of Queer Students of Color is imperative.

Next, intersectionality also advanced scholarship by causing individuals to consider the complexities that exist within individual and group identities (Dill & Zambrana, 2009). This intervention relates to Crenshaw's (1991) analysis of political intersectionality and how she interrogated notions of identity politics. When groups advocate for a particular social category (e.g., queer individuals), they oftentimes default to the majority even within this minoritized community (e.g., white gay individuals). As Rogers and Lott (1997) underscored, "Oppressed groups struggle not only against the boundaries dividing them from privileged groups but also against boundaries constituted by mixes of privilege and disprivilege within their ranks" (p. 445). Therefore, intersectional theorizing challenges individuals to scrutinize considerations of within-group differences, asking them to instead foreground the most marginalized within minoritized groups. Attending to this intervention required me to make intentional decisions around sampling (see the Methodological Appendix for more information) and to reveal the complexities within Queer Students of Colors' identities (see Chapter Five for a description of the within-group differences present in this study).

The third intervention of intersectionality, and perhaps the most important, necessitates comprehending how structures of domination fashion the lives of minoritized individuals in society. Crenshaw's (1989) main contention was not simply that Black women hold intersecting identities relative to their race and gender, but rather that they "experience double-discrimination – the combined effects of practices which discriminate on the basis of race, and on the basis of sex" (p. 149). Thus, intersectional scholars must worry about their analysis "turning inward," language advanced by Collins (2009b, p. ix) to depict what occurs when people focus on identities and not systems of power. In speaking with the Queer Students of Color who participated in this research, I hence needed to move beyond their reflections on identity broadly and instead implicate the ways that manifestations of power both within and outside of their institution influenced their exploration.

The final intervention honors the history of activism that led to the introduction of intersectionality into scholarly discourse (Hancock, 2016). Specifically, it is the belief that theorists should employ intersectionality with the ultimate goal of changing the social conditions that oppress minoritized groups. Of note, Crenshaw (1989, 1991) identified the intersectional erasure experienced by Women of Color and Black women in particular in the hopes of shifting how courts thought about disciplinary justice for these individuals. As a researcher, this is perhaps the intervention that I struggled with the most, reflections that I provide both in Chapter Eight and in the Epilogue in this text. In the end, I sincerely wish that by reading the stories of the participants in this study, faculty and staff who work at HWIs are better equipped to reimagine institutional practices and policies with Queer People of Color in mind.

Considerations in Using Intersectionality to Research Identity

By surveying the scholarly landscape of intersectionality, I saw the potential that this framework had for the questions that had long intrigued me as someone who works on college campuses. However, at the same time, I came to learn about some possible tensions that would exist in leveraging intersectionality to research matters of college student identity. Characteristic of the third wave of student development, I set out to use a framework not created with higher education in mind (Jones & Stewart, 2016). Therefore, I encountered two major quandaries that I needed to rectify in order to engage in this work: what it mean to use a power-based lens to research identity and the relationship between intersectionality and queer studies. However, I did so embracing the positions of intersectional scholars like Nash (2019) who encouraged Black feminist thinkers to open up the possibilities of the framework by resisting rigid applications of intersectionality.

The Tension Between Power and the Study of Identity

Mentioned previously, one of the significant interventions of intersectional theorizing involves its intentional foregrounding of a power-based analysis. Connected to this point, scholars have engaged in a debate to determine whether intersectionality can be used in research about identity at all with the fear that such scholarship would obscure its focus on structures of oppression. In fact, these theorists contend that people should only employ intersectionality to interrogate macro-level issues and policies. As Staunæs (2003) described, intersectionality was not intended to examine the "lived experiences of concrete subjects" and actually needs another theory paired with intersectionality should scholars want to understand issues of identity (p. 101). In a likewise fashion, Cho et al. (2013) also argued that intersectionality is more directed toward "the way things work rather than who people are" (p. 923). Yet, I assert that using intersectionality in the study of identity can accomplish both goals: *understanding the ways things work by seeing who people are.*

To frame this argument, I reference the work of Vivian May, an intersectional scholar who has explored the epistemological and ontological projects of the framework. In May's (2015) reading of intersectionality, she stated that theorizing from an intersectional lens actually can bridge identity and structures of power:

> A more thorough reading of intersectionality literatures would reveal that a both/and approach to (multiple) identities contextualized within myriad social structures and attendant to the relational nature

> of power and privilege within and between groups is (and has long been fundamental) to intersectionality.
>
> (p. 114)

With this statement in mind, I believe that intersectional theorizing lends itself to the study of identity because structures of oppression inherently inform how people view their identities. Thus, the knowledge gained from people's perspectives on identity showcases how systems of inequality function in society.

Student development theorists have similarly embraced this same position as they have argued for the increased use of intersectionality in college student development research (see Jones & Abes, 2013; Jones & Stewart, 2016; Torres et al., 2009; Wijeyesinghe, 2019; Wijeyesinghe & Jones, 2014). Doing so requires the field of higher education and student affairs to think differently about the nature of identity altogether. Illustrating this point, Wijeyesinghe and Jones (2014) put forward the following question:

> Can identity truly be an individual experience when people embody social identities that carry meaning in society and result in differential access to resources and control of various domains that fundamentally influence a person's life, regardless of whether he or she [or they] acknowledges the existence or influence of those identities?
>
> (p. 14)

Utilizing an intersectional lens in research on identity requires scholars to see the construct of identity in a different way, as suggested by Wijeyesinghe and Jones (2014). Yet, in approaching it from this new light, scholars effectively bridge the gap between intersectionality and matters of identity.

Intersectionality's Relationship With Queer Studies

In addition to the debate on power and the nature of identity, I also see it important to discuss intersectionality's relationship with queer studies. Namely, in researching the lives of *Queer* Students of Color, I need to provide some clarity on how queerness is treated in this text. This is particularly relevant given that theorists have asserted that queerness can be used to explain different concepts, including an identity, practice, and politic (see Burford & Allen, 2019). Although I designed this research thinking about queerness largely as an identity describing those who are minoritized on the basis of their sexuality, I use this following section to interrogate the dis/connections that exist between intersectionality and queerness in more expansive ways.

Intersectionality and Queerness: Claims of Who Is Intersectional

To begin, post-intersectional thinkers have critiqued intersectionality for having a narrow lens that is solely applicable to interrogate intersecting forms of racism and sexism (Hutchinson, 1997, 2001; Kwan, 1997, 2000; Mutua, 2013; Valdes, 1995, 1997). These scholars represent another area of critical legal studies, alleging that intersectionality's analysis does not account for certain social locations. A large portion of post-intersectional scholarship, for example, declared that intersectionality is insufficient to comprehend the ways that systems pertaining to sexuality intersect with other structures of domination, especially salient in the context of this investigation. Kwan (1997) stressed this critique when he stated,

> It is not just that intersectionality slighted issues of sexual orientation . . . but that by focusing, for example, on the particularities of black women's experience, intersectionality stands in danger of pushing to its margins issues of class, religion, and able-bodiedness, as well as issues of sexual orientation.
>
> (p. 1276)

Additionally, Mutua (2013) found an issue with intersectionality, contending that it was limited in its capacity to analyze systems of privilege like those tied to masculinity. This perceived flaw of intersectionality has led these groups of scholars to propose their own alternatives including but not limited to "inter-connectivities" (Valdes, 1995), "cosynthesis," (Kwan, 1997), and "multidimensionality" (Hutchinson, 2001).

However, these claims put forth by post-intersectional scholars are flawed in numerous ways. First, May (2015) articulated that though the framework has origins in Women of Color feminism, intersectionality can apply beyond an analysis of race and gender: "Intersectionality . . . uses 'both/and' thinking to underscore how Black women's experiences are not delimited in their relevance only to Black women" (p. 26). As a theory, intersectionality seeks to understand how larger interlocking structures of privilege and oppression impact individuals based on their social location. Hence, academics have stated that the framework can examine the lives of multiple groups, not just Black women (Carbado, 2013; Cole, 2009; Goodman, 2014; Kendall & Wijeyesinghe, 2017; May, 2015). Since everyone is positioned within systems of power, intersectionality can function as a lens for the study of many communities. Furthering this critique of post-intersectionality, Cho (2013) argued that in moving away from Crenshaw's (1989, 1991) framework, some legal theorists have failed to center power in their analysis: "Kwan's concern about whether intersectionality properly accounts for the straight White male or disproportionately centers Black women suggests that he might favor an approach that would be inattentive to power or the specificity of actual political struggle" (p. 393). Thus, post-intersectional scholars should critically consider what might be lost in their departure from intersectionality, especially as it relates to the framework's goal of social change.

Second, another troubling phenomenon connected to this body of research involves the furthered erasure of Black women's labor when naming work as post-intersectional. On one hand, by asserting that sexuality has remained on the margins of intersectional thought, these legal scholars render the contributions of Queer Women of Color that led to the creation of intersectionality invisible (see Combahee River Collective, 1977/1983). On the other hand, the approaches that post-intersectional scholars take to understand interlocking systems of power and oppression almost always resemble that of intersectionality (Dhamoon, 2011; May, 2015). Therefore, post-intersectionality repackages Crenshaw's (1989, 1991) framework but in its place moves away from its genealogies attached Women of Color feminism. In particular, Carbado (2013) argued that it obscures the labor of Black feminists and "is part of a larger ideological scene in which Blackness is permitted to play no racial role in anchoring claims for social justice (p. 814). Carbado's (2013) words thus serve as a reminder to post-intersectional thinkers to consider the epistemological ramifications that arise when reproducing similar forms of analysis without paying homage to intersectionality's genealogy. Nonetheless, one final concern that needs to be addressed is intersectionality's relationship with scholarship in queer studies that resists pre-determined social categories.

Intersectionality and Queerness: The Nature of Identity, Practices, and Politics

Despite the problematic nature of post-intersectional claims that sexuality is non-existent in intersectionality, this body of scholarship does bring up the question of how the field of intersectional studies relates to queer research. Specifically, queer studies diverge from intersectionality in some key ways, especially as it pertains to their epistemological foundations. According to Fotopoulou (2012), intersectionality proposes a systematic way to understand social oppression and identities while queer research has attempted to resist static categories of identity. Therefore, intersectionality might advance a perspective that differs from queer theory's poststructural view of identity as inherently fluid. Yet, intersectional scholars have challenged the notion that the framework treats identity as static entities (Collins & Bilge, 2016; Gedalof, 2013; May, 2015) and consequently, reject the belief that intersectionality is inherently at odds with queer studies. As Gedalof (2013) observed, identities "are not straightforward descriptions of pre-existing realities but are discursive constructs that continually produce the realities they claim to describe" (p. 119). When theorists understand identities not as fixed, but as discursive constructs, then the possibility for queer studies and intersectionality to exist in relationship with each other increases.

In fact, queer scholars and intersectional researchers have a great deal to learn from one another (Bilge, 2012; Christensen, 2018; Collins & Bilge, 2016; Duong, 2012; Olive, 2015; Rahman, 2010). In Bilge's (2012) chapter proclaiming a need for queer intersectionality, she wrote that queer studies can help intersectionality resist "neoliberal diversity mainstreaming" (p. 23). Bilge (2012) elaborated on this idea by stating that "queer must be understood as a political metaphor without a predetermined referent that serves to challenge institutional forces normalizing and commodifying difference" (p. 23). Queer studies can subsequently inform intersectionality because of its aims to challenge systems that create normative ways of being and that regulate identities deviating from the status quo. Similarly, Rahman (2010) underscored queer theory's challenge to universal ideas of identity, discussing the ways that power functions as a "disciplinary force in the construction of identities" (p. 952). Consequently, queer theory provides another vantage point of how power operates in society to marginalize others seen as deviant. These arguments thus open up the possibilities for intersectional scholars to continue to reimagine notions of political solidary and how power reinforces categories of identities. In doing so, intersectional theorists can incorporate queer studies' mission to oppose normalization in their research and practice.

In writing up the stories of the participants for this book, I thought critically about my use of intersectionality as a framework in the original study. In particular, I weighed what it meant to use intersectionality in lieu of other "intersectional" frameworks created to capture the realities of Queer People of Color like Queer of Color Critique (Ferguson, 2004) and Quare Theory (Johnson, 2001). Though each contribute different perspectives to matters of identity and the lives of Queer Students of Color (Duran, 2019d; Duran & Jackson, 2019), I came to understand how these bodies of scholarship can inform one another. As I elaborate on in Chapter Eight, I consider how intersectionality and queer frameworks could provide nuanced perspectives on how structures like racism and heterosexism posit Queer People of Color as deviant on college campuses, in addition to showcasing how these individuals remain resilient and practice agency despite these oppressive systems.

Conclusion

To move the study of college student development into the third wave requires that researchers carefully attend to the critical and poststructural schools of thought that they employ in their scholarship. In the case of the research I conducted with Queer Students of Color, I had to reflect thoroughly on my mobilization of intersectionality as a framework. How would I honor its histories? How do I attend to its focus on power and not reduce it to a theory of intersecting identities? How do I put it in conversation with queer studies? All of these questions circulated in my mind and continue to do so. Although I do not profess to have done this work perfectly, I offer my process so that others interested in doing work alongside Queer People of Color may consider similar issues. In particular, I return to these tensions and possibilities in Chapter Eight of this text, offering implications for intersectional theorizing in higher education.

2 Centering Queer Students of Color

Setting the Stage for the Study

Though college student development research on Queer People of Color is lacking, higher education scholars have progressively shone a light on the experiences that these individuals have on college campuses (Duran, 2019d; Duran et al., 2020; Lange et al., 2019; Rankin et al., 2019). This literature not only includes examinations of the lives of Queer People of Color at HWIs (e.g., Blockett, 2017; Duran, 2019b, 2019c; Goode-Cross, 2009; Goode-Cross & Tager, 2011; Harris, 2003; Holloman & Strayhorn, 2010; Mitchell & Means, 2014; Strayhorn, 2012a) but also attention to sites such as Historically Black Colleges and Universities (Mobley & Johnson, 2015; Mobley & Hall, 2020; Patton & Simmons, 2008) and Hispanic-Serving Institutions (Vega, 2016). Indeed, the field of higher education and student affairs has come a long way. Although Renn's, (2010) state of the field acknowledged a glaring omission of research on LGBT students of color, the academic scholarship on Queer Students of Color grew in subsequent years (see Duran, 2019d for a systemic literature review on the topic). However, important to note is that a shortage of research on Transgender Students of Color persists (see Garvey, Mobley, Summerville, & Moore, 2019; Jourian, 2017; Nicolazzo, 2016 for exceptions). This growing body of literature on Queer Students of Color has shown their unique realities on college campuses that warrant the attention of scholars and practitioners alike.

To help set the stage for the study at the heart of this text, I review the body of research that has emerged recently about Queer People of Color in higher education using themes that I discovered in a previous systematic literature review (Duran, 2019d). First, with intersectionality's focus on how structures of domination shape the lives of minoritized individuals, I survey the scholarship on the oppressive experiences that Queer Students of Color face at HWIs. Following this, I examine issues of institutional resources and representation for this demographic of students. Next, I describe the formative support networks that have been documented in the literature on Queer College Students of Color. I then honor intersectionality's attention to within-group differences (Dill & Zambrana, 2009) by bringing to light other salient identities that Queer

Students of Color may hold. With this foundation, I conclude this chapter with a brief overview of the research project that provided the data for this text.

Oppressive Experiences at Historically White Institutions

As stressed in the introduction to this text, HWIs have long legacies of racism (Museus, Ledesma, & Parker, 2015; Wilder, 2013) and heterosexism (Graves, 2009, 2018; Nash & Silverman, 2015). Hence, it comes as no surprise that these campuses can be particularly oppressive for students who hold multiple minoritized identities, including Queer Students of Color (e.g., Blockett, 2017; Harris, 2003; Strayhorn, 2012a; Strayhorn, Blakewood, & DeVita, 2010). Beyond experiencing marginalization on an institutional level, Queer Students of Color also face the manifestations of political intersectionality (Crenshaw, 1991) where they face exclusion from groups on campus dedicated to serving racially minoritized groups *or* queer communities. Namely, their status as multiply minoritized leads to marginalization in siloed identity groups (Duran, 2019c, Goode-Cross & Good, 2009; Strayhorn, 2013).

Oppressive Experiences on an Institutional Level

To begin, research has shown the minoritization that Queer Students of Color encounter while navigating HWIs (e.g., Blockett, 2017; Duran, 2019b, 2019c; Goode-Cross, 2009; Gresham, 2009; Harris, 2003; Holloman & Strayhorn, 2010; Mitchell & Means, 2014; Strayhorn, 2010, 2012a). One example of this can be seen in Blockett's (2017) research on Black queer men participating in a peer-support group at an HWI. Blockett (2017) documented how these Black queer men needed to labor in order to create a space of support within a larger institutional context that others those who are sexual minorities and People of Color. Describing a participant's reflection, Blockett (2017) noted that his "intersectional identities exist within a system of oppression that he explained promotes both white supremacy and heterosexual dominance" (p. 809). Because of interlocking systems of domination, these Black queer men reported feeling their identities and selves devalued at their institution.

Other scholars have underscored the issues that Queer People of Color have in attempting to navigate their intersectional identities in contexts that perpetuate racist and heterosexist norms (Duran, 2019b; Harris, 2003; Miller & Vaccaro, 2016; Strayhorn, 2012a, 2012b, 2013, 2014; Strayhorn et al., 2010). For instance, in a study on Queer Students of Color at a Midwestern predominantly white institution, Duran (2019b) shared how participants did not feel a sense of belonging and lacked a connection to their university because of the minoritization they experienced. Since they did not believe their intersecting identities were affirmed, these students were disconnected from their institution as a whole. Importantly, researchers communicate that the way that Queer Students of Color navigate their identities differs from their peers with only one of these minoritized identities (i.e., white queer students or Heterosexual People of Color). Harris (2003) communicated this point when she observed, " 'White privilege' provides white SGL [same-gender-loving] males with a 'coat of armor' that homosexual males of African descent are devoid of on PWCU [predominantly white colleges and university] campuses" (p. 48). Because Queer People of Color lack the privilege that their white queer peers or Heterosexual Individuals of Color have, they are exposed to unique forms of minoritization at HWIs, realities that people working on campuses must recognize.

Oppressive Experiences in Siloed Identity Groups

Beyond experiencing minoritization on an institutional level due to the presence of white supremacy and heterosexist ideologies, Queer Students of Color also must contend with the oppressive behaviors and attitudes they face within siloed identity groups. In particular, siloed identity groups capture communities on college campuses that are intended to serve a minoritized community, but that may consciously or unconsciously center those who hold other majority identities (e.g., heterosexual students in a group dedicated to the uplifting of Communities of Color). To describe the experiences that Queer People of Color face, Strayhorn (2013) depicted this phenomenon as being " 'betwixt and between' . . . two worlds, neither in which they were able to integrate fully" (p. 114). Put simply, Queer Students of Color are regularly disenfranchised because of the heteronormativity that may exist in Groups of Color or because of the racism that exists in queer organizations. In failing to attend to those with intersecting identities in siloed identity groups, these spaces engage in a process of intersectional erasure that makes invisible the needs of Queer People of Color.

To begin, queer spaces and organizations on college campuses have regularly been critiqued for their perpetuation of whiteness and white supremacy (Duran, 2019c; Duran & Pérez, 2017; Goode-Cross & Tager, 2011; Miller & Vaccaro, 2016; Vaccaro & Mena, 2011). For instance, students in Vaccaro and Mena's (2011) study on Queer Activists of Color commented that the queer student organization at their predominantly white institution seemed to reproduce the very systems present on campus as a whole. Namely, they felt underserved in the queer student group due to the presence of whiteness that undergirded the organization. Similarly, participants in Goode-Cross and Tager's (2011) research on African-American gay and bisexual men at a PWI noted that they were completely segregated from the white gay community on campus and "did not perceive the predominantly white LGBT community as a source of adequate support" because of the ways people in these spaces treated them (p. 1244). Evident from these examples, Queer Students of Color do not only experience being targeted because of their race on their campuses as a whole, but also in queer communities that would seemingly embrace them.

These sentiments of exclusion reported by Queer Students of Color are then often replicated in Communities of Color due to the heteronormativity that often permeates these groups (Goode-Cross, 2009; Goode-Cross & Good, 2008; Narui, 2011a, 2011b; Strayhorn, 2013; Strayhorn et al., 2010; Strayhorn & Mullins, 2012). For Asian/American gay, lesbian, and bisexual students in Narui's (2011b) research, for example, they shared how homosexuality was not often talked about or culturally accepted in Asian/American student organizations at the predominantly white institution they attended. In a like fashion, Black gay male students in Strayhorn and Mullin (2012) reported visual harassment or even physical altercations with other Black students in their residence halls. Necessary to state here, however, is that Communities of Color are not more inherently homophobic as some may argue but that the ways they position queer individuals as deviant stems from histories of conforming to standards of respectability created by white supremacy, as well as anti-Black racism (Clarke, 1983). Nevertheless, Queer Students of Color inevitably deal with these effects in siloed identity groups on campus.

(A Lack of) Resources and Representation for Queer People of Color

Beyond reporting experiences of minoritization on campus and in siloed identity groups because of interlocking systems of oppression, Queer Students of Color often have fewer resources available to them at higher education institutions (Duran & Pérez, 2017; Goode-Cross & Tager, 2011; Goode-Cross & Good, 2009; Harris, 2003; Johnson & Javier, 2017; Mitchell & Means, 2014; Squire & Mobley, 2015). As Johnson and Javier (2017) articulated, "Although campuses have made strides toward providing services for students of color or have created spaces for queer students, little to no effort has been made to best serve students at the intersections of these identities" (p. 2). Lacking an understanding of the needs of Queer People of Color, campuses offices regularly fail to program in ways that attend to these students.

For instance, LGBTQ Centers at higher education institutions have been the subject of criticism due to the fact that they uphold a veil of whiteness through their initiatives, hiring, and spaces (Johnson & Javier, 2017; Mitchell & Means, 2014). Consequently, Queer Students of Color rarely feel as though they can access resources in these centers and as though these services actually pertain to them. On a similar note, centers dedicated to racial groups also face similar challenges (Johnson & Javier,

2017) with scholars like Harris and Patton (2017) pointing to the difficulty of attending to students' intersectional identities due to a lack of funding provided to these offices. Even though Queer Students of Color would assume to find a place of affirmation in these spaces, these offices are still behind in their ability to support those with multiple minoritized identities.

Aside from identity centers, scholars have also pointed to the mental health challenges of Queer People of Color when they lack institutional resources and how campus counseling centers are ill-equipped to assist these students. Without having opportunities to explore their intersecting identities, Queer Students of Color can have negative mental health experiences (Strayhorn et al., 2010; Strayhorn, 2014; Vaccaro & Mena, 2011). Moreover, participants in Strayhorn et al.'s (2010) study on Black gay males at PWIs found that these individuals had a shortage of counseling services that could help them navigate their intersectional identities on campus. Findings such as these led Chan, Erby, & Ford (2017) to note that "college campuses have to be able to address the specific mental needs of QPOC, and college counseling centers and other college student personnel with counseling backgrounds have to be intentional in reaching QPOC" (p. 9). Yet, college counseling services still have a way to go before they reach a place where they can adequately support Queer People of Color.

Finally, Queer Students of Color not only report a shortage of resources dedicated to their intersecting identities, but they also indicate that higher education institutions lack a large representation of faculty and staff who identify as Queer People of Color (Aguilar & Johnson, 2017). This dearth in representation is concerning given the literature stating that Queer People of Color are more likely to feel connected to their institution if they have the ability to create relationships with those who hold similar identities (Goode-Cross & Tager, 2011; Strayhorn, 2012b). Without others who identify as Queer Individuals of Color on campus, students may lack guidance on how to navigate oppressive experiences or to process through important questions of identity (Vaccaro & Mena, 2011; Washington & Wall, 2010). Consequently, the issue of representation is another vital one that Queer Students of Color face, especially at HWIs.

Formative Support Networks in Higher Education

Though the scholarship on Queer Students of Color in higher education is rife with examples of how these individuals encounter adverse circumstances, it is vital to share that these people still maintain a sense of resilience despite these oppressive experiences (Duran, 2019c). Additionally, research shows that college campuses may be the first opportunity that Queer Students of Color have in order to ask crucial questions about their intersecting identities (Higgins, 2015; King, 2011; Strayhorn, 2013, 2014; Strayhorn, Blakewood, & DeVita, 2008). As Strayhorn (2014) communicated in his study on Korean American gay college students, postsecondary education was their initial chance to "live out" (p. 589) due to the heteronormative environments they had occupied prior. While on campus, Queer Students of Color are also often able to form valuable connections with peers, faculty, and staff, a pattern highlighted in the literature. Furthermore, student organizations may also themselves function as sources of support for these students.

As mentioned, peers, staff, and faculty on campus have the ability to provide crucial assistance to Queer Students of Color living out their identities on campus. Although I detailed previously the risk factors presented by siloed identity groups, some Queer Students of Color do develop formative relationships with those who only share one of their minoritized identities. For instance, literature has shown how white gay peers (Goode-Cross & Good, 2008; Strayhorn, 2013; Strayhorn et al., 2010; Strayhorn & Mullins, 2012) and Heterosexual Peers of Color (Strayhorn, 2013; Strayhorn & Mullins, 2012; Strayhorn & Tillman-Kelly, 2013) can be instrumental in the success of Queer People of Color. Aside from peers, researchers also point to the important connections that Queer Students of Color form with faculty and staff (e.g., Goode-Cross & Tager, 2011; Means & Jaeger, 2013; Strayhorn, 2012b), with some scholarship showing how Queer Individuals of Color develop chosen family relationships with higher education professionals (Duran & Pérez, 2017, 2019).

Beyond these more informal relationships with peers, faculty, and staff, the research on Queer Students of Color has also commented on the positive influences that student organizations (both identity-based and non-identity-based) can have in these individuals' lives. For instance, on the subject of identity-based student organizations, Queer People of Color across various studies do report developing support networks within groups that focus on issues of sexuality or on race/ethnicity (Goode-Cross, 2009; Goode-Cross & Good, 2008; Means & Jaeger, 2013; Narui, 2011a, 2011b; Strayhorn, 2012b; Strayhorn et al., 2010). Though singular identity groups may be limited in their ability to affirm those with multiple minoritized identities, some Queer Students of Color end up forming valuable relationships in these spaces. Additionally, the scholarship has investigated the benefits that Queer People of Color express when they become part of a student organization specifically dedicated to those minoritized at the intersections of race and sexuality (Duran, 2019b; Duran & Pérez, 2017; Miller & Vaccaro, 2016; Vaccaro & Mena, 2011; Vaccaro & Miller, 2017). Yet, Duran (2019b) also cautioned against seeing QPOC-student organizations as the end-all, be-all for Queer Students of Color as some of them may not connect with others due to personal interests.

Relatedly, researchers have also named interest-based student organizations as other places that Queer People of Color seek out in the search for support. Though Queer Students of Color in these studies still want their intersecting identities to be validated by others in the group, they also enjoy connecting with people based on their personal and professional interests (Carter, 2013; Chan, 2017; Duran, 2019b; Garcia & Duran, 2020; Harper, Wardell, & McGuire, 2011). One example of such a student group includes sororities and fraternities that create positive environments around matters of sexuality (Chan, 2017; Garcia & Duran, 2020; Harper et al., 2011). Importantly, not all fraternal cultures are affirming of queer individuals, but those that are can lead to the formation of positive relationships for Queer Students of Color.

The Within-Group Differences Present in Queer Communities of Color

One final theme that exists in the literature on Queer Communities of Color is that these students hold other salient identities that influence their lived realities. Queer Students of Color are thus not monoliths, an argument that Johnson and Javier (2017) advanced when they wrote, "Much of the discussion around QPOC is broad and generalizes all racial groups as if it is one unified community with the same challenges" (p. 4). Seeking to add complexity to the study of Queer People of Color, there has been an increase in research that investigates the within-group differences that are present in these communities by exploring how specific racial and sexuality intersections lead to differences in student outcomes (BrckaLorenz, Duran, Fassett, & Palmer, 2019; Garvey et al., 2019). In addition, research has also highlighted how salient identities like gender and religion may shape how Queer Students of Color navigate college campuses.

To begin, religion is a common topic that appears in literature about Queer Students of Color due to the potentially tense relationships that they hold with faith traditions (Poynter & Washington, 2005). Poynter and Washington communicated this reality when they stated, "Multiple-identity LGBT people have to contend with racism and religious intolerance from within the LGBT community and from homophobia within the various heterosexual minority and religious communities" (p. 44). Knowing this, it is not shocking to learn that religion frequently comes up as an influence that shapes how Queer People of Color think about their race and sexuality (e.g., Chan, 2017; Means, 2017; Means & Jaeger, 2015, 2016; Narui, 2011a, 2011b; Poynter & Washington, 2005; Strayhorn, 2012b; Strayhorn et al., 2010; Strayhorn & Tillman-Kelly, 2013). However, religion is not always a negative force in the lives of Queer People of Color. For instance, the work of Darris Means (2017) highlights how Black gay and bisexual male college students can participate in a reclaiming of their faith and actually find solace in their spirituality. Consequently, it is unfair to say that religious identity and contexts altogether produce turmoil for Queer Students of Color; instead, their faith experiences are themselves complex.

In addition to religion, gender identity also emerges as another identity of interest for Queer Students of Color. Specifically, the literature on Transgender Students of Color is few and far between with only a few of exceptions existing (Garvey et al., 2019; Jourian, 2017; Nicolazzo, 2016). Furthermore, only a small amount of research in higher education has focused on Queer Women of Color (e.g., Hughes, 2015; King, 2011; Patton & Simmons, 2008; Revilla, 2010; Vega, 2016). What this subset of scholarship does reveal is that Queer Women of Color contend with not only racism and heterosexism, but also the manifestations of patriarchal systems and sexism on campus (Revilla, 2010). For instance, Patton and Simmons' (2008) study on Black lesbian women at an HBCU shared that Queer Women of Color had to deal with the comments made by men who targeted them because of their gender, as well as sexuality. Although more perspectives on gender are needed, these studies showcase how considerations of gender identity must also be integrated in research about Queer People of Color.

Introducing the Study

With this scholarship on Queer Students of Color serving as a knowledge basis, I set out to engage in my dissertation research. Though more information on my study design can be found in the *Methodological Appendix* of this book, I see it important to offer a brief introduction to this project in order to set the stage for the subsequent chapters. Mentioned in the *Introduction* to this text, I was particularly interested in understanding how Queer Students of Color explored their intersectional identities at HWIs. Specifically, I used constructivist grounded theory (Charmaz, 2014) as the methodology to guide the research because my ultimate goal was to develop a theory that professionals in the field of higher education and student affairs could reference in order to guide their practice. Constructivist grounded theory thus made sense because it equips researchers with the ability to systematically analyze data and to generate a theory that explains how a social process (e.g., identity exploration) occurs (Charmaz, 2014).

After solidifying my process of interest and other significant study details, I needed to recruit participants who could speak to their experiences and the ways that they navigated matters of identity during their college years. I thus placed a call for participants on social media avenues like Facebook, Twitter, and Instagram. To my surprise, I had a great deal of interest with more than 40 individuals expressing their desire to participate. Of note, I had set 20 as the initial number of participants I wanted to recruit. With this pool of individuals, I then made decisions on who would be a part of the study. I employed what is referred to as maximum variation sampling (Mertens, 2015), a procedure that I used to compile a sample of individuals who represented different social identities and institutional types. Specifically, I wanted to avoid having a particular demographic overrepresented in the research. For instance, because the majority of research on Queer People of Color focuses on Cisgender Men of Color (Duran, 2019d), I did not want the same to be the case in this project. Thus, I paid attention to the sexualities, races, and other identities of people who expressed interest. Finally, because the role of context is central to constructivist grounded theory as well as intersectionality, I hoped to have different types of institutions in the sample. To make these determinations, I asked interested individuals to share whether they attended a public or private HWI, what geographic region in the country they were in, and how large the institution was. After trying out many different configurations, I selected the sample of 20 individuals. Although I will introduce these people more thoroughly in the stories I offer in the following chapters, I invite readers to see Table 2.1 for demographic information about these Queer Students of Color.

Following the selection of the participants, I held three individual interviews with each of them, together with engaging them in a reflection journal activity in between the first and second interview. Of note, both E and Mirella Blackwell discontinued their participation after the first interview due to time though they both consented to have their stories represented in the research. The conversations that I had with these 20 participants were inspiring and enriching, a point that I illustrate throughout the book. I reflected thoroughly on these interviews and reflection journals as I analyzed their stories, discovering how they all coalesced to provide a view on how Queer Students of Color explored their intersecting identities at HWIs. The result was a conceptual model detailing the process that Queer Students of Color undergo as a part of this identity exploration (See Figure 2.1).

And yet, I wanted these participants to be known beyond the model itself, leading me to write this text. In the chapters that follow, I capture some of the valuable insights that I gathered from these Queer Students of Color. I highlight topics like how manifestations of power shaped their identity exploration, how navigating their campuses allowed them to ask questions about identity, and what hopes they had for their futures. It is my desire that readers pick up their stories and use them to positively impact the lives of Queer People of Color as a way of honoring these participants' narratives.

Table 2.1 Participant Information (Disclosed on Demographic Form)

Pseudonym[1]	*Pronouns*	*Race & Ethnicity*	*Sexuality*	*Gender*	*Do you identify as having a disability?*	*Institutional Characteristics*	*Class Year*
Alejandro (Alejo)	he/him	Hispanic/Latinx – Salvadoran American	Bisexual	Man	No	Large public HWI in the Southeast	Fourth
Avery Demán	it/its[2]	Multiracial (Hispanic and white) – Mexican American	Gynysexual	Demi-femme	Anxiety and PTSD	Small public HWI in the Northwest	Fourth
Carmen	they/them	Mestiza - Mexican	Queer	Non-binary	Mentally ill	Large public HWI in the Mountain West	Third
Dash	she/her	Asian American - Korean	Queer	Woman	Able	Large public HWI in the Southwest	Sixth
E	they/them	Black – US and Nigerian	Pansexual	Non-binary	ADHD	Large private HWI in the Midwest	Fourth
Ezekiel	he/him	Latino – Mexican American	Gay	Cisman	*Left Blank*	Large public HWI in the Southwest	Third
gentle-breeze	she/her	Black and Asian – American and Japanese	Bisexual	Cis woman but also ???	Depression	Large private HWI in the Midwest	Third
John Doe	he/him	Black – African American	Bisexual	Man	N/A	Large private HWI in the Midwest	Third
Levix	he/him or they/them	Latino	Bisexual	Man	*Left Blank*	Large private HWI in the Southeast	Fourth

Max Aguirre	they/them	Latinx – Mexican	Queer	Gender fluid/ non-binary/ trans	ADHD	Large public HWI in the Midwest	Fourth
Mirella Blackwell	she/her	Black – African American	Demisexual	Woman	Anxiety	Small private HWI in the Southeast	Fourth
Ness	they/them	Asian American – Vietnamese	Pansexual	Non-binary	*Left Blank*	Large public HWI in the Southeast	Fourth
Oliver	he/him	Latinx	Gay	Cisman	N/A	Large public HWI in the Southwest	Fourth
Parker	he/him	Biracial (Filipino and white)	Gay	Man	No	Large public HWI in the Midwest	Third
Richard	he/him	Asian – Nepalese	Queer	Man	No	Large public HWI in the Southeast	Sixth
Rosa	she/her	Asian - Chinese	Bisexual	Ciswoman	No	Large public HWI in the Northeast	Third
Rose E.	she/her or they/them	Black – African American	Queer, bisexual	Black femme, Black woman	No	Large public HWI in the Southeast	Third
Sarah Ray	she/her	Black	Queer	Woman	No	Small public HWI in the Midwest	Third
TJ	she/her	Black – African	Asexual biromantic	Woman	No	Large public HWI in the Midwest	Third
Wren	he/him or they/them	African American - Black American/ Creole	Queer	Non-binary boy (boi)	*Left Blank*	Small public HWI in the Midwest	Fourth

1 Participants selected their pseudonym via the demographic form.

2 Throughout this book, I use it/its pronouns for Avery Demán. In particular, Avery's "more unconventional pronouns" (as it stated) allowed it to resist dominant norms pertaining to gender identity. Still, I acknowledge the potentially objectifying nature of referring to people using it/its and would encourage readers to practice pronoun usage that aligns with how people identify.

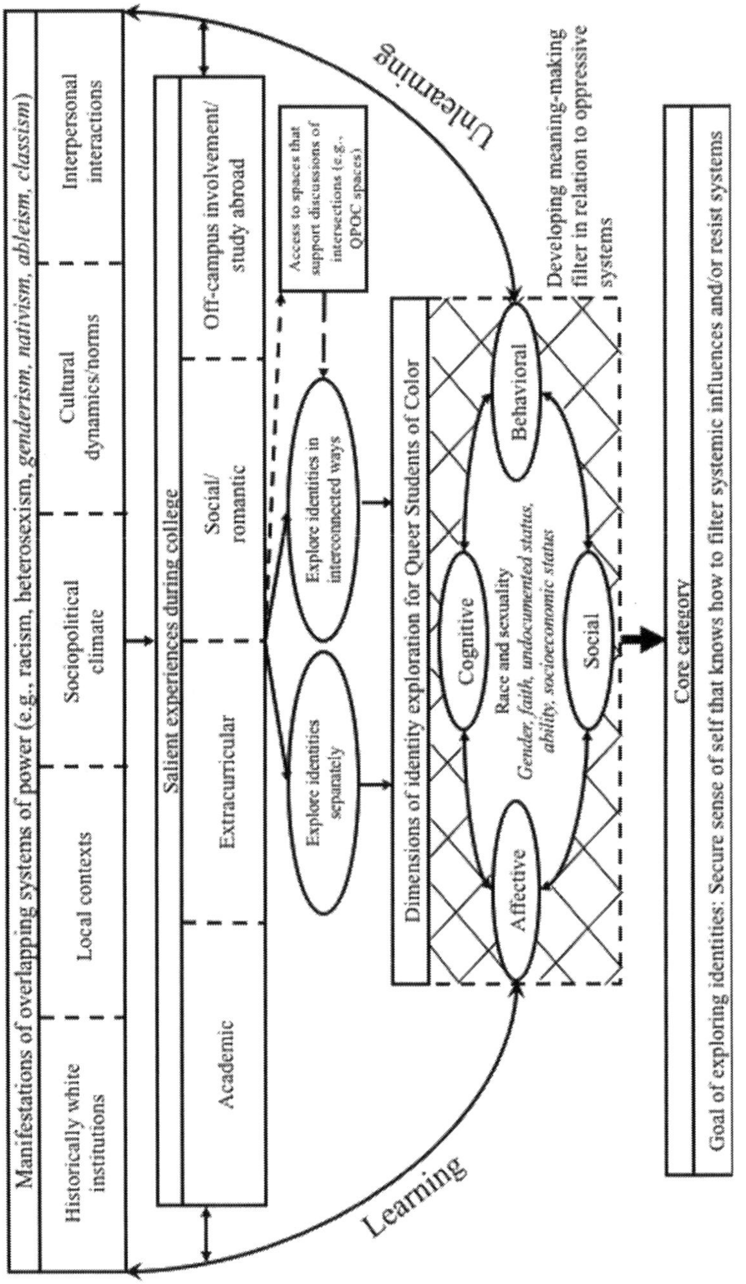

Figure 2.1 The Intersectional Model of Identity Exploration for Queer Students of Color

Conclusion

Research centering Queer People of Color continues to increase in higher education (Duran, 2019d; Duran et al., 2020; Lange et al., 2019; Rankin et al., 2019), showing the diversity of experiences that these students face on college campuses. A substantial amount of this scholarship focuses on Queer Students of Color enrolled at HWIs, showcasing the oppressive experiences they encounter and the vital supports they form despite this marginalization. However, those in higher education and student affairs still require more knowledge specific to student development for Queer Students of Color. As a result, the following chapters showcase how Queer Students of Color underwent significant developmental journeys as they navigated their intersecting identities at their HWIs.

Part 2

Exploring the Intersections

3 Intersectional Influences

Manifestations of Overlapping Systems of Power

Wren's Story

A person who always approached their decisions and life with intention, Wren was a fourth-year student majoring in sociology at a small public HWI located in the Midwest. Though this particular college was initially low on their list of schools to attend, the financial aid package was too good to pass up for Wren, leading them to visit the campus to see what it would be like to be a student there. Immediately, they noticed booths for organizations that illustrated what the campus would have to offer. Specifically, Wren recalled seeing a booth for the Gender and Sexuality Center on campus, as well as noticing Black-led booths as well. "Hoping some intersectionality would come from that," Wren began to feel more comfortable with the idea of attending this institution, as they believed that it was going to be a "pretty safe space" for them as an African American queer non-binary boi. However, when Wren arrived on campus in the fall of their first year, they encountered substantial issues that caused them to question the motives of those working at this HWI.

Wren came into college having gone to a predominantly white high school, an environment that caused them to feel "disconnected from other Black people." Therefore, Wren's journey at their HWI involved them wanting to explore their Blackness, as well as their queer identity. Though they initially sought out connections in student organizations that centered on queer issues, Wren eventually made the decision to leave these groups, growing "very, very, very wary of white spaces." As Wren described it, they had unknowingly become the token Black person in white queer activist communities, which caused them to think critically about how anti-Blackness manifested in their life. Commenting on this experience, Wren shared that they had developed a "weird and disgusting feeling of pride" in being one of the few Black bodies among white activists. To put it plainly, Wren stated, "It was pride of being Black but only because of being close to whiteness and white people in these cases." This moment of revelation caused Wren to seek connections with other Queer People of Color as they disinvested in their relationships with white people.

Connecting with other Queer People of Color proved to be invaluable for Wren: "I think my friendships with Queer People of Color have really been this space of growth for me, and just being able to discuss certain things that we all have in common, that has been a good space for me, as the person that I am." Notably, Wren acknowledged that these informal friendships were more positive for their identity than any "institutionalized space." In fact, it was the conversations they had with other Queer People of Color that challenged Wren to think critically about the role that institutions played in their life. In going on this journey of exploration, Wren gained the awareness and language to challenge how structures like those present at their college existed to oppress queer Black bodies like theirs.

As Wren spoke about their HWI, they shared how they felt a sense of "heaviness" moving through a campus that did not care about them. Wren stated that the institution itself was "very impersonal," making students "feel like they're a commodity for the school." Though they initially saw messaging communicating that the HWI cared about minoritized populations, they quickly realized that this was "inauthentic." In essence, Wren felt commodified by their institution, an experience they "tied to colonialism and capitalism specifically." Their body was desirable to the HWI, a reality that caused Wren to distrust the campus.

This snippet of Wren's story showcases the journey they experienced during their years as a college student. My conversations with Wren were always thought-provoking, as they shared the ideas that they had been working through relative to how power functioned in society and on campus. Notably, they had a seemingly heighted sense of awareness about the ways that dominant groups perpetuated oppressive ideologies and systems. For instance, it was not unsurprising to hear Wren share how they perceived colonialism, capitalism, and anti-Black racism to be at play within their collegiate environment. Beyond simply seeing these structures of domination manifest, however, Wren also articulated how they had to resist internalizing these influences as they once did in high school. It is in this recognition that this first theme comes to light.

In my conversations with the Queer Students of Color in this research project, they described how they saw systems of power like racism and heterosexism (among others) manifesting in five different sites: (a) their HWIs; (b) the local contexts in which their HWI was situated; (c) in the sociopolitical discourse; (d) in the cultural dynamics and norms they encountered in queer communities and Groups of Color; and (e) their interpersonal interactions with faculty, staff, and peers. Yet, what is unique about their comments is that they not only stated how they experienced these oppressive influences, phenomena already documented in the literature (e.g., Blockett, 2017; Duran, 2019b, 2019c; Goode-Cross, 2009; Gresham, 2009; Harris, 2003; Holloman & Strayhorn, 2010;

Mitchell & Means, 2014; Strayhorn, 2010, 2012a). Instead, these Queer Students of Color articulated how these structural inequalities influenced their exploration of their identities. In the following sections, I expand on each of these sites and how they shaped how Queer Students of Color explored their identities like race and sexuality.

Historically White Institutions

In my initial interview with John Doe, he spoke about how he experienced his institutional environment as perpetuating white ideals, feeling excluded on the basis of his Black bisexual identities. When I asked him to speak about the influence this had on how he saw his intersecting identities, John Doe shared, "I am what I am because of the institution I attend." John Doe's short, but important, comment points to the salient ways that HWIs shaped how Queer Students of Color navigated and explored their identities on campus. Even more specifically, participants mentioned how they noticed racism, heterosexism, and other oppressive systems manifesting at the institutional level that in turn, informed how they saw their worth and sense of self on campus. Namely, they noted the feelings of exclusion felt because of the campus climate, the lack of funding and recruitment efforts for minoritized populations, together with an overall erasure of Queer People of Color in student affairs initiatives and in classroom spaces.

Campus Climate for Queer People of Color

As a whole, the Queer Students of Color in this study saw the campus climates at their HWI to be largely white and heteronormative, which in turned influenced how they viewed their own identities. For instance, Parker attended a large public HWI which had a reputation of catering to an affluent student body. When I asked about his experiences at the institution, he shared, "Being a non-white person at [the institution], you can see a lot of racism occurring throughout the years. . . . The institution and the people in it, and the cultural local context here, is definitely a major influence on how racism and heterosexism plays out." Specifically, Parker pointed to the students themselves as the main perpetrators of racist ideologies, believing that they punished those who were "open about who they are." In hearing this, I asked Parker to comment on how this environment may have informed his own identities as someone who was biracial and gay. He commented:

> It definitely limits how I can explore my identity and how other people can explore their identities, because yeah . . . it's always nice to hear that the people who run [the institution] are trying, but it's not

> comforting when the people around you are causing fear, or uneasiness, or just any negative feeling about it.

In Parker's statement, he once again emphasized how his peers pushed back against those who were different, playing a substantial role in how he perceived his own minoritized identities. Even though the institution did display a desire to create resources for diverse populations, Parker still felt the effects of a student body that upheld standards of whiteness and that were heteronormative, limiting his attempts of exploration. Other participants shared similar perspectives to Parker on the oppressive attitudes of students at HWIs. Ezekiel, for example, attended a HWI in the Southwest and also perceived the same exclusionary behaviors that Parker saw at his HWI: "I just think it's a campus-wide groupthink thing that if you perform your identities in other ways than what we have heard already then it's not a welcoming environment." In their largely homogenous student bodies, Queer Students of Color inherently felt othered and targeted for their social identities.

Nevertheless, it is imperative to acknowledge that these oppressive ideologies were not only a product of the student body, but that participants saw these issues manifesting on an institutional level as well. Rose E. conveyed this reality as she spoke about the large public HWI that she attended. In her third year at the time of the interviews, Rose E. commented on how she had experienced the institution's president refusing to denounce a racist campus act, the presence of conservative speakers giving lectures, and an overall lack of Black individuals (i.e., staff, faculty, and students) at the HWI. All of these led Rose E. to assert that the institution was complicit in racism, a disappointing fact because Rose E. initially expected the HWI to be affirming: "They tell you when you first get here about the resources you have available, how you get treated, you'll get respected and all these different things." This sharp realization that Rose E. experienced on campus led her to assert that the institution did not value her and her identities. Specifically, Rose E. noted,

> It always makes you question, "How much do you really value me being here? And what does me being here do for you?" It makes me think 'bout how the world perceives me based on my race, how the world engages with me, particularly at institutions themselves.

The practices that the institution perpetuated played a role in how Rose E. viewed herself, a concerning reality for those hoping to support Queer Students of Color. Like Rose E., Levix also regarded his Catholic HWI as perpetuating heterosexism since they actively pushed against any "mainstream understanding of sexuality and identities." Levix, in particular, offered an example of when the HWI did not speak out against a conservative student organization that furthered anti-queer and -trans messages on campus. Levix then remarked that this had a significant influence on how he thought of his place at the institution: "I mean in general, I can't turn to the institution to help me think about my identities. . . . I have to look more internally, look to personal relationships and discussions I have with friends." What comments such as Levix' underscore is that how these students encountered racism and heterosexism then affected this vital process of identity exploration.

Funding and Recruitment for Minoritized Populations

Beyond commenting on campus climates broadly, Queer Students of Color also observed oppressive ideologies manifesting in the ways that the institution funded and recruited minoritized populations, or rather, the lack of effort behind these practices. Though I initially (and perhaps naively) did not expect these individuals to talk about the connections between funding and their identity exploration, this was a comment that manifested across participants like Alejo, Carmen, Ezekiel, Max, Ness, Oliver, Richard, and Wren. Notably, most of these statements were contextualized by students noting a reduction of budgets for services on campuses dedicated to underserved groups. Ezekiel spoke specifically to this phenomenon as he started to notice programs designed for minoritized communities disappearing at his HWI:

> If you get rid of Latino Student Services, Native American Student Services, Asian-American/Pacific Islander Student Services, and LGBTQ lounge, and the gender and equality center then you're basically saying, "Oh, your guys' identities don't matter. You're not important enough for us to continue to fund."

In this statement, Ezekiel captured the sentiments of many Queer Students of Color in this study. For instance, Max noted how the land-grant institution they attended in the Midwest "doesn't really formally engage in the LGBTQ Center and gives [them] a very small amount of money that doesn't make up a quarter of the budget." Like Max and Ezekiel, Carmen noted how at their public institution "the different cultural and diversity centers are funded the least," which led to them feeling "forgotten" on campus.

However, this lack of funding also extended into the academic programs at these HWIs. For instance, Oliver felt particularly dismayed at the fact that the Mexican American studies major that he cared about was almost disbanded at the Southwestern HWI he attended. When I probed about how he made sense of this relative to his own perceptions of his identities, Oliver stated the following: "It made me feel like, because of having these identities, there wasn't really a space for me. It made me feel like all the school wants from me is my money and that's it." By failing to provide the necessary resources to support the identity exploration of these Queer Students of Color, these individuals felt the same sense of commodification that Wren commented on in the introductory vignette to this chapter.

Relatedly, these participants also critiqued their HWI's recruitment efforts, as they rarely saw other people who held similar identities to them. This lack of representation then had deleterious effects on their identities, for as Carmen observed,

> And so, it makes you feel invisible in a way. But, I think it just makes it more complicated to truly accept yourself in all identities and also which one do I focus on. 'Cause, like, do I focus on me being a brown person during this time, especially, at a really white campus, in a really white city. Or, do I focus on me being queer here, or, how do I focus on both?

In this excerpt, Carmen asserted the following: by nature of the interlocking systems of oppression at the institution and the shortage of people who identified as Queer Individuals of Color, they felt as though they must select one salient identity (i.e., their race *or* sexuality) to focus on at a time. These sentiments were even replicated when these participants saw individuals who shared one of their minoritized identities. For example, Rose E. stated,

> I think also, at a PWI, sometimes you feel that, or at least I feel that . . . I know there's more QTPOC people, but I feel that a lot of the LGBTQ people that show up and show out are not QTPOC, so I wish we had more diverse of a campus here too.

What Rose E. emphasizes that it is not enough to think about identities in monolithic ways, because she still felt disconnected from groups that only attended to one aspect of her identities. Thus, institutional agents at HWIs needed to attend to students' intersecting identities in matters of representation and funding when attempting to combat oppressive systems.

Intersectional Erasure in Programming and Curricula

One final way that systems of power manifested in the lives of Queer Students of Color navigating HWIs involved the nature of what was covered in academic coursework, as well as in student affairs programming. Notably, participants observed the intersectional erasure of Queer

Communities of Color in courses that did and did not focus on matters of identity. For example, Avery shared how even in classes designed to talk about social groups, they rarely attended to within-group differences that exist within communities. Avery elaborated on this observation by noting,

> But especially in the anthropology classes where it's all about culture and life like that, that would be a really good time to express that like hey, this is what it's like for this kind of group. This is how they're marginalized. . . . You get by so far with just talking about things and just not letting it be the silent elephant in the room.

Referring to multiply minoritized people as the "silent elephant in the room," Avery struggled with the lack of representation they saw in classes that, in theory, would allow them to broach important questions of identity.

However, these intersectional failures also extended to instructors who approached teaching from an identity-neutral standpoint. Dash provided this perspective when she reflected on her experiences as a math and meteorology double major at her HWI. In talking with Dash, she disclosed to me, "I feel like meteorology classrooms are all about the science and all about focusing on that and not focusing on basically anything else, just focusing straight up on what you're learning and stuff." Like Dash, Richard also perceived instructors in his STEM major to be overlooking the role that students' identities play in their experiences in and outside of the classroom: "I don't think they help or center on anyone's identities. And I never got a chance to take any classes that were more able to delve into such stuff like that." Though academic spaces can be one way that students explore their identities, a reality further explored in Chapter Four, these participants believed that instructors and educators were missing out on vital opportunities to assist people with minoritized identities.

This type of experience also manifested in student affairs offices on campus designed for minoritized individuals. In my conversations with Avery, it shared a particular poignant reading of this reality. Thinking about its exploration of its intersecting identities at its small public HWI, Avery commented, "We do have a QPOC week on campus where both identities meet but that's around the only time I see that kind of happen and coincide today." In this statement, Avery implicates both the LGBTQ center and diversity affairs office as failing to attend to its race and sexuality on any other week other than one that occurred in the year. When prompted to identify the potential effects this had on how it viewed its identities, Avery mentioned, "It makes me feel like I have to pick and choose. Like I can't be authentically myself because both parts play a role in who I am. . . . And it adds to the fight of how to identify in everyday situations." Because student affairs offices failed to attend to the needs of multiply minoritized individuals, they limited the places where Queer Students of Color could go to in order to seek out advice related to identities. This pattern appeared time and time again with individuals questioning identity centers on campus and their ability to assist in their exploration.

Local Contexts

Nevertheless, HWIs were not only the only places where Queer Students of Color reported the presence of racist, heterosexist, and other oppressive norms. Of particular interest, participants also discussed how the local towns and cities where they attended college also played a role in their identity exploration process. This phenomenon was especially salient for those who attended college in the South – Alejo, Dash, Ezekiel, Levix, Mirella Blackwell, Ness, Oliver, Richard, and Rose E. – who reported fearing the oppressive beliefs held by some in the surrounding area. Rose E. explained this by stating that "social exploration looks different for Queer People of Color in the South versus in the North or the West." An example of this came up in my first interview with Mirella Blackwell, a Black demisexual woman enrolled at a small private HWI in the South. In particular, Mirella Blackwell shared,

> Being in the south it's still kind of scary to just be open because there have been a few people on campus who are open about not accepting that kind of thing. They'll say that they think it's wrong or that it shouldn't happen.

Expanding upon this comment, Mirella commented that she "wouldn't try to date a girl" anytime soon because of the potential homophobia that she would face, especially as a Black individual.

Though this was possibly heightened for those who attended school in the South, participants across different geographic regions oftentimes drew a distinction between their institutional environment and the local context. In fact, numerous students used the language that their HWI represented a "bubble" from the town or city. As a queer Asian woman, for instance, Dash stated that the town she lived in was different in its acceptance of these identities than her HWI:

> So yeah, living in that, it makes you, at least in the local community, not always feel comfortable with being out. And not in the sense that you're not proud, but in the sense of for your own safety, I guess, just 'cause there's a lot of things, like a lot of people say things, a lot

> of people will suggest certain things, and that kind of can sometimes stunt your exploration or stunt your ability to grow and move past, because of fear and other factors.

Though Dash was more comfortable with sharing her sexuality as a queer Asian woman on campus, she felt more limited in doing so when she left the collegiate space because of the heterosexism she perceived. In addition, other participants like Wren mentioned the racism they noticed in their surrounding context. Namely, Wren referenced a number of anti-Black instances (like the constant blaming of robberies on Black people), which in turn caused them to say, "Being in that environment, it's hard to find spaces where you can . . . hard to find spaces that really help you grow if that makes sense." Undoubtedly, Queer Students of Color were subject to racism and heterosexism as they navigated their identities off of campus, serving as another influence in their exploratory journeys.

Sociopolitical Climate

In addition to implicating the spaces they moved through, these participants also commented on the sociopolitical discourses tied to their identities as another way that oppressive systems shaped their experiences. Important to note is that I conducted this research in the Fall of 2018, meaning that these students had been through the 2016 presidential election in their college years. Based on the ways that the 2016 election served as a catalyst for racist, heterosexist, nativist, sexist, transphobic, and other oppressive manifestations of power, students had more trepidations in exploring their minoritized identities. At their HWI, for instance, Max mentioned how "shit got bad" with people having "no shame" about their oppressive behaviors. In fact, in one of the most harrowing moments I shared with a participant, Max disclosed that they were once sent a picture of President Trump, complete with imagery of the KKK and a burning cross. Though they never found out who sent it, they knew it was "extremely identity based," which made them fear for their safety. Thus, Max had to be careful in seeking out spaces where they could explore their identities.

Other Queer Students of Color shared how they felt wary when they would encounter people who supported President Trump or who wore symbols associated with his presidency. Parker was in his first year at his HWI in the Midwest when the election occurred. During this time, he was particularly cognizant of those who wore red Make America Great Again hats:

> Me exploring my own identities during this current political climate has definitely made me very cautious almost, because if I see someone

> wearing a red hat I'm like, "Oh, shit. There they go. They probably voted for. . . . No. They definitely voted for Trump, but are they homophobic? Racist? Sexist?" Whatever.

In a similar fashion, TJ discussed how at her Midwestern HWI, she paid attention to which classmates expressed support for the president. TJ expressed that President Trump's presidency dissuaded her from being too open about her sexuality, given that she was already oppressed on her visible Black identity:

> It's definitely made me more vigilant, just because I see a lot of, well not a lot but more than I would like to see, support for the current president, so that tells me who to stay away from and makes me . . . I don't know, it kind of makes me loath to explore the intersection because I already feel like a potential target due to my race. I don't want to add sexuality onto that.

Because TJ already encountered anti-Black racism, the sociopolitical discourse surrounding Trump's presidency made her less likely to be open about her asexual biromantic identity, fearing the potential marginalization that may ensure from this disclosure.

Of note, Carmen and Oliver were two participants who expressed a heighted awareness of this sociopolitical climate given their undocumented and DREAMer statuses, respectively. More than any other event, Carmen asserted that the 2016 presidential election was the most significant time that shaped their perception of themselves as a Queer Person of Color. As Carmen described, "I didn't feel safe, I didn't feel safe sharing my identity as being queer or my identity as being undocumented." Because of the racist nativism perpetuated in conjunction with the heterosexism Carmen observed, they were cautious about sharing their identities with others:

> So, it made me want to hide again, and I think it took a little bit longer . . . to be able to say, "Oh, like, this is who I am." I feel like it made me take steps back to what I was doing from my freshman year.

Like Carmen, Oliver noted "the federal, national level telling people 'we don't want you and you don't belong,'" leading him to feel "especially targeted." Oliver was consequently hesitant to talk about his DREAMer status with others. As seen in these narratives, the sociopolitical climate was an oppressive influence in the lives of Queer Students of Color, but it was especially harmful for those who encountered the effects of racist nativism.

Cultural Dynamics/Norms

The fourth site in which oppressive ideologies manifested in the lives of Queer Students of Color and then had negative effects on their exploration involved the minoritized communities in which they held social group membership. Echoing the experiences that Crenshaw (1991) noted in regards to political intersectionality, these participants encountered marginalization in groups intended to serve queer individuals and in Communities of Color. To begin, individuals often brought up the fact that queerness is rendered invisible in Communities of Color, causing them to hide this part of themselves. Richard conveyed this point when he reflected on sexuality in Asian American communities:

> Well, I would say that the Asian cultural norms that I associate with, queerness kinda just doesn't exist. It's not even talked or thought about or put into play. That is a huge suppression where it's just not there. It's just like this doesn't exist. It's just not talked about or even seen.

Because of how queerness was erased in the Asian American spaces Richard was a part of, he believed it "took longer" for him to explore what it meant to be a queer Asian individual. TJ also mentioned how she perceived Black culture as not acknowledging the presence of queer individuals. It is not that TJ saw Black communities as disparaging queerness, but rather, she stated, "It's just like it's not something you do." Because of the ways that queerness was not spoken about in the Black communities she navigated, TJ saw it as "not having acceptance . . . so that kind of made me put a damper on exploring it because of that."

These experiences then translated to their campus contexts. For example, Ness referenced the Asian American student organizations they were involved with as perpetuating "very much cis-heteronormativity." As Ness described it, "I could feel that heterosexual energy when I walked into culture org meetings. . . . In that space, I didn't feel welcome as a queer person." Rose E. reported a similar sentiment in Black spaces at their HWI, feeling encouraged to "put your Blackness first" while erasing their queer identity. Though Ezekiel indicated the same reality about Latinx communities on his own campus, he cautioned people from seeing this as an issue inherent to Communities of Color: "I think maybe POC have been so policed by white communities that they . . . basically reinforce that whole, like, policing and self-governing thing." Because of the ways that whiteness dictates respectability politics in Communities of Color, these Queer Students of Color reported encountering heteronormative ideals in these spaces.

Yet, these participants noted that the same within-group marginalization manifested in queer communities as well. Ness stressed this point when they talked to me about the whiteness that permeates queer spaces and groups:

> The whiteness of what I would consider queer culture has jarred me in a lot of senses. Every face I see on media that is LGBT is white. I didn't feel LGBT enough because I kept seeing white faces, and sometimes even the individualized actions of what is considered "queer culture" quote unquote, they're very much things I would never see myself doing out of shame, or something? But I see queer white people doing them all the time, so I'm like, "Okay, that's probably a white thing to do."

Because of the fact that the "white queer community can be super reductive" to People of Color, Ness had to contend with how whiteness informed how they thought about their Vietnamese identity. However, Ness was not the only one who had this experience.

Parker was another person who felt deeply how racism manifested in queer communities, influencing his perceptions of his biracial identity. Parker indicated that others had rejected him on dating apps such as Grindr simply because he was biracial (white and Filipino). Parker conveyed the impact it had on himself: "I just self-deprecate more than I usually do . . . it just makes me feel like I wish I wasn't who I was. Whether it was . . . I wish I was all white or I wish I was not gay or both." Parker's statements struck me, showcasing how Queer Students of Color experienced the harmful effects of racism within communities that seemingly should accept them.

Interpersonal Interactions

Queer Students of Color in this research lastly spoke about the interpersonal interactions they had on campus, in which they were the subject of microaggressions and other oppressive comments. In these instances, Queer College Students of Color had to reconcile the messages shared by higher education professionals or peers with their own views of self. Several participants discussed how they had faculty who themselves perpetuated oppressive messages. For instance, Oliver recalled an instructor they had for one of their history classes. In particular, this faculty member would always tokenize Oliver, asking him to represent the beliefs of all Latinx individuals:

> There was always this thing where if anybody who was Latinx was brought up . . . I remember at the time Marco Rubio was running

> for office. When he would mention anything that related to Latinos and whatnot, he would immediately go to me and be like, "What's your opinion?"

Understandably, Oliver felt extremely uncomfortable in these moments contrasting it to the sentiments of pride he had in his Mexican American studies courses. In this history classroom environment, Oliver remembered thinking, "Why am I being called out, isolated, right now?"

Unfortunately, numerous participants could point to a particular faculty member that furthered racist and/or heterosexist logics in class. Sarah Ray offered another example of this when she talked about a theater class she had with a white gay instructor. Though the course was largely comprised of white people, the instructor had them sing spirituals specific to the Black community: "He thought that because he was gay, he could do no harm to People of Color. And there was this thing where the choir is singing Negro spirituals." Though Sarah Ray herself tried to educate the faculty member on why this was problematic, he did not listen to her. Sarah Ray then described how this shaped the view she had of her own self as a member of the class and a student at the HWI: "But, it's still difficult, 'cause I'm like, I don't want these horrific experiences to shape my understanding of my identity, but I know that they are. . . . Cause he's like, 'I have more power than you.' " In this reflection, Sarah Ray explicitly calls attention to how the instructor exercised his power as a white man despite also identifying as queer, which inevitably influenced how she saw herself.

Aside from faculty, Queer Students of Color could also name peers who microagressed them on the basis of their race, as well as their sexuality. For instance, white students at Carmen's HWI would target them by telling Carmen comments like, "Say little things [in Spanish]." These statements made Carmen feel extremely uncomfortable. In further debriefing these comments with Carmen, they noted, "It makes me feel kind of shameful. . . . It makes me feel ashamed that I'm a Person of Color or that I'm an immigrant or things like that." These interactions caused discomfort for Carmen, leading them to retreat and to avoid disclosing their Mexican identity to others. Avery also experienced microaggressions, offering an example of a time when someone called it out for being "too gay." Avery divulged that this was a short statement that had a powerful impact on how it thought about its identities:

> That one was a surprisingly hurtful one ["too gay"]. Even at the institution, I've had that too where I feel like I'm being silenced or just being told to tone it back. I get that a lot where it's like, "It's really great what you bring to the table, but we were hoping you could just dial it back. Don't be quiet, just dial it back."

Racist and/or homophobic microaggressions like the ones reported by Avery and Carmen had a profound influence on how secure they were in displaying and exploring their identities at HWIs.

Reflections on Identity

Employing an intersectional lens (Crenshaw, 1989, 1991) to view the stories of these Queer Students of Color reveals vital novel reflections on the nature of identity for these individuals. Because many theories on social identity development originate in fields outside of education, they lack specific mention of how collegiate environments shape identity (Patton et al., 2016). This is especially concerning given that it has been decades since Knefelkamp et al. (1978) encouraged student development theorists to understand how colleges "encourage or inhibit" growth (p. x). The narratives and analysis provided previously thus serve as an intervention in the student development literature by offering specific examples of how HWIs inform identity.

Specifically, the students in the study articulated that HWIs perpetuate oppressive practices, policies, and structures that negatively influenced their identity exploration. Therefore, when approached from a viewpoint attentive to the role of power and oppression, colleges are not altogether positive in the developmental journeys of students. Of note, Queer Students of Color contended with overlapping axes of oppression as they explored their intersectional identities at HWIs. By bringing to light how systems of power shaped their realities, this chapter showcases the potential that third wave frameworks have to push the study of college student development and identity forward (Abes, 2016; Abes et al., 2019; Jones & Stewart, 2016).

However, what was also made clear by the participants is that racism, heterosexism, and other forms of oppression were also present in their local contexts and in identity groups present off campus. Consequently, these Queer Students of Color also experienced the impression of these sites as they engaged in matters of exploration. As Duran and Jones (2019a) argued, third wave student development theorists must expand their analyses of contextual influences beyond college campuses, recognizing how other environments impact identity considerations. This chapter hence contributes to the field of higher education and student affairs' understanding of identity by shedding a light on the oppressive structures both at and beyond HWIs that have a bearing on how Queer Students of Color view themselves.

Conclusion

For Queer Students of Color navigating HWIs, manifestations of racism, heterosexism, and other forms of oppression are omnipresent. Whether it is recognizing the intersectional erasure that occurs in curricula/programming or in the ways that funding operates, Queer College Students of Color receive messaging devaluing their identities. These forces inevitably affect how able these individuals feel to broach important questions of identity during these formative college years. Additionally, they contend with these same oppressive systems outside of the collegiate environment. These stories serve as a call for those working on campuses to take intentional steps to address the manifestations of structural inequalities in order to assist Queer Students of Color attending HWIs.

4 Navigating Historically White Institutions and Beyond

The Role of Salient Experiences During College

Ness' Story

An individual who paved the way for other queer Asian American individuals on their campus and who was increasingly growing into the label of "student activist," Ness was in their fourth year studying biochemistry at a large public HWI in the Southeastern region of the United States. When searching for colleges, Ness believed that they did not have many options on where to attend, not having performed strongly in their academics as a high school student. This reality, tied with their limited financial aid, led them to search for a school in the state where they grew up. Their selection process was "haphazard," according to Ness, having never visited any campuses where they applied. In the end, they selected their institution because they knew many people from their high school enrolled at the other large state university, wanting to avoid clinging to the friends they had made previously.

Before their first year at college, they had rarely given thought to their social identities. Ness remarked, "I knew I was some kind of label under the LGBTQ umbrella in high school, and I identified as Asian American, Vietnamese American, but I didn't really put a specific purpose to those labels before high school." Thus, they had not searched online or in-person for any resources dedicated to these communities before starting at their university. It was not until they attended an event for first-year queer students that they realized how white the institution and the queer communities on campus were: "It's most likely because I saw that everyone, pretty much 90% of the people there were white and had this sense of humor that I couldn't click with." This awareness led them to feel "kind of empty" after this instance. However, in February of their first year, Ness learned of a student organization specifically dedicated to Queer and Trans People of Color, which changed their trajectory.

Although the group was small, this space motivated Ness to learn more about their identities: "I think being around them really sparked my interest in queer studies. Not necessarily just queer studies, but just exploring my queer identity." The following years saw Ness getting more and more involved with identity-based movements on campus, including Asian American groups as well. However, it was not until they attended Creating Change, a conference that dealt with queer issues, that they thought more critically about what it meant to be a pansexual, non-binary Vietnamese person specifically. This was because they took part in Asian American workshops that encouraged them to "do critical thinking of what it means to be both Asian American and queer at the same time." Though the QTPOC organization allowed them to reflect on issues facing those who were both racial and sexual minorities broadly, their time at Creating Change challenged them to focus in on the unique experiences they faced as someone who was Asian American, as well as pansexual and non-binary.

Following this experience, Ness was driven to continue to learn more about the intersections between queerness and their Asian American identity. Specifically, as an executive board member of both an Asian American organization and the QTPOC group, Ness took the initiative to learn about the histories tied to their identities. Ness commented that a lot of this work had to be individual given the lack of classes at their HWI that centered on these identities. Their commitment to these issues led to their reputation as a strong advocate and activist. Although they did not find many others at their institution who were like them, lacking the ability to "cultivate a big enough Asian space" on campus, they still maintained strong connections to the people they met at the Creating Change conference. These relationships, as well as their continued learning, assisted Ness in furthering the exploration of their identities.

Ness' experiences moving through their HWI showcases how one's college years can serve as a spark for identity exploration. For instance, Ness arrived on campus their first year having reflected very little on their minoritized identities. Though they recognized that they were part of the queer community and that they were Asian American, they associated very little meaning to these labels. As Ness started to get more involved on campus, the relationship that they had with their identities quickly changed. In fact, Ness' story exemplifies major patterns that emerged across each of the Queer Students of Color. That is, several collegiate experiences existed that were particularly salient to these students' identity exploration, allowing them to ask important questions about their social groups.

Although the preceding chapter communicated how HWIs and other sites perpetuated oppressive ideologies that shaped how Queer Students of Color explored their identities, these individuals also commented on the potential that experiences had if they affirmed their intersecting identities. Of note, they discussed how they theorized identity in curricular spaces, as well as in their co-curricular involvement. Additionally, the social and romantic relationships they formed during their college years were similarly formative to their exploration. Finally, Queer Students of Color highlighted how off-campus involvement opportunities, as well as study abroad participation, were also helpful. Ultimately, the following sections reveal the benefits that result when collegiate experiences validate students' multiple minoritized identities.

Curricular Experiences

One of the first places that Queer Students of Color learned about their identities were the classes they took on campus. When instructors constructed their courses to allow for this exploration, participants experienced the ability to interrogate the meanings they attributed to their race and sexuality. For example, though Max faced numerous instances where they felt out of place at their HWI, they felt embraced in particular classes where they could read about minoritized communities: "I think being at a large research institution that's also extremely academically competitive I feel like my exploration was definitely influenced by that kind of academia culture, and that a lot of it is started with the classroom." Similarly, Ness acknowledged how they had appreciated learning about their intersecting identities through their academics despite having few changes to do so:

> Yeah I think a really instrumental part of having, exploring identity, having spaces be much more affirming to our generalized identities is having that institutional support through academia. Having social spaces isn't enough because you have to engage in spaces a little more critically than just having, than just a regular social space. You can talk about interpersonal kind of experiences but definitely having that academic experience on it too I think is super super helpful.

In this excerpt, Ness underscored the unique contributions that coursework made to the exploration process of Queer Students of Color. Having the opportunity to explore both through academics, as well as through the relationships they formed was particularly beneficial for Queer People of Color.

The reason why classes played a valuable role in matters of identity for these participants stemmed from the fact that it was oftentimes the first instance where they read material centering the perspectives and knowledge of Queer and Trans People of Color. For example, E commented on how their gender studies allowed them to explore the interconnections between their race, gender, and sexuality by exposing them to bodies of work that theorized the three together:

> I always am getting into like different political theories. . . . I focused on post-colonialism. And so my identity really guided my academic

> explorations also because I was sort of looking for something that I could focus on and use both academically and artistically to ground myself that had something to say about the connection between Blackness and queerness and transness, and like post-colonialism, post-colonial theory definitely does.

By reading post-colonial theories, E finally had the language to describe how Blackness, queerness, and transness were interconnected in their life. Like E, Carmen also reflected on the relationships between their race, gender, and sexuality as a result of a women's studies course they took. In this class, they read a poem in which the author showed how Latinx cultures minoritize women. In reading the line – "How am I supposed to love someone else's vagina if I don't live mine?" – Carmen reflected on their own Mestiza and queer self. To this point, Carmen noted, "I started thinking about how I viewed myself in the past, and how my culture and being part of two cultures impacted me." For many of these students, encountering material that spoke to their experiences as multiply minoritized individuals led them to explore questions of identity for the first time.

In addition to the class content itself, participants shared how course discussions themselves contributed to their exploration. One noticeable example of this emerged in my conversations with Sarah Ray as she recalled a gender studies course she enrolled in during her first year in college. The readings assigned in this class included the work of Black feminists like Audre Lorde and bell hooks with conversations oftentimes veering into topics such as the intersections between Blackness and women identities. In describing her experience in the class, Sarah Ray commented, "I don't know how to explain it, but maybe that was leading me, and she [the instructor] didn't even know she was leading me." Specifically, Sarah Ray greatly benefited from these conversations as they served as the catalyst for her to relate to her identities and the structures of power surrounding them by "actually doing something about it, and fighting for [her] existence, identity, instead of just being like, 'This is it. This is how life is going to be.'" Like Sarah Ray, Parker who spoke fondly about a women's studies course he once took. Parker thought highly about this experience because the environment validated him to the point where he could discuss how he moved through life and campus as someone who is biracial and gay:

> We also talked a lot about sexuality too and me being the only other gay person in that class, apart from my professor, I have a lot of my own opinions too on this and then I would always talk about how my racial identity and my sexual orientation shape who I am. Then, we ended up talking about how Queer People of Color have definitely been through a lot of oppression and how they're treated. How

> society has stunted where they are in life and it really got me thinking about who I am as Filipino and gay, but also everyone I know that's queer and/or a Person of Color.

This women's studies class was different than other classroom spaces that Parker had been in previously. Though Chapter Three portrayed instances where faculty perpetuated oppressive beliefs, these stories showcase how educators can in fact be positive influences.

Co-Curricular Activities

Outside of the classroom, Queer Students of Color also had the chance to reflect on their identities as they accessed services on campus for minoritized individuals. This included identity centers on campus like LGBTQ centers or those attending to racial groups. Moreover, participants also connected with student organizations, places that led to vital reflections on their identities. Important to note is that these spaces were imperfect, underscored in Chapter Three's analysis showcasing that these resources frequently failed to address within-group differences. Nevertheless, many Queer Students of Color still derived value from these co-curricular activities.

Identity Centers on Campus

First, several participants including Alejo, Avery, Carmen, E, Max, Oliver, Parker, Richard, Rose E., and TJ developed ties to the identity centers that existed on their college campuses. Because these centers were explicitly founded to serve minoritized individuals, it was not a surprise that students took advantage of their staff and the orchestrated initiatives in order to explore their intersecting identities. For instance, TJ initially stayed away from the LGBTQ center that existed at her Midwestern HWI, perceiving it to be too white. However, she eventually became a resident assistant for a gender-inclusive housing community, which always had a strong relationship with the LGBTQ center. Consequently, she eventually visited it for the first time and realized that it was different from what they had expected. TJ took notice of how they attempted to program for those who came from different racial backgrounds, a sentiment captured in the following statement:

> I guess it made me feel more accepted because I knew that I was in fact accepted in that space and they put a lot of effort into making it intersectional so . . . I never really felt like I didn't belong there and that kind of helped me explore my identities, because I didn't have to focus so much energy on the fear of potentially not being accepted.

Because this LGBTQ center made an intentional effort to attend to the within-group differences in the LGBTQ community, TJ felt validated and affirmed, which in turn encouraged her to explore her identities.

Similarly, Carmen viewed the LGBTQ center at their institution to largely cater toward white individuals. Yet, this did not dissuade Carmen from visiting it, especially in a time when they wanted to "come to terms with [their] queer identity." Because someone connected Carmen specifically to the Assistant Director of the LGBTQ center who also identified as a Queer Person of Color, Carmen saw it as a space that "would honor" both their race and sexuality. For those who accessed identity centers on campus, it was not uncommon for them to find mentors in these spaces. Rose E. was another example of this, naming both the LGBTQ center and the Black Resource Office as formative to her identity exploration. Notably, both directors of these centers were Queer People of Color, which led Rose E. to say, "[It is] really important to be able to have a conversation with someone who you know is within your community to ask for advice, ask for guidance." In providing them with a space and with relationships where they could bring up their intersecting identities, these centers proved to be strong influences for Queer Students of Color.

Student Organizations

Apart from identity centers, participants named the student organizations they engaged in as other collegiate experiences informing their exploration. For Mirella Blackwell, an organization named "Exploring Gender and Sexuality" (EGS) was particularly important because she did not have an LGBTQ center at her small private institution in the South. By being involved with the organization, Mirella felt affirmed despite the lack of other spaces on campus that did the same:

> With EGS, it's kind of helped me normalize it because you just, surprisingly there are a lot of people interested in it so seeing all these people who either identify as gay or people who just support it and want to show their support for it, it helps to just make sense of it and say that it's normal. It's just like anyone else. It's just a different sexuality.

In normalizing different sexual identities, Mirella developed a more positive view on her own demisexual identity.

Within these identity-based student organizations, Queer Students of Color regularly took on leadership roles, which motivated them to explore matters of identity. As introduced in the beginning vignette to this chapter, Ness was one example of someone who used leadership positions as a way to learn about their race, sexuality, and gender. Though

Ness saw classroom environments to be significant in broaching questions of identity, there were no courses on campus that were about queer Asian American topics specifically. Thus, Ness mobilized their executive board positions into opportunities to examine the histories connected to their identities:

> When I realized that the curriculum wasn't offering anything that I wanted, I had to do that research myself. And in doing that research for my organization, Asian American Association, that's how I politicized myself. That's how I explored my identity. I empathized with the struggles of the people who created my identity.

Little did Ness know, this student organization involvement would eventually lead them to be a strong advocate for their communities, all beginning with the initial research they did relative to their race, sexuality, and gender.

Yet, the student organizations did not have to be focused on sexuality or race as long as Queer Students of Color had friends in these clubs that validated their multiple minoritized identities. Dash, for example, had deep connections with those who were a part of the Ultimate Frisbee team on campus, as well as with her sorority. In talking about her sorority, Dash mentioned,

> I found that just being a member of a sorority with very open and incredibly caring members definitely gave me a community along with a safe place to discover how my sexuality affected me as well as a place to be comfortable with myself and the person that I was becoming.

Dash's sorority sisters provided Dash solace from the surrounding local context where she feared being her holistic self. Namely, her sorority sisters showed Dash that she was a valued member of the group and that they respected her identities (including her sexuality). Another participant who spoke about a non-identity-based student organization was Richard who was a member of a dance team. Richard found it ironic that his dance team proved to be a place where he established relationships with other queer Asian people:

> For some reason, also, a huge amount of the dance team community is just Asian, in other campuses and colleges, and non-collegiate affiliate team. Like I said, that's where I met most of the queer people in my life. That's a big space I feel like I've met a lot of queer Asian people, and we've all explored that a little bit together.

Because of the presence of people who were like him, Richard considered his dance team to be one of the main ways he explored his multiple minoritized identities.

Social and Romantic Relationships

Though many Queer Students of Color formed relationships through their co-curricular activities, others developed informal connections with people who would go on to be formative to their exploration. Notably, participants described the centrality of relationships with Queer People of Color in their identity exploration. Furthermore, these students named romantic relationships as prompting them to investigate how they viewed themselves.

Social Connections

Participants in the study named a variety of relationships as significant as they navigated their HWIs. Yet, these individuals largely referenced bonds with other Queer People of Color as being beneficial for their exploration. John Doe communicated this belief as he emphasized the necessity for spaces consisting of Queer People of Color in one of our interviews together:

> It means that I have safe spaces in which to properly explore my identity: with people, not a vacuum. For QPOC without such spaces, life will be more difficult because they do not have the official space in which to safely explore their identities. They must defend themselves against everyone else, an overbearing majority that will usually seek to assimilate, and thus eliminate, their identities.

When surrounded by other Queer Individuals of Color, participants frequently experienced a judgement-free zone to inquire about issues pertaining to their identities.

In my conversations with Parker, he echoed this view as he ruminated on a relationship he had with someone who similarly identified as queer and with Filipino heritage. Sharing these commonalities was rare at a HWI, which made Parker value this friend even more:

> I talk to her a lot and that's great. We have similar families. Her dad immigrated here when he was in his early 20's and was very, very culture shocked. We always talked about how it is between our families and how it is especially with our sexuality. Like, "Oh, is your Filipino side of the family okay with you being bi?" She would ask me if my family is okay with me being gay and then we would just

> talk about that, so that's one of the areas that I have actually talked about me being biracial and gay.

Other individuals who held different racial identities or sexualities might not have been able to comprehend the cultural nuances that affected how Parker related to his family. Thus, this social relationship played a positive role as Parker thought about this during college. TJ underscored the importance Queer Communities of Color hold for individuals, saying that a bond such as this one "helps explore identity and leads to a better knowledge about yourself . . . and what it means to be a QPOC."

Beyond giving them a space to ask questions, forming ties with other Queer People of Color was significant because it allowed participants to decompress after facing oppressive incidents, especially those that occurred at HWIs. Max brought this fact up during one of our conversations. They observed:

> I think surrounding myself with Queer People of Color [is important] because they tend to be very supportive of each other and we just check in with each other, and we share so much so we can even share "Today I'm really down. This is what happened to me" and there's been someone who's gonna tell you, "No, you are a beautiful human being, and this is probably just some internalized stuff, or this is something that caught up with you today."

Importantly, other Queer Individuals of Color were the only ones who could help participants like Max because they shared the same vantage point and had also experienced the internalization of structural oppression. Like Max, Wren also searched for relationships to Queer People of Color and namely, Queer Femmes of Color. Because their identity exploration journey involved recognizing their prior proximity to whiteness, these newfound friendships were a welcomed change for Wren:

> That's really the energy I need to be in right now to heal. I think that's really what I'm trying to do at this point, just take time and space away from as many white spaces as I can, logistically to just heal from all this, to maybe bounce back.

When surrounded by other Queer People of Color, Wren had the ability to explore their identities without struggling overtly with whiteness.

Romantic Relationships

For Queer Students of Color like Alejo, Avery, E, Levix, Richard, Rosa, Rose E., and Sarah Ray, their romantic partners also caused them to critically reflect on their race, sexuality, and other salient identities. This occurred either because their partners had similar interests and identities or because they differed in terms of their degrees of privilege. E, for instance, described how their partner held similar interests as them, meaning that they followed these points of intrigue together: "They're an international student from Pakistan, and we both started to, I think, also get interested in some of the same things, post-colonialism and the way that has implications for specifically Queer and Trans People of Color." E's relationship with another Queer and Trans Person of Color hence allowed them to do the work of exploration in close proximity with another person.

However, when Queer Students of Color dated partners who identified different racially, they had to negotiate their different social locations, which in itself prompted a form of identity exploration. This point came across when I chatted with Avery about its partner. Although Avery had hoped to find a "unicorn," someone who identified in similar ways as it, its fiancé was only "two-thirds of the equation, because he's missing out on that other part, the cultural part." Avery's fiancé was half Mexican, but he did not learn about this part of his identity growing up. Therefore, Avery did not believe that its fiancé could fully understand its racial culture. This resulted in Avery thinking about how it had unique experiences as someone who is part of the queer community but who also has strong ties to its racially minoritized identities. Rosa explained an experience that resembled that of Avery. Specifically, Rosa was dating a white transmasculine bisexual person. In talking about their relationship, Rosa shared,

> Cory's white, so it reminds me that I'm not white, because sometimes they're very conscientious of when other people say stupid or ignorant things that are racist towards me. I don't really recognize it, so dating him kind of made me recognize a little bit more of prejudices that people have.

In dating a white individual, Rosa became hyperaware of her Chinese identity based on how people interacted with them differently.

And in some instances, it was partners themselves who perpetuated oppressive attitudes in the lives of these Queer Students of Color. Levix was a key example of this happening. In his interviews, Levix brought up the emotionally abusive relationship that he was once in with a white man. He referenced the relationship by observing,

> I found within that relationship, power dynamics coming into play. Him being older, him having more income, him being white, there was just so much disconnect. Yeah, my boyfriend was sort of, not

> sort of, he was racist and he would make racist comments, racist jokes, and I – every time I'd tell, ask him about it, he'd be, "Oh that's sort of how I grew up, like in the South." And I tried to have a discussion with him, but he'd always turn it away.

Because of his ex-boyfriend's racist behaviors, Levix gained the awareness that he was differentially positioned to his partner because of his racial identity. This situation caused him to recognize the unique struggles he would face as a Queer Person of Color, leading him to also fear engaging in romantic relationships moving forward. Unfortunately, Levix' story showcases the traumatic experiences with partners that may spur identity exploration for Queer Students of Color.

Off-Campus Involvement and Study Abroad

The final set of salient collegiate experiences for Queer Students of Color exploring their identities involves connections with organizations off campus (whether local or national), as well as study abroad participation. This pattern reveals how forces beyond college campuses can be instrumental to these individuals' identities. To begin, several participants in the study including E, Sarah Ray, Rose E., and Wren sought out local organizations catering to their minoritized communities. Seeing their time in college as one of their first opportunities to connect with queer individuals, E found an organization that focused on sex education in the Midwest city in which they lived that "was very queer focused." Namely, E referenced this space with other Queer People of Color as having a substantial impact:

> There are things that we would be aware of happening in the city, and it's interesting because I do think that people tend to feel like [this city's] queer scene is like really racially segregated. Like I really feel like almost all the queer people that I know are Queer People of Color, and so I think you sort of get the sense that you're like becoming part of this scene or like community. And I think that was like really important to me, to my identity.

Aside from exploring their intersecting identities through coursework and through their romantic partnership, E named the bonds they developed through this grassroots organization as a significant collegiate experience that shaped who they were.

In a like fashion to E, Sarah Ray considered their involvement with a local organization comprised largely of queer Black women as formative to her holistic development. It was in this group that Sarah Ray learned the value of collective organizing and what it meant to fight for liberation:

> Then we have leaders or people who have been teaching us a lot of the content who identify as queer as well. They don't even consider . . . they wouldn't even call themselves authority figures. But having people who are leading you and guiding you and helping you figure out things, especially when it comes to the liberation of all people. Somebody who I can see myself in, that really helps me.

In seeing the leaders in this group seamlessly embracing their roles, but also their social identities, Sarah Ray reconciled her status as a queer Black woman in the face of interlocking structures of domination. She communicated this reality when she stated,

> I honestly think that it's a brave decision to even have both as a part of your identity, because I'm already a Person of Color, I'm a woman, and I'm now accepting another title as a queer person. I think just having all of these marginalized groups intersect, it's scary at times, because I know that some people are gonna hate me because I'm this, and now people are gonna hate me because I identify this way.

Although she recognized that embracing her intersecting identities was brave given how society marginalizes queer Black women, it was the connections she made in this local group that infused a sense of confidence in her necessary to explore these aspects of herself.

Other participants like Dash, Ezekiel, Levix, Rose E., and Ness looked beyond their local contexts and instead tapped into national professional organizations as part of their exploration. Ness' opening vignette communicated the value of Creating Change in their life. In their conversations with me, they also mentioned a conference on queer Asian communities as providing a similar benefit to their navigation of identity. For Ness, it was life-changing to spend time with people who could understand the unique realities they faced as a queer and trans Asian person:

> Before I went to [this queer Asian conference] or the Asian American all-day event at Creating Change, I didn't get the chance to have that room for specifically queer Asian topics. Like I was just never engaged in those topics before, or at least in a critical setting. 'Cause it's one thing to read about it online, but there's a second thing to say it out loud. And that's what was so transformative about that space for me . . . It was because I got to put words into those things that I was thinking about all the time.

Because they did not "have any trans Asian friends," these spaces led to a "super deep connection" as a result of Ness having desired friends who came from the same cultural background as them. When Queer Students of Color could not find these connections at their HWIs, they could instead locate them in places like these national organizations.

Finally, another off-campus experience that individuals like Alejo and John Doe discussed involved participating in study abroad. Alejo traveled to a country in South America as a part of his study abroad experience, which was especially meaningful due to his own Latinx heritage. During his time in this country, Alejo noticed "more intersectional representation and expression of Latino LGBT life that is sometimes very lacking" in the United States. In seeing queer Latino individuals hold hands on the street or kiss in public places, Alejo gained a new perspective on how to view his own bisexual Latinx identities:

> I think the most important thing is I felt more normal I guess. There was so many other people like me that I didn't feel like an outcast. . . . I think that's why it was easier to come out here at [my institution], because in college a lot of people are able to find themselves, explore themselves. And finally, I embraced my sexuality after potentially suppressing it for a long time before college.

By traveling to another country in which he could see what it would look like to publically embrace queer Latinx identities, Alejo acquired more confidence in exploring and disclosing his own bisexuality when he returned to the large public HWI he attended. Alejo's narrative exemplifies how experiences like studying abroad in college encouraged them to examine their intersecting identities, learning how they would navigate oppressive contexts in and outside of higher education.

Reflections on Identity

Though the previous chapter revealed participants' experiences of racism and heterosexism, among other forms of oppression at HWIs, the stories detailed earlier reveal that collegiate environments can in some ways contribute positively to identity exploration for Queer Students of Color. As a result, those reading this chapter will be able to know how relationships and practices in college inform identity development, a necessary area of understanding (Patton et al., 2016). When reading this current and the preceding chapter together, it is clear that these environments only have beneficial impacts when they are implemented with intention and by explicitly addressing the role of structural inequalities. Furthermore, readers are encouraged to think about how they can connect students to the informal influences that emerged (e.g., social/romantic relationships or off-campus organizations).

Importantly, the experiences that participants detailed typically involved the recognition and affirmation of their multiple minoritized identities. What this pattern indicates is that scholars and practitioners in higher education need theories that attend to students' intersecting identities to guide their practice. Though examples of such perspectives exist (Abes et al., 2007; Jones & Abes, 2013; Jones & McEwen, 2000; Reynolds & Pope, 1991; Wijeyesinghe, 2012), more work is needed for specific social identity groups. In the case of this text, these narratives fill a needed gap that bridges what is documented in the research on sexual identity (Dillon et al., 2011) and on racial identity (e.g., Cross & Fhagen-Smith, 2001; Gallegos & Ferdman, 2012; Horse, 2012; Kim, 2012; Renn, 2003, 2004), making professionals better equipped to work with those who identify as both queer *and* People of Color.

Conclusion

Although Queer Students of Color noted that HWIs are central sites where they encounter oppressive behaviors and attitudes, the spaces that exist on these campuses can serve as beneficial influences when designed well. For instance, participants showcased how academic spaces were helpful when they saw themselves represented in the literature or when student organizations recognized the needs that came with their multiple minoritized identities. Similarly, Queer Students of Color formed valuable social and romantic connections to others that produced spaces where they could reflect on their identities. These, alongside the other findings highlighted in this chapter, showcase the potential that the college years have for Queer Students of Color as they ask major questions about their intersecting identities and learn about themselves in the process.

5 Race, Sexuality, and More

The Intersecting Identities of Queer Students of Color

Carmen's Story

Each participant interview began with the question, "Tell me about yourself. What is important for me to know about you?" Carmen began by sharing the following: "I guess I'll start with my identity. I identify as queer, non-binary, undocumented, born as a female, and mentally ill. I think all of these identities have shaped who I am together." These intersecting identities were particularly salient for Carmen, having informed the ways they navigated campus and the world. Now in their third year as a psychology major at a large public HWI in the Mountain West region of the country, they shared how college had allowed them to reflect critically on all of these areas that comprised their social location. In fact, before enrolling at their university, they had "never been given information about what it means to be queer or even a Person of Color." This quickly changed when they started as a first-year student.

Carmen began to question issues tied to identity and systems of oppression when they realized that they were "one of the only People of Color in [their] dorm hall freshman year," a residence hall where they did not have "one single Black individual." Thus, they immediately felt like the "only one," a sentiment that was amplified in their psychology classes that also consisted of mostly white individuals. Due to these experiences, Carmen looked for groups where they could be surrounded by people who looked like them. This journey led Carmen to a Latinx mentoring group on campus known as "La Familia." It was here that Carmen "got a little bit of home away from home." Their first year was also when Carmen came out as queer since they felt that "something was still missing." When they disclosed their queer identity to the mentor they had in La Familia, this person then connected them to the LGBTQ center and specifically, the assistant director who was also a Queer Person of Color. As a result of these experiences, Carmen considered their first year at this HWI to be extremely formative.

However, despite making vital connections as a first-year student, Carmen still felt different from the people they met at La Familia or those who spent time in the LGBTQ center. It was not until they took a women's studies course that they recognized, "Oh, I'm an immigrant. That's why I have different views than other people." This realization served as a reminder to Carmen that their experiences were unique because of their undocumented status. Subsequent instances at their HWI solidified this reality. In fact, Carmen remembered an instance that occurred during the 2016 election where a group of Republican students built "a Trump wall out of cardboard boxes" on campus. Interestingly enough, this happened during National Coming Out Day. Carmen reflected on this by stating, "I'm trying to celebrate one identify of me, like coming out day. The other one, with the elections and everything, it was like this identity is still very vulnerable." As a product of the harmful sociopolitical discourse present on campus and in U.S. society, Carmen's undocumented status significantly shaped how they thought about their other intersecting identities.

From the beginning of their interview, Carmen was especially attuned to several of their social identities. Notably, Carmen drew attention to their gender, undocumented status, sexuality, sex assigned at birth, and disability status as forming their holistic self. Their experiences at their HWI only served to solidify the salience of these identities. In fact, Carmen observed how they were one of a few People of Color in their residence hall, which in turn led them to find other Latinx individuals in a mentoring program on campus. All the while, Carmen was also exploring what it meant to be queer and non-binary, having the assistance of a staff member at the institution's LGBTQ center.

Carmen's story begins this chapter because it shows how the Queer Students of Color in this study were by no means the same. Each of the participants who engaged in this research held different racial identities, sexualities, and additional salient identities. Although they shared some commonalities in how they explored their race and sexuality, their other intersecting social identities uniquely informed their exploratory process. This chapter thus highlights how identities such as gender, faith, ability, undocumented status, and socioeconomic status shaped how Queer College Students of Color in this research engaged in the process of identity exploration. Moreover, another relevant finding was how participants perceived the relationship between their race and sexuality. Of note, two main patterns emerged. On the one hand, nine Queer Students of Color believed they had explored their race and sexuality separately, seeing them as interwoven only occasionally. On the other, the remaining 11 individuals stated that they thought of their race and sexuality as intricately connected, meaning that they could not explore one without the other. I examine these two identity patterns in greater detail in the next section, offering a potential reason for why they emerged.

Identity Patterns Tied to Race and Sexuality

In my conversations with the 20 participants, I began to notice an interesting distinction in the ways that students thought about their race and sexuality during their college years. The first group consisted of those who thought that their race and sexuality did not largely influence the other. Therefore, the opportunities they participated in to question matters of identity were different for their race from their sexuality. An example of this emerged in my conversations with Ezekiel who differentiated his sexuality from his racial identity. When I asked him to offer his thoughts on how these two related to one another, Ezekiel shared, "I would say that they're exclusive from each other. I would never put them together . . . because I feel like every interaction I have always focuses on one of the identities and never all of them." In this statement, Ezekiel communicated that he had never really encountered a space or formative moment on campus when he had to think about what it meant to be both gay *and* Latino. However, Ezekiel himself acknowledged that this could potentially change in the future. Like Ezekiel, Parker offered how he saw his biracial identity differently than being gay:

> I feel like they aren't so dependent on each other . . . they don't exclude each other as well, because they're both part of me. But I feel like the fact that I'm gay is a whole different circle than me being biracial or half Filipino.

In a similar fashion to Ezekiel, Parker did not readily see situations in which both his biracial identity and sexuality were salient together (sans his experience with his friend who identified similarly), leading him to disassociate the two. Although they were still a part of his whole self, he conceived of the two as distinct most of the time.

Another participant who was also in this particular identity pattern was TJ. In our discussions together, TJ acknowledged that she had not explored her Blackness in conjunction with her asexual biromantic identity. When I asked her to explain why this might be the case, TJ communicated that her racial identity is more visible to others, and because of the ways that anti-Blackness operates, she is more likely to "experience oppression on it day to day." Her asexual biromantic identity, on the other hand, does not lead to a "lot of backlash" since it is more of a "personal identity," one that is not seen by those around her. Therefore, though Ezekiel and Parker spoke broadly about a lack of instances that would cause them to think simultaneously about their race and sexuality, TJ located her comments within experiences of marginalization specifically. Because she had not encountered many instances in which she was aware of oppressive attitudes or practices on the basis of her race *and* sexuality, she distinguished the two in her mind. TJ's comments might resonate greatly for other Queer People of Color as they navigate HWIs where their racial identity might be more apparent to others compared to their sexuality. Hence, unless confronted with an experience in which both are called into question, Queer Students of Color may not conceive of their race and sexuality as interconnected.

And yet, 11 participants in the study did articulate how the exploration of their race and sexuality was intricately related. Carmen who provided the opening vignette for this chapter underscored this point, using the analogy of a painting to depict the relationship between their identities: "I couldn't disconnect any of the identities from one another. I couldn't just place one here, place one here because all of them are melted together like in a painting." Similar to their opening statement in the first interview, Carmen saw their identities as inseparable, all contributing to their holistic self. Sarah Ray offered a comment similar to that of Carmen when commenting on her Black queer women identities: "I just see them all like layers. I don't think it's like one that comes first, because I'm like, 'They're all presented at once.'" Interestingly, like TJ previously, Sarah Ray used logic tied to how she experienced oppression to explain how she thought about her identities. However, unlike TJ, Sarah Ray believed that the minoritization she encountered was on the basis of her intersecting identities with each compounding one another. Sarah Ray communicated this by arguing, "I don't think somebody's like, 'Oh, today I'm going to oppress the Black part of you.'" In hearing this comment, I wondered what led to the difference in Sarah Ray's and TJ's identity patterns. After all, they both used the language of oppression to justify how they saw the relationship between their race and sexuality.

What emerged from Sarah Ray's story, as well as the other ten participants, was that these students often had strong connections to Queer Communities of Color where they had the chance to consider how these intersecting identities together shaped their realities. For instance, returning to Sarah Ray, she was particularly passionate about her involvement with a local grassroots organization comprised of a significant amount of queer Black women. In discussing how this organization influenced her identity exploration, Sarah Ray mentioned that it gave her the confidence to state that she was a queer Black woman instead of simply saying, "I'm a Black woman." This was especially important based on how Sarah Ray described the predominantly Black communities she was previously a part of where they "only talk about being Black but [they] don't talk about queerness." Thus, for Sarah Ray, surrounding herself with other queer Black women led to the perception that her race and sexuality were intricately connected.

In my interviews with Richard, he summarized this reality by stating the following:

> How like back in the day when I was in my Asian organizations that was the main focus, and now when I'm surrounded by queer people that is the main focus. Definitely the people around you, the places that you put yourself into are a huge identifier of which identity you're kind of gonna be exploring. But also having things that help me explore both at the same time is similar in the same way. Being surrounded by queer Asian people really helps that out. Having that. It's just like I can relate with this and this. We're one!

Richard's comment poignantly captures the role that contextual influences play in how Queer People of Color view their identities. Notably, having the space to spend time with others who identify as queer and Asian encouraged Richard to explore both of these identities at the same time, which differed from his previous years at the HWI he attended. As illustrated in previous chapters, this was also the case for Ness after they attended workshops at the Creating Change conference focused on queer Asian American issues. When they returned to campus and to their Queer and Trans People of Color organization, Ness asserted, "[The club] had me cognizant of the fact that, when I talk about my queer identity, I will always talk about it in the context of being a Person of Color, or more specifically, an Asian." Captured in Ness' statement was the centrality of Queer People of Color spaces to these students, which serves as a potential explanation for the two identity patterns that emerged.

The Role of Other Intersecting Identities

In addition to noticing differences in how Queer Students of Color described the relationship between their race and sexuality, participants brought up how their experiences navigating their intersectional identities also depended on other salient identities. Some of the most common identities that these individuals brought up involved gender, faith, ability, undocumented status, and socioeconomic status. In the particular instances that students referenced these identities, participants commented on how these identities played a role in how they viewed their race and sexuality, together with how others interacted with them on campus. Therefore, this also meant that Queer Students of Color encountered other forms of oppression on the basis of these salient identities, a reality further explained below.

Gender

The questions in this study largely focused on students' race and sexuality; yet, in talking with several participants, they noted how their gender identity substantially informed how they explored their intersecting identities at their HWI. E was one example of a participant who sought out opportunities to explore how their gender related to their race and sexuality. As a gender studies and theater double major, they often did so through their coursework. In fact, college represented one of the first times they could theorize the connections between all three identities: "I got even larger than that, larger than thinking about theories related to transness and related to gender, was theories that were connecting gender and queerness and transness, and race." Doing so allowed them to feel "grounded" and to understand how societal norms affected these three identities in conjunction with one another.

Connected to this, participants who also identified as trans attempted to reconcile how oppressive gender norms informed how they viewed their sexuality and race. Ness shared comments exemplifying this point as we spoke about the relationship between their non-binary identity and pansexuality. Specifically, Ness mentioned,

> I still have body image issues with being trans-non-binary. I still think of . . . sexuality is still like . . . the people I have been with recently still don't . . . I still haven't told them that I identify as trans-non-binary yet. They still think of me as female, so therefore they think of me with a female body, and that has given me some insecurities in a lot of ways.

In addition to thinking of Ness in a particular gendered way, their partners also believed that Ness was straight. Therefore, the ways that trans oppression operated in their life led them to also worry about coming out as pansexual to their partners. For Ness, the presence of gender-oppressive norms thus limited their ability to also disclose their pansexuality, a reality that they still grappled with at the time of our interviews together.

Like Ness, Carmen also had to deal with what it meant to be both queer and non-binary in Communities of Color. Namely, Carmen discussed how they tried to figure out how to explain both of these identities to their family:

> That's why I didn't want to come out as non-binary because I didn't want to make it complicated. Like okay, I'm a woman. I'm gonna use she, hers. But then I started thinking, "No, this is me. I have to be me." And yeah, so I think that it just makes it more complicated, I guess, adding my culture into my sexual orientation and my gender identity.

Carmen initially only came out as queer to their immediately family, telling their mom that they "liked a girl." Hearing this and also seeing a change in Carmen's appearance after they cut their hair, Carmen's mother feared that they "wanted to be a boy," which caused Carmen to stray away from disclosing their non-binary identity. As Carmen stated in the earlier quote above, negotiating matters of their sexuality and gender identity was particularly complicated by their Mexican identity as well.

Faith

Beyond gender, participants such as Alejo, Avery, Carmen, John Doe, Levix, Max, and Sarah Ray all talked about how their faith background informed the process of identity exploration. For instance, Avery posed the following question in one of our first interviews together: "Well, how can I have this intersectional identity of being a person of faith, and also a person who is queer, and also who is gender non-conforming?" In asking Avery to elaborate on this question, it stated that it had previously thought it had to "give up [its] faith in order to have the other two." Yet, Avery was by no means the only participant in this study who initially saw their faith as irreconcilable with their intersecting identities.

One participant who spoke at length about their religious background was Levix. As we conversed about how he explored his sexuality in college, Levix made connections to his faith background as hindering his early attempts to do so: "My struggles came out of trying to reconcile it [sexuality] with my faith being originally, when I grew up, our church was founded within the Latino community as a Baptist church." Though Levix found opportunities to process through these feelings, he did comment that his identity exploration could be described as a "journey of trying to reconcile" his sexuality, faith, and race. Coming from a Latino religious community which preached anti-queer messages, Levix had to consciously combat these messages as he came to explore himself as a bisexual man. Dash was another example of a participant who drew connections between sexuality and faith. Specifically, Dash described how the Southern context in which her HWI was located led her to constantly hear the belief that "being gay seems like or is a huge sin." When I asked her to potentially connect this comment to her identity exploration, Dash commented, "I think it's hindered some of my exploration." Because of the prevailing messages that Dash heard about queerness in this Southern religious context, she felt limited in her ability to examine this part of her identity thoroughly.

Rose E. was one participant who stated that she had no desire to reconcile a religious background with her sexuality, causing her to divest from the Baptist tradition in which she was raised. Instead, Rose E. identified as agnostic, an identity that made her "feel more comfortable to explore queerness." This was because agnosticism was in stark contrast to the statements that she had heard from Baptists like "you can't be queer and Baptist. You can't love God and be queer." Nevertheless, agnosticism was not without its challenges for Rose E. and her exploration. Of note, Rose E. described the term agnosticism as being very "white," leading to an internal struggle as she made sense of this relative to her Black identity. Although it was all that she "had to play with right now," Rose E. still expressed some discontent in our conversations together concerning these connections between faith, race, and sexuality.

Ability

Ability status and ableism also came up in my conversations with participants including Carmen, gentle-breeze, Max, Ness, and Parker. These participants drew connections between their disabilities and their ability to explore their other social identities. Of note, these individuals shared how Communities of Color were hesitant to engage matters of mental health. Ness articulated how "mental health in Asian communities is not something you talk about" and Max also shared how "mental health is something People of Color don't engage with." The result of this in ability to talk thoroughly about mental illness meant that participants like Ness and Max kept themselves isolated or hindered their ability to comprehend how their disabilities would continue to structure their lives. Max captured this point when they commented that they wanted to learn how ableist systems in addition to other forms of oppression like racism, heterosexism, and trans oppression would impact them: "Not like as a Person of Color, then as a queer and trans person-but as a poor queer and trans Latinx individual and how that shapes my connection to mental illness, and my communities." In this quote, Max underscores that it is impossible to consider their mental health challenges without also considering their race, sexuality, gender, and class.

Other participants commented on matters of mental health by stating that it precluded them from forming connections with others that may have otherwise proved valuable for them as Queer People of Color. For instance, Parker disclosed to me that he experienced depression and that this influenced how he related to others: "I can have a poor self-image and I don't have the confidence to talk to people. . . . So it prevents me from doing things and getting my experience out there, and living my life, and exploring." Experiencing depression resulted in Parker "holding back," leading him to feel particularly afraid to seek out romantic and social relationships. This, paired with the white norms he saw perpetuated on apps like Grindr, led Parker to feel inadequate as a biracial gay man. Therefore, for him, his mental health combined with the oppressive norms present on virtual spaces affected his ability to explore his sexuality and race in ways that other Queer People of Color would.

Undocumented Status

Two participants in this dissertation research identified as undocumented: Carmen and Oliver. As documented in Carmen's vignette, identifying as undocumented was formative to how they viewed themselves. At one point during their interview, Carmen underscored the unique ways this impacted them by stating, "I know that me being undocumented changes many things. . . . I'm not just a Person of Color. I also don't have papers so that adds a whole other layer." Oliver also echoed this reality when he introduced himself to me: "I'm also a DREAMer student; that's a big part of me and who I am and shaped how I navigated through college." Both Carmen and Oliver then elaborated on specific instances that they saw their undocumented status playing a role in the exploration of their identities.

An example of this came up when Carmen discussed how heteronormativity, gendered norms, and their undocumented status intersected. In particular, their mom would often tell Carmen that they had "to get married" so that they could "get papers." Because of this message from their mother, they instilled in their mind that they could only like men in order to eventually secure citizenship for their mother. Carmen internalized this up until when they arrived to their HWI where they were finally able to push back on this train of thought: "So then getting into college kind of separated me from that belief that I have to hide myself and I have to be this way and that way." Thankfully, Carmen eventually found support for all of their identities in the campus diversity center, a welcomed departure from past educational experiences:

> In high school, I thought I was alone that nobody wanted to help undocumented students, nobody wants to help queer students, that if I came out, people would just be like, "Oh you're weird, what are you doing?" But I think being able to voice this is who I am, even within the diversity center's helped a lot realizing, "Oh. People care about you and your identities."

Though Carmen found this space, this did not fully eliminate the stress that resulted from nativist systems and beliefs.

Oliver faced similar issues as he considered his DREAMer status and the potential implications of disclosure. Specifically, Oliver brought up how his DREAMer status also affected how he thought about making romantic connections. He feared the potential of blackmail, comparing disclosing his DREAMer status as a "second coming out." He shared, "If I tell them, could they use that against me? Or will they actually support me?" Consequently, Oliver found himself limiting his potential for romantic relationships because of nativist attitudes that potential partners may hold. This worry was amplified by the experiences Oliver had with other People of Color, stating that "even among other Latinos, a lot of them don't get it when they hear about DREAMers." Furthermore, he had not yet reached a point where he could "even shar[e] that among queer spaces yet." For Oliver, his DREAMer status was a substantial factor in how he related to other racial and sexual minorities, which inevitably influenced his exploration of his intersecting identities.

Socioeconomic Status

Finally, socioeconomic status was another identity that played a role in how certain participants including Levix, Parker, and Wren approached their exploration. Parker, for example, was forthcoming about his background as a working-class individual. When he shared this with me, I asked him if it potentially influenced his ability to explore his identities. We had a hearty laugh when he jokingly shared that he "could pick up more guys" if he did not have to spend time working. And yet, Parker also did mention that he missed out on opportunities that he saw other queer peers engaging in, such as going out, which he believed limited his exploration. He also worried that potential romantic partners may not "accept or notice" him as someone who is from a working-class background. Like Parker, Levix also drew connections between SES and his sexuality, as well as race. Levix shared that he foregrounded needs attached to his socioeconomic status instead of attending to his sexuality. To make this explicit, Levix informed me of a time when he saw a major difference between him and friends:

> There was a big difference because of socioeconomics. Most of our peers talked about not really having a space or the ability to explore sexuality because of harsh parents. That was an essential part that we could not really explore because we had other socioeconomic factors that we really had to take into account. While other friends were, since they don't have to worry about socioeconomics, they had a little more positive experiences with their sexuality.

In debriefing this experience, Levix asserted that he believed that his finances had to take priority whereas others did not have to expend this same amount of energy, which then freed them up to attend to the exploration of their sexuality.

Reflections on Identity

The previous stories illustrate substantial differences in the ways that Queer Students of Color thought about and explored their intersecting identities. This chapter thus exemplifies the potential that intersectionality has to interrogate the complexities of group identities (Dill & Zambrana, 2009). Moreover, the presentation of these narratives also displays a resistance of the inclination to treat Queer People of Color and the experience they have at higher education institutions in a monolithic way (Johnson & Javier, 2017). Like other scholarship in student development research on intersecting identities (e.g., Abes et al., 2007; Jones & Abes, 2013; Jones & McEwen, 2000), these Queer Students of Color showed how social identities intersect and differ in salience depending on contextual influences.

From an intersectional lens, it is clear that a major contextual influence involves the manifestations of oppressive behaviors and attitudes. For example, Carmen's undocumented status was particularly integral to how they explored their race and sexuality based on the nativist sociopolitical rhetoric present during the 2016 presidential election. In other words, Carmen could not think about their race and sexuality without also considering the nativist attitudes that accompanied experiences of racism and heterosexism. Similarly, the presence of oppressive gender norms also played a role in how a select group of Queer Students of Color engaged in identity exploration. Consequently, it is imperative to acknowledge the heighted sense of marginalization that some Queer People of Color face at HWIs because of the systems of power connected to their other salient identities.

Conclusion

Although I set out on my dissertation research attempting to develop a unifying theory that would describe how Queer Students of Color explored their identities at HWIs, my conversations with these individuals led me to also comprehend the beautiful diversity that exists in Queer Communities of Color. No Queer Person of Color will experience their campus context in a way exactly the same as another. As a result, professionals in higher education must be in tune with this reality when seeking to support these students, especially at HWIs. Furthermore, attending to these complexities will also allow faculty and staff on campuses to consider and combat the ways that systems of oppression are interconnected in order to move toward more liberatory practices.

6 Who Am I?

(Un)Learning and Identity Exploration

Richard's Story

Describing himself as a "super senior of some sort," Richard was in his sixth and final year studying data analytics and computational modeling at a large public HWI in the Southeast – a fact that he was extremely happy about. In his time at the HWI, Richard had taken advantage of a number of different communities, including creating connections to Asian-interest organizations, a dance team, and the LGBTQ center on campus. These diverse involvements seemed to mirror his life before college, having lived on three different continents, which gave him a "lot of experience with different types of people." When searching for a college to attend, Richard enjoyed the particular town in which his HWI was located, seeing it as "slightly secluded" from everything else in the state. Moreover, he noted a "variety of people" when he toured the university in contrast to another institution he visited where "white people was all [he] saw." This difference in experiences led him to enroll and start his college years at his HWI.

When he first arrived onto campus, Richard searched for opportunities to explore his Asian identity, identifying as a Nepalese person specifically. Though he recognized that he was not straight, he gave little thought to his sexuality in his first two years in college. In fact, he shared that he thought he was asexual for a period because he did not see "any of the people around as heavily attractive." He also worried about being seen as anything other than straight. It was not until he joined his dance team, one of his primary forms of involvement, that he met someone whom he felt connected to on a romantic level. It was in that moment that Richard thought, "I'm some sort of queer," giving him some semblance of peace and ownership over this part of himself.

During his initial years at the HWI, Richard saw his communities as "bubbled off," which then had an influence on how he saw his identities. Of note, Richard noticed that the Asian community on his campus was very "self-sufficient within their own bubble . . . [and] same with the queer community." Consequently, the two groups rarely interacted with one another, leading Richard to conceive of his identities separately: "The first two years, I was very heavily focused with the Asian community here. I was part of, like, an executive member for many orgs and clubs here. But I kinda missed out on all the queerness 'cause I was so focused on that." After a while, Richard felt compelled to explore his queerness by getting involved at the LGBTQ center, eventually getting a student worker job in the office. As he connected with these communities, he learned new perspectives on what it meant to be a queer Nepalese man. However, the experiences were not always easy, as Richard described. Notably, he recalled having to unlearn sentiments of shame and trauma as he started to explore his intersecting identities at the HWI. In fact, he had once been told that "white is right, straight is great," a message that he began to push back on as he made connections in different groups on campus.

This brief look into Richard's story leads me to discuss a significant theme that emerged in the study. With my interest in identity exploration, I was keenly aware of Richard's experiences in his siloed identity communities, especially given the identity patterns that I covered in Chapter 4. However, Richard's story also stood out to me because of the harrowing message that he shared in one of our interviews together. He communicated that at one point, someone had used the phrase, "white is right, straight is great." Unsurprisingly, this oppressive statement stuck with him, informing how he thought about his queer Nepalese identities. Nevertheless, the groups he connected with on campus showed him a new perspective on his identities, serving as vital influences for his exploration.

Ultimately, Richard's vignette exemplifies the fact that identity exploration for Queer Students of Color involves a concurrent cycle of (un) learning. In the process of exploring their identities, participants detailed how they learned new thoughts, actions, emotions, and connections relative to their social identities. They also simultaneously had to unlearn the negative influences they previously internalized due to systems like racism and heterosexism. This cycle of (un)learning occurred in four different dimensions: cognitive, behavioral, affective, and social. Whereas the cognitive dimension encapsulated the ideas and thoughts that Queer Students of Color had about their social identities, the behavioral dimensions articulated the actions and behaviors they engaged in order to examine different possibilities. The affective dimension involved the feelings and emotions Queer Students of Color encountered in exploration. Lastly, the social dimension described the ways that these students connected to their social identity groups. Importantly, attending to one of these dimensions inevitably influenced the others. In these sections, I offer examples from the participants to illustrate each of these points in the (un)learning process.

(Un)Learning in the Cognitive Dimension: The Role of Thoughts

For Queer Students of Color in the study, one of the central characteristics of identity exploration involved the thoughts and views they had of their intersecting identities. As they learned new ideas about their social identities (e.g., gaining knowledge about systemic oppression, seeing identity as fluid), they also unlearned the harmful stereotypes they once internalized about their racial identity as well as their sexuality. Therefore, unlearning required the resistance of oppressive messages.

Unlearning: Stereotypes and Oppressive Messages

To begin, Queer Collegians of Color at HWIs detailed how they began to divest from racist stereotypes that stemmed from whiteness. For instance, in my conversations with Oliver, we spoke about the ways his Latino studies courses changed his perspective on his Latino identity. It was only by taking these courses that Oliver realized the ideas he had grown up with that he subconsciously believed had an ounce of truth:

> And you know, I've always known harmful stereotypes like a lazy Mexican, and you know just a lot of messages that indicate that Latinos, specifically Mexicans, are not . . . you're just kind of meant to be working at fast food restaurants, janitorial positions, stuff like that. So for me, I had to unlearn those stereotypes.

Having heard the language of being a "lazy Mexican" particularly resonated with Oliver because he had also been told that "Latinos don't belong in higher education." However, he clearly was enrolled in a postsecondary institution, meaning that these stereotypes had no semblance of truth to them. Consequently, Oliver realized that he needed to learn and develop a new way of thinking about his Latino identity, something he gained through his Latino studies classes.

For other participants, unlearning involved the intersections of their race and sexuality. For example, TJ and I discussed their asexual biromantic identity as it related to this unlearning process. Specifically, TJ had mentioned that initially asexuality was not an identity they wanted to embrace, because people had taught her that it was "something that only young white people experienced." Yet, when TJ came across a music artist who was a Person of Color and asexual, she began to push back on this stereotype as well as the sentiments of embarrassment they once attached to the label. Like TJ, Max offered an example of how they unlearned a message that was inherently racialized. Namely, Max pushed back against the thought that their gender and sexuality were distinct identities. As they began to learn more about their Latinx identity through courses at their HWI, Max came to a new place of understanding: "If you are queer that means that you are probably also gender not normal. And so that gave me the space to let me explore what gender identity means to me." Explaining this point further, Max believed the idea that "gender and sexuality are completely separate" is in fact "pretty Eurocentric." In taking courses centered on identity, they had the chance to question how whiteness shaped how they had previously thought about their queerness relative to their gender fluid/non-binary/trans identity. For example, Max shared how they wrote a paper on the topics of *marimachas* (a Spanish term for lesbian women who are more masculine-expressing), leading them to engage in unlearning.

Other Queer Students of Color in the study unlearned the racism they had been exposed to in queer communities and the heterosexism present in their Communities of Color. For Ezekiel, for example, masculinity was a topic that appeared throughout his interviews. In fact, he had long reflected on it because of his participation in a fraternal organization at his HWI. However, in a particular part of our conversations together, Ezekiel named how he struggled with masculine ideals present in his Latinx culture. As Ezekiel put it, he had internalized dominant norms he had grown up with, which caused him to be "always kind of anti-effeminate men, like femme phobia." However, by moving away from home and being able to reflect on these messages, Ezekiel had grown to question this femme phobia. He commented,

> Growth has happened, and unlearning, I don't know, I think it's the toxic masculinity part of the identity too because even if I do accept an openly gay identity, which I do, masculinity is still such a huge part in the identity. Masculinity, machismo is so huge in the Latino culture that I still feel the effects of the learning that has been done onto me, the teaching that I have to undo and be okay with men that are not masculine.

Ezekiel's process of unlearning thus required him to push back against the heteronormativity he had come to associate with Latinx culture, which manifested in ideals about masculinity. However, Ezekiel was not the only participant who unlearned concepts that originated from the Latinx community. Avery shared how it had to unlearn the statement, "Latinas aren't queer," as this was a phrase that had been ingrained in its mind as it grew up. Similarly, Levix also wrestled with "the cultural dynamics that come with gender" as he explored whether he identified as pansexual or bisexual. Like Ezekiel, Levix had long followed scripts that placed a major emphasis on hypermasculinity, but in college, he started to learn that gender did not "have to be such a duality." Consequently, Levix began to question whether pansexual would be a more apt term to define his sexuality. Highlighted in these stories, unlearning messages they had come to accept as true in the cognitive dimension was a key part of exploration for these Queer Students of Color.

Learning: Systemic Oppression, Fluidity, and Language

As they unlearned stereotypes and oppressive lessons, these Queer Students of Color also learned new thoughts and ideas that informed how they viewed their intersecting identities. To begin, one of the major new concepts that participants reported learning was about the role that systemic oppression played in the lives of minoritized individuals, including themselves. For many participants, this recognition came as a result of taking classes that focused on social identity groups. When referencing her gender studies courses, for example, Rose E. named how she had gained new perspective on her own identities as someone who was a Black queer woman:

> A lot of that happened through my gender classes, classes that are for women and gender studies, and I think a lot of that came from that. Learning about history definitely helps me see the trends and patterns of things, and learn that things don't just happen. People don't just get injured or shot, and people don't just – I don't know, develop this unique sense of queerness. A lot of times they're influenced by people.

Because of her academic coursework, Rose E. understood how oppression targeted at women, queer people, and other minoritized individuals not only manifests interpersonally, but is instead a structural issue that is deeply historical. Wren came to a similar point of reflection as they spoke to me about the social construction of identities that leads to real and material consequences. Namely, Wren commented,

> I feel like that kept reinforcing how I view my gender and . . . not my gender. Specifically, my gender and sexuality, more so. Then even my race and how I move along this world as a raced person, and as a Person of Color, being my specific race. . . . All these traumas and all that stuff is generational, and it is based in stuff, but the basis of that is faulty.

In learning from feminist theories courses, Wren began to think about their own non-binary queer identities. They learned that all of the oppression that they face is based upon a socially constructed system that inevitably benefits those with dominant identities. Though the basis of marginalization "is faulty," pointing to the irrational logic that people used to justify the systemic exclusion of people, these structures still affected how Wren saw their gender, sexuality, and race.

For people like Max, this process of learning new ideas about their identities also provided them the chance to challenge the very genesis of stereotypes they had accepted as true. The specific stereotype that they spoke about was the fact that Mexican communities are highly homophobic, a point that was taken up by other participants. However, Max learned that the homophobia present in the Mexican community was actually a product of systems of white supremacy and settler colonialism. Max' classes showed them the following:

> So thinking about why the particular community that I grew up in of Mexican folks was pretty homophobic, and very outwardly homophobic and just acknowledging that queerness was a thing prior to colonization. . . . Realizing it [colonialism] creates a system within itself in that like, "Okay, we're all oppressed as Latinx people but there's a hierarchy cause I'm straight and cis. So you're the other in that case."

Learning in the cognitive dimension showed Max that the very ways they had thought about their communities stemmed from whiteness and colonization, thus shifting Max's relationship with their sexuality and gender, as well as their race.

In addition to recognizing how systemic oppression manifested in their lives, participants learned that their queer identities were fluid. Participants like Alejo, Carmen, Ezekiel, gentle-breeze, Ness, Richard, and Wren all discussed how their classes and interactions with queer peers encouraged them to see that identities were not binary in nature. In talking about a course that focused on matters of culture, gender, and violence, Alejo described how he started to see his own identities as existing on a greater spectrum:

> I think we talk a lot about orientation and gender and it made me realize we've always lived in a very binary world and just very focused on categories. Having to fulfill those categories, or if you don't you have to fix it, like fix the problem almost. People have always treated me as abnormal, not being on that straight path, and so I think that class in particular has taught me so much about how fluid sexuality can be. How fluid gender can be, or sometimes you don't have to be that fluid with your orientation.

Rather than seeing his gender and sexuality as static, Alejo learned that these identities were more complex than he previously thought and that they were ever-shifting. Carmen offered a similar perspective when they referenced the lessons they learned from a Queer Person of Color student organization at their HWI. Their involvement in this club created space for them to embrace themselves as someone who identifies as a Mestiza queer non-binary person:

> That I feel like, when I was first coming into terms with my identities. Because then also that was one thing with the Latinx community, that if you have a girlfriend, you're a lesbian. And then, if you get a boyfriend, like, why aren't you a lesbian? And, so I was always scared of that. Like, "Oh, what are people gonna think of me?" So then, I think talking to people and realizing "Oh, no, it's fluid, it can be whatever you want it to mean too."

Rather than focusing too rigidly on what others would think about them, Carmen recognized that the perceptions of others, especially in the Latinx community, stemmed from binary forms of thinking. By connecting to other Queer People of Color, Carmen recognized that this was an inherently flawed school of thought.

Beyond learning about systemic oppression and the fluidity of identities, participants' exploration involved gaining knowledge about language pertinent to their minoritized communities. For instance, Rosa shared how they learned about the numerous terms that exist to describe queer people. She stated that one of the primary ways she explored her bisexual Asian identities was by simply being exposed to language:

> I would say in the sense of what I guess I identify as, I mean thinking about queer that it can go beyond the labels that are currently in existence, which I think is interesting. I also didn't think that was possible, but you know, sometimes we just build boxes for ourselves and say, "You have to go in the box." But there's a world outside the box.

For Rosa, encountering new labels for those in the queer community prompted them to consider what meaning they ascribed to their own bisexuality. Other participants emphasized similar experiences to Rosa.

For example, Oliver shared how he acquired a broader understanding of identity through his participation in a mentoring program for racially minoritized people and through cultural centers on campus:

> I think with queer culture it's become, it's helped me learn more about different sexualities. Like beforehand I basically only knew like gay, straight, bisexual, or maybe even asexual. But then there are all these other kinds of identities for sexuality and gender as well. So I think that's helped me really become like I said more proud of my queerness but more of an ally to people of differing queer identities.

Oliver personally identified as gay, but he still gained a great deal from learning how others identified. Notably, it caused him to reflect on why gay was a label that he felt comfortable with and what it symbolized for him. Echoing both Rosa and Oliver's comments, Levix communicated the following in our conversations together:

> I guess I'm always going back to the language, how new language that I could use to understand myself, understand others around me, be able to communicate with others about my experience or be able to understand others better about their own experiences.

Levix' statement perfectly captures the value of learning in the cognitive dimension. By acquiring new ideas and perspectives through their coursework, involvement on campus, or their peer relationships, Queer Students of Color ruminated on the nature of their intersecting identities.

(Un)Learning in the Behavioral Dimension: The Role of Actions

However, it is important to note that thinking through possible alternatives was not the only way that these Queer College Students of Color explored matters of race, sexuality, and other identities. In fact, their exploration involved them engaging in certain actions that affected how they viewed their identities. As a part of this process, these students also pushed back against how their dominant norms had previously regulated their bodies and behaviors.

Unlearning: Challenging Assimilatory Norms

Characteristic of the behavioral dimension, Queer Students of Color commented on the ways that they unlearned patterns of behavior that they enacted in order to conform to dominant society. Max' comments offer one example of this type of behavioral unlearning. Navigating their HWI showed Max how they previously would remain subservient in an attempt to assimilate to gendered norms. Max shared the following:

> I think for me it's been beneficial . . . because I am able to speak up for myself in ways that I grew up not being able to. Like, being an AFAB [assigned female at birth] person in Latinx culture is very much, "Be quiet, do what you are supposed to do, don't talk back to elders," things like that. I'm learning this through academic [spaces]. I have a voice. I'm going to use it kind of thing.

When they arrived on campus, Max knew that they had to be unapologetically proud in their identities. Their academic coursework thus gave them the confidence necessary to unlearn the inclination they would have had to be quiet in their academic spaces, now not being "afraid to speak up and challenge peers." Carmen felt similar to Max, commenting on how they had been taught as a Person of Color to "speak less in classrooms, or even ask less questions." Yet, Carmen found themselves attempting to unlearn this inclination, stating:

> If you felt different, you wouldn't really say anything so now I'm trying to unlearn that and be more comfortable with raising my hands and saying my opinions without being afraid that if I say, "Oh actually this is wrong," a white person next to me is gonna be like, "Oh no, what do you know?"

By surrounding themselves with other minoritized individuals, Carmen recognized that their silence in white spaces made them complicit to white norms, which inspired them to push back on this behavior.

Another form of unlearning in the behavioral dimension involved how Queer Students of Color expressed themselves through dress and appearance. For example, Richard shared in his interviews that he enjoyed dressing in different ways, including liking to "wear heels like crazy for no reason just because . . . they look great." Though he now felt comfortable going out in his college town in heels, Richard mentioned that this was itself a process of unlearning dressing in a masculine way in order to conform to others' sensibilities. This idea was "pushed" by his parents, but when Richard arrived to college, he wanted to express his queerness in this way: "Nowadays, [I wear] just whatever the heck I want. Things that more people generally would see as queer as outfits and choices. I just full out on that." Finally, other participants described their unlearning behavior in relationship to language usage. Ness provided one example of this, commenting on how their time in an LGBTQ issues class led to an increased feeling of comfort to use the term "queer." Their initial feelings of discomfort stemmed from the fact that they believed they were not "qualified enough to reclaim" the term. They expanded on this argument when they observed,

> I know people who do reclaim the slurs and are taking back the power that the oppressors have previously used on that slur against us. I didn't do enough with my queer identity to feel like I could reclaim the slur, but now that I've done a lot more research on the history, even outside of the class, I read articles and I talk with other people about it. I take part in a lot of discussions and stuff. I think I now have a much better understanding of what it means to be queer, of what it means to move through spaces as a non-cishet person in general.

Though Ness previously drew a distinction between them and others who were qualified to use the term queer, their behavioral unlearning broke down this distinction. Now, they had a sense of confidence in being able to use language like "queer."

Learning: Seeking Out Connections and Adopting New Behaviors

In the process of unlearning dominant behavioral norms, Queer Students of Color engaged in new actions that allowed them to explore their identities. One behavior that Queer College Students of Color engaged in included looking for chances to connect with those who also identified as Queer People of Color. Doing so moved them these individuals from seeing their identities as labels to instead understanding how their identities impacted how they moved through the world. Avery, for instance, communicated this when it commented,

> I started asking questions. I started not just trying to live in my head and trying to make sense of it to myself . . . I thought, "I'm gonna need more help so I need to ask more questions. I need to be curious about that."

Avery's spark in curiosity challenged it to find people on campus who allow it to ask questions about its identities as a multiracial gynysexual demi-femme person. Carmen also mentioned how they benefited from the counsel of people, leading them to actively seek these individuals out:

> I think talking to people, going places that have people that share similar experiences or ideas or views of the identities. They don't have to identify the same way as you but they might know more things and to just talk it through, I guess, and feel a little bit more validated too that it's not just in my head or I'm not going through a phase, like it's actually like, "Okay, these are my identities and this is how I am and how I go on about the world."

Through their connections to cultural centers on campus, Carmen made their identities and the issues affecting them more tangible, exploring these questions with others.

Importantly, these Queer Students of Color did not simply search for any connections, but instead they desired relationships that would be different from the racism and heterosexism they experienced on campus. Oliver underscored this reality by stating,

> I had gone to the queer affinity groups that they have here at [the institution]. And then I also went to the Latinx Cultural Center here

> and there. So I don't know, it's just been a mix of visiting spaces where I can feel more comfortable as opposed to just the overall, just feeling like . . . sort of ostracized I guess in a PWI.

By going to cultural centers and identity-based student organizations, Oliver hoped to find people who understood what it was like to hold minoritized identities at a HWI.

Aside from developing relationships with other minoritized people, participants spoke to the centrality of acting upon their queer desires as a part of their behavioral exploration. gentle-breeze commented on the importance of queer encounters as she reflected upon her first time kissing a woman. In processing through this experience, she noted, "In subsequent months, years, I would be better able to identify possibilities for queer intimacy, and how I wanted to interact with girls or otherwise, and working theories in my head of how interpersonal things work." Having this initial encounter allowed gentle-breeze to wonder about their bisexuality and what this identity would mean moving forward. In a similar way to gentle-breeze, Levix explained to me that the primary way he explored his queerness was through his sexual behaviors:

> My journey figuring out my sexuality I think was first rooted in trying to understand my desires. And I mean those manifested in what I was able to understand easiest, and what I kind of culturally received from media or discussions with other gay individuals. How it was sort of hyper-sexualized, that queerness is expressed through sexual desires. And, I mean, from those sexual desires manifest romantic desires. So in a way, it was sort of seeing, okay, is this what I really want? Is this what my queerness manifests in?

Although Levix initially associated queerness with hypersexuality, his sexual encounters caused him to pause and question what his queerness really meant.

Wren was another participant who talked explicitly about how sex was in itself an exploratory act: "I wouldn't say I ever have sex because I want the pleasure. I feel I have sex because I want to explore, and I want to learn different things." However, as Wren began to examine what their sexuality meant in relationship to his Black identity, they also identified that race played a role in their exploring of queer desires. They noted,

> Whenever I have sex with white people, a part of my soul, especially with certain white people and the way I see them. . . . I've had sex with white gays that has been not fulfilling and I feel I'm doing a detriment to my soul, my ancestors. . . . . I can feel my lineage looking at me being like, "What?"

In this moment, Wren thought critically about their queer identity and race as a result of having sex with white people. They questioned how they furthered contributed to the dominance of whiteness by engaging sexually with white people, a point of inquiry that was especially salient to them as a Queer Person of Color.

(Un)Learning in the Affective Dimension: The Role of Emotions

Though the importance of cognitive and behavioral exploration has been documented in the literature on identity exploration (Kroger & Marcia, 2011), the narratives provided by the Queer Students of Color in this study pointed to additional complexity that defined this process. Of note, these individuals not only described the role of formative thoughts and behaviors as they explored their identities; instead, they also showed how identity exploration involved an affective dimension, resembling other research on social identities (Phinney, 1993). Specifically, their stories consistently revealed the significant emotions they felt as they broached important questions of identity. Their (un)learning process involved first resisting feelings of self-hate, shame, and trauma which in turn, led them to embrace healing and pride.

Unlearning: Self-Hate, Shame, and Trauma

Threaded through the participants' stories was a continual need to divest from oppressive influences and messaging. Although this necessitated a cognitive and behavioral reframing, it also meant that they underwent a significant emotional journey relative to systemic oppression. As a part of this, Queer Students of Color recognized how they had internalized self-hate, shame, and trauma. Richard captured this sentiment in his final interview when I asked him to reflect on his years at his HWI:

> I had to unlearn shame. Shame would be a big thing because you're conditioned I think by society and people from a young age that white is right, straight is great. I think that's what someone told me once. And it is unlearning all those self-harmful thoughts like this is bad, you shouldn't be like this. . . . But for me mostly it's not a matter of unlearning, it's a matter of learning more things too. Because I feel like I grew the more I learned. And I didn't have that much of a basis of stuff that was – other than just people and society telling me this is better or this is the way to strive for. It's mostly me exploring stuff, learning more about myself, history and such. And being more me.

By getting involved on campus, especially through his Asian American clubs, the dance team, and the LGBTQ center, Richard realized that he had come to associate his identities with racist and heterosexist norms. This association resulted in the deep feelings of shame. However, it was in his ability to identify these feelings that he was finally able to move away from them toward embracing his queer Nepalese self.

Rose E. also went on a similar journey to Richard's, in which she attempted to push back against "personal self-hate or self-disgust or things [they] picked up from that convention of racism." To illustrate her point, Rose E. talked to me about the relationship that she had with her hair. Initially, she unknowingly was "going for Eurocentric features in a Black experience, low key," but when she realized this was what was occurring, she acknowledged the need for a change. Because she "had a lot of self-hate about hair," she decided to cut it off altogether. In doing so, Rose E. felt liberated and as though she no longer had to experience the self-hate she had developed because of white norms. Gaining an awareness of how oppressive systems impacted their emotionality allowed participants to reimagine the relationship they had with their identities. Max emphasized this connection by explaining,

> I think just exploring them to a point where I did unlearn a lot of things that I was taught to be shameful of, or to navigate through the lens of whiteness. Unlearning those made me feel very affirmed in my own experiences. Feeling like, well, these ideas of shame, or having to assimilate to whiteness is all kind of systemic and problematic. Letting go of those things let me really be myself, and be really confident in that. I guess, even decolonizing the way that I view myself.

As in the case with the other dimensions (i.e., cognitive, behavioral, and social), the affective unlearning process directly related to the manifestations of structures like whiteness.

Learning: Healing and Pride

As alluded to in the previous quotes provided by participants, the shift from feelings such as self-hate or shame resulted in more positive affective relationships to one's identities as a Queer Person of Color. Specifically, individuals mentioned how they engaged in healing or developed a newfound sense of pride by exploring their identities. In talking with Max about their experiences navigating their identities as a college student, they acknowledged that their process involved the following:

> Definitely a lot of healing. Some of my classes really turned me onto works by Queer Women of Color like Gloria Anzaldúa, bell hooks, Audre Lorde, and I read these works and it's very much . . . I mean Audre Lorde in general just talks about self-care as being an act of

> resistance. . . . Reading those has helped me opened up to sharing my own experiences and feeling like they don't have to just sit there in the back of my head. Really trying it unpack the trauma that I typically avoid. Like okay, let me piece it together. How does that still affect my life now? Does that make me afraid to do certain things? What systemic forces influence that?

For people like Max, the identity exploration process represented a form of healing, an affective component that emerged. By learning the perspectives of Queer Women of Color, for instance, Max gained the awareness of how people had addressed and resisted racism, sexism, and heterosexism. Ness' connection to the queer and trans Asian American people they met at Creating Change, in addition to those who were affiliated with a national organization focused on queer Asian issues, resulted in the same effect:

> I really do think seeking a community, that's how it made me realize seeking a community is so healing in a lot of ways. It's important to develop. I very much think finding a community of people who share marginalized identities with you is a really good way of discovering yourself and to heal yourself, too.

As highlighted in Ness' words, having a "tangible" community allowed them to heal from past trauma. Ness mentioned that having people they could actively consult with questions was particularly meaningful in conjunction with having the ability to read more "theoretical and academic stuff."

In addition to healing, these Queer Students of Color reported developing a sense of pride and confidence by exploring their identities. In speaking with Dash, for example, she reflected on her time with her Ultimate Frisbee team and sorority, both representing spaces where Dash felt her sexuality and racial identity embraced. Because of the validation she felt in these groups and in college broadly, Dash mentioned that she felt more prideful:

> My time at [my institution] has only helped me accept and flourish as a Queer Person of Color. I've found that the fears I had coming in to college and the things I so often wanted to repress became defining traits of who I was as a person and deserved to be celebrated instead of tucked away. The people I surrounded myself with and their constant encouragements helped me to gain confidence and take a stand against my negative experiences.

Though she initially saw her social identities as points of shame or embarrassment, being surrounded by individuals that she met through these student organizations transformed these sentiments into pride. In a similar fashion to Dash, Oliver grew more confident in his identities through his involvement on campus. He explicitly referenced his time as a mentor in a program focused on matters of diversity and inclusion when he stated,

> I just felt like I've grown to be more proud to be Latino and queer. It's given me more spaces to have conversations. . . . It's just nice because bit by bit those kind of help me develop and be more comfortable in my skin, being more outspoken about issues that affect me personally, or people like me.

What is clear from these examples is that when Queer Students of Color have access to affirming spaces, they are likely to experience positive manifestations of affect like pride, confidence, or healing.

(Un)Learning in the Social Dimension: The Role of Connection

Importantly, the perspectives disclosed by Queer Students of Color revealed one final dimension that defined their identity exploration. These individuals shared that by exploring aspects such as race and sexuality, they no longer felt as though they were the only one on campus or in the world who experienced issues tied to these identities. As they dissociated with these ideas of being the "only one," they developed strong bonds to other Queer People of Color, including some examples where participants felt connected to historical figures.

Unlearning: Beliefs of Being the Only One

Prior to exploring their identities, participants often felt that they were the only person who experienced the unique effects of racism and heterosexism, among other forms of oppression. For instance, TJ commented on this sentiment when she noted,

> I guess searching for them independently reflected my. . . . It reflected me thinking that there's not much out there. I don't know. I guess sometimes it feels like I'm the only one who holds these identities. I know that's not true, but at times it does.

At the beginning of her exploration, TJ had not yet met others who were Black and asexual. Though they cognitively recognized this was not the case, it was difficult to escape this belief. It was not until they formed bonds with other Queer People of Color through spaces such as the LGBTQ center at their HWI that they moved away from this thought.

Like TJ, Oliver also mentioned that his academic coursework generated a shift in how he related to other queer individuals or People of Color. To this point, he shared the following in one of his interviews:

> It is not until you take specific ethnic history courses or queer history courses that you finally get to have the aspect of "I'm not the only one." But also, that there's been other people before me who have made an impact on the face of the planet because of who they are.

By being able to unlearn these sentiments through his academic coursework, Oliver felt a weight off of his shoulder: "It kind of makes me feel more at ease about them, because, like I said, a lot of it is like that anxiety of there being no one else or not that many other people share my identities." Therefore, this unlearning in the social dimension was intricately connected to the ideas he had about his identities, as well as the feelings he had throughout this process. Echoing this reality, Carmen noted that by engaging with others also led to feelings of solidarity: "I think it's definitely helped to see that we are out there. Well, that there's more people out there than I thought." Carmen's comment then leads into the learning component of the social dimension.

Learning: Connections to People in Contemporary and Historical Times

In the process of exploration, Queer Students of Color articulated how they felt part of a larger collective comprised of Queer People of Color. When reflecting upon their experiences in college, Rosa stated that she formed bonds with people who were like her:

> I feel like initially you have feelings and then you go to explore them and now you search for meaning and understanding in your own feelings, doing that research and trying to seek out actively information, that information leads you to other people who are either seeking the same thing, so now you've found someone, or it leads you to a bigger group or a resource that brings you closer to other people, who are also undergoing similar feelings or who identify in a similar way.

It was not only meeting these individuals that was significant, but that she felt a social tie to them that extended beyond a typical relationship. Further emphasizing this pattern, other individuals commented on the unique nature of the connection they developed with Queer People of Color. Rose E., for instance, spoke about her involvement in a local grassroots organization present in the city where she attended college, in addition to referencing the professional conferences she went to in her academic discipline where she met other Queer Individuals of Color:

> At least the communities that I'm in, I feel like I have a whole lot of reciprocity with them understanding. So that's something that's new to me and something that I'm really grateful for and it makes me wanna give back in different ways. It makes me wanna be a leader, it makes me wanna take some of my money and give to different organizations and makes me wanna give back because I know it's given to me in so many ways. So I think the feelings that come from that would be like love, appreciation, and gratitude.

In this excerpt from one of Rose E.'s interview, what stands out is the novelty that results from relating to other Queer People of Color. As she put it, "Just knowing that when people know that you're a Queer Person of Color and they also are, I feel like there's a recognition emotionally." For people like Rosa and Rose E., they conveyed a powerful connection on the basis of their social identities.

However, these ties not only emerged with individuals that these participants knew, but they also disclosed that this social dimension involved historicizing their identity. In other words, these Queer Students of Color shared how they had a sense of association with historical figures who identified in similar ways. Avery was an example of a participant who showed how this manifested. Specifically, Avery learned that Frida Kahlo, a revered Mexican painter, was also bisexual. In reflecting upon this recognition, Avery stated,

> They're still recognized as this big important person in the history of this country, like Mexico and just in general the world as the self-portrait painter that she was. That was really cool learning that in the grand scheme of things, I'll also be a part of that bigger picture. I've just added another puzzle piece or another color to a painting that makes up being gay and being ethnic. It was validating having that like, okay, I'm really not the only person that's possibly gone through this journey, has made those decisions, all that. It's affirming.

Avery beautifully painted a picture of how it saw itself as a puzzle piece fitting into a broader portrait, representing the ties it had to Queer Communities of Color. Ness similarly portrayed these historical relationships as they thought about their exploration: "Myself finding appreciation for my histories in each of my identities and maybe the intersections of those histories . . . I think has helped me finding meaning with what I could also do with my identity." Ultimately, Ness used this bond they had with history to strive to create better futures for other Queer People of Color to come, stating,

> To take that founding, the need for that space, what they have had in mind for that space and to translate that into what I could do now with the privileges I do hold, even if I am one of those Queer People of Color, making . . . being as loud as I can.

Hearing Ness disclose this desire to contribute to change for other Queer People of Color displayed to me the power that this social dimension of identity exploration has, underscoring the interconnectedness that resulted from doing the work of personal self-reflection.

Reflections on Identity

The insights highlighted previously showcase how Queer Students of Color experience the process of identity exploration in unique ways. Specifically, I undertook this research hoping to extend the work of Marcia (1966, 1994) who framed exploration as an important developmental task that many encounter in their lifetime. Described as a period of exploring meaningful alternatives (Kroger & Marcia, 2011), the stories that the Queer Students of Color offered suggested that in order for people to try out new perspectives, they must first unlearn ones that they had internalized prior. Hence, it is not enough to learn new ways of viewing, performing, or relating to one's identities; instead, Queer Students of Color must also do the work of unlearning the oppressive influences they had encountered due to racism, heterosexism, and other structures of domination. This simultaneous cycle of learning and unlearning thus becomes integral when researchers use frameworks like intersectionality (Crenshaw, 1989, 1991) to investigate college student identity because this finding underscores that individuals come to campus believing oppressive societal messages about their identities.

In addition to revealing new perspectives on identity exploration broadly, the experiences that the 20 participants had also revealed that exploration is a more complex process than previously thought. Specifically, initial conceptualizations of identity exploration framed it as involving a cognitive and behavioral dimension (Marcia, 1966, 1994). Subsequent research then asserted that an affective dimension was also present (Phinney, 1993). The stories of the Queer College Students of Color in this research affirm the presence of an affective component of exploration, pointing attention to the emotions that they experience in this process. Additionally, I argue that a social dimension to identity exploration also exists where Queer Students of Color negotiate their relationship to social identity groups, showcasing a connection to social identity theory (Tajfel, 1978, 1982; Tajfel & Turner, 1979). In this social dimension, Queer Students of Color reevaluate their membership in a larger social group, strengthening their bonds to groups present in their lives as well as with historical figures. All four of these dimensions – cognitive, behavioral, affective, and social – more accurately capture the nuanced experiences of Queer Students of Color exploring their identities.

Conclusion

With the construct of identity exploration being at the heart of the study that led to this book, this chapter offers vital insight on how this process occurs for Queer Students of Color at HWIs. As Queer Students of Color unlearn previously internalized oppressive messages, behaviors, and sentiments, they learn new ways of viewing, performing, and relating to their identities. This also results in a stronger connection to the minoritized groups that they are a part of, shaking off the belief that they are the "only one." Therefore, readers should be particularly attentive to the implicit messages that they may communicate, aspiring to contribute to positive lessons that Queer Students of Color adopt as they explore these ever-important questions of identity.

7 Moving Forward

Hopes Shared by Queer Students of Color

Max's Story

A passionate advocate for trans healthcare, a student worker at the Rainbow Center on campus, and a person with a love for the work of Gloria Anzaldúa, Max Aguirre was in their fourth year at a large public HWI in the Midwest. Having been a "military brat," Max had a great deal of comfort with moving around and navigating different towns. They enrolled at their institution to escape being close to home, having a tense relationship with their abusive mother, but also to benefit from the reputation of a school known for its science programs. Eventually, they hoped to train medical professionals on how to best interact with trans patients and how to make a more trans-affirming healthcare system. In our first interview together, Max mentioned that they wanted to "make folks feel more comfortable that they're figuring out what their needs are when they're going to see a physician or any kind of medical professional." Max wished that they would go on to get their Ph.D., seeing their thesis on primary healthcare for gender nonconforming people as one of the steps that would take them there.

Before starting at their institution, Max was living in the Southwest, surrounded by those who looked like them, sharing the "same kind of cultural understandings." However, their new Midwestern environment proved to be a bigger adjustment that they had initially thought. The bridge program they had attended the summer before their first year made them believe that they would be surrounded by other People of Color when the semester began, but this did not turn out to be the case at an institution that felt like a "sea of white." They often spoke about missing hearing Spanish spoken on the street or encountering others who were from Latinx communities. Yet, Max saw potential for their college years. This was to be a place where they can display their Latinx identity because not talking about it would be "harmful" to them. Max also knew this would be an opportunity to explore who they were as a queer gender fluid/non-binary/trans individual, not being out at home. For them, it was important to be as out as possible and "be super visible," finally getting the chance to explore these parts of themselves. They leaned into this by finding texts that spoke to their queer Latinx identities, taking classes explicitly about trans identities, and connecting with other Queer People of Color at their Rainbow Center. In fact, they vividly recalled happening upon the Rainbow Center in their student union when they noticed a rainbow rug in an office. They immediately thought, "That's me."

Max's story is filled with many journeys. It was only after some time at the institution that they finally embraced their QTPOC identities as being interconnected, seeing power in embracing their queer, trans, and Latinx identities as informing each other. In the beginning, being new to a HWI isolated them, making exploring all of their identities "too much to handle." Relatedly, Max was open about their mental health challenges, having reflected thoroughly on the need to embrace this aspect of their being and encouraging others to do the same. As they put it, the "traumas and experiences" they had influenced how they related to their "ethnicity, gender identity, and sexual orientation." To put it plainly, Max stated, "It just shapes every aspect of my life." Max encountered many an instance that would negatively affect them during their years at their HWI, from being deadnamed in a class or constantly being microaggressed and misgendered. It was their moments with other Queer People of Color "that just get it" that allowed them to remain resilient in the face of racism, heterosexism, and trans oppression and process through these experiences.

As a result of these connections, Max retained hope and found healing. In fact, they shared: "I always hope to grow, to learn more about myself, to learn more about the ways the systems of oppression manifest." It was through the exploration of their identities that they both acknowledged the role of power but also grew to embrace every part of themselves. Guided by hooks' (2000) All About Love, they wanted to move forward in life with the intention to change the world for others, as well as for themselves. "Learning that it's not selfish, and it's actually quite powerful, and very much wanting to heal and survive is like sticking it to the man," Max stated.

Max's narrative felt like a fitting way to enter into the final theme that emerged in my conversations with the Queer Students of Color in this project. Though the previous chapters detailed plenty of instances where participants encountered the manifestations of oppressive systems at their HWIs, they imagined futures where they would continue to love themselves fully despite the presence of structural inequalities. This anticipation was the fuel that these students used to continue exploring who they were, seeking out resources as well as communities on and off campus. Of note, each participant mentioned that they had hoped to develop a more secure sense of self, a goal that they were already moving toward based on the experiences they had at their colleges and universities. This chapter further elaborates on this central hope that all of the Queer Students of Color shared, communicating what they thought their futures would look like and how they wanted to get there.

Though participants universally strove to acquire this secure sense of self, two major patterns emerged about how they defined this aim, especially when considering the role of systems of power. Namely, for all participants, having a secure sense of self would mean being able to filter out negative influences that would have previously made them feel less than others. From an intersectional perspective (Crenshaw, 1989, 1991), being secure in one's self takes the form of acknowledging racist, heterosexist, and other oppressive behaviors and being able to embrace one's identities despite the manifestations of these systems. Nevertheless, other participants went further in their assertions. For them, a secure sense of self would entail being mobilized to push back against systemic oppression, changing conditions for Queer People of Color to come. With Max's words in mind, I expand on both of these patterns in the next sections.

A Secure Sense of Self: Resisting Internalizing Systemic Influences

In my seeking to understand how participants explored their intersecting identities in a society that perpetuates oppressive ideologies and systems, I also came to learn their why. In other words, I gained the insight of why people would even want to explore their identities in the first place. As our interviews together progressed, I began to hear the term "secure sense of self" over and over again, which immediately peaked my interest. For instance, during an interview I had with Dash, I asked her to describe a goal that she had for herself. Taking some time to pause and reflect, Dash then shared with me the following:

> I think my forever thing is to be able to find a secure sense of who I am without letting anyone care, like my goal is always to be someone who myself likes and not worry about what others think or what others are trying to push onto me, and being able to stand strong in that. I think by exploring both identities, I can do that because as I accept them more and move through them more, they're not things that nag me. They're just things that I become more proud of.

Hearing this reminded me of Dash's previous stories where she detailed that by her exploring her identities, it would allow her to assist others as well. In fact, she consistently spoke about finding a sense of pride as a queer Asian American woman. In the process of doing so, she noted how important it was to resist the negative messages that she had previously encountered. Examples such as Dash's exemplify the goal that the Queer Students of Color had for themselves.

When I asked follow-up questions to Dash and others, I learned that attaining a secure sense of self would require more complex ways of making meaning. Specifically, they hoped to reach a place in their lives where they could actively manage what others thought about them and the messages they received in society. For instance, TJ provided some insight on this hope by integrating lessons that she learned as a psychology major:

> In my opinion and experience, I don't think it would necessarily make you just not care about what people think. I think it would, I definitely think it can bring you an amount of peace, but it's . . . I don't know. It feels like since we are social animals you would still care at least a little bit about other people's evaluations of you despite or regardless of how at peace you are about it. That being said having peace in your identities might kind of flip the switch a little bit. Before if you were uncomfortable with your identity it might be a negative thing all the time, but afterwards it might be like, yes I am here. This is who I am, and I know people might be judging me but that is a little bit empowering in certain contexts.

Although she initially arrived to college thinking, "Please don't look at me," TJ's exploration led her to acknowledge that she will forever be hypervisible as someone who was a Black queer woman. However, because of the experiences she was having during her years as an undergraduate student, she was coming to a place where she was empowered, and not discouraged, by her identities.

Similarly, Rose E. and I spoke at length about the wishes that she had for her future. Though she considered herself a very confident individual, Rose E. was still making sense of the ways that anti-Black racism and heterosexism influenced how she thought about her intersecting identities. When she brought up the concept of a secure sense of self, I asked Rose E. to explain what she thought this looked like, to which she responded:

> I think it means to be able to consistently know that those systems exist but to know that your existence is not imperfection or cannot be defined by those systems. Does that make sense? Yes. So, you can't not acknowledge those systems, 'cause you're gonna have a hard time. You have to acknowledge those systems, understand critically why they're there, but also understand that in your existence, you're gonna be a contradiction to those systems and that is okay. And that is your perfection actually. And that's how I have come to understand that. If I am to obtain that secure sense of self, I have to

> constantly work on this in the "I am perfection." And I'm constantly trying to do that with my exploration.

Like TJ, Rose E. asserted that systems of oppression will always be present; yet, the relationship she had with these structures would be different. Rather than seeing her identities from a deficit standpoint, Rose E. believed that her being as a Black queer/bisexual individual would be a beautiful contradiction to the negative influences she had previously internalized.

This journey would be complex, a reality that Rose E. herself mentioned. She went on to state,

> The systems are the problem. So it's a constant battle in that relationship of understanding them, understanding the racism, understanding the sexism, understanding how they're evolving, become more implicit in how they're evolving to become more serious. These things are not just stopping. They're continually evolving and there won't be something to stop them. I can't just ignore them and I think I'm becoming more secure in myself, I actually have to become more aware of them in order to see that I am perfect in all that I am.

By sharing this perspective, Rose E. solidified the need to become adept at recognizing oppressive external influences. As she put it, racism, sexism, and other systemic forms of marginalization will forever shape her life as a Queer Person of Color. Yet, she desired more complex ways of making meaning in order to embrace her perfection in the presence of these structures.

Levix shared a perspective that resembled Rose E. as he reflected on the fact that racism will be a constant force as he moves forward beyond his collegiate experience:

> It is understanding that racism has implications that have hurt people in the past, that has hurt their ability to become their own selves. It's limited people to become their fullest self. Racism exists. . . . For me it's going beyond not caring about all these things. It's not having to rely on these systems and just building genuine connections to identities.

In a likewise fashion to TJ and Rose E., Levix named how systemic oppression, and specifically racism, is inescapable as he continues to move through and beyond his HWI. Nevertheless, he strives to achieve a place where he does not "rely" on these systems to inform how he views his identities. Comments such as these signal a desire to develop complex cognitive structures that would allow these Queer Students of Color to obtain a sense of self not susceptible to the messages that will continue to follow them in a racist and heterosexist society.

Though many participants put this in the language that suggested cognitive complexity, Max offered insight that clearly connected to their appreciation of bell hooks' (2000) *All About Love*. Specifically, their comments related to the affective dimension that is a part of identity exploration:

> A lot of my motivation in doing this work is just wanting to feel good in my own skin and my own head, feeling that kind of validity and a love for myself because a lot of the ways that these identities are constructed, it comes with a lot of negative messages that you just kind of internalized. Even if you're not actively internalizing them against yourself, they're there. They're still like a back feeling of shame. The more I explore how these identities are constructed the more I can feel like there's nothing inherently wrong about me being me. That's actually a very beautiful thing.

Quotes like these speak to the real emotionality that Queer People of Color encounter as they navigate their intersectional identities. Though Max had experienced numerous instances of trauma in the process of doing so, their exploration also led to a "lot of healing," as they discovered more positive ways of perceiving their queerness, racial identity, and transness. Like Max, Wren had hoped to reach a place where they had the ability to determine which influences would impact their "spirit." They stated, "It might not even be possible. Like, ever even, in a lifetime. But, that choice is there and it takes a lot of work to get to." Though Wren saw this as potentially impossible, participants sought to approach the cognitive and affective effects of oppressive systems from a more complex manner, reducing the impacts that they had long encountered. Of note, however, several participants shared that a sense of self that could filter out negative external influences was not their only goal. For these Queer Students of Color, their identity exploration journey would lead them to be fierce advocates against the manifestations of racism, heterosexism, and other forms of marginalization.

A Secure Sense of Self: Pushing Back Against Systemic Oppression

In my conversations with Alejo, Ezekiel, gentle-breeze, Max, Ness, Oliver, and Sarah Ray, they all described futures where they would feel confident to resist the ways that systemic oppression operated in their own lives, as well as others. Though some of these individuals were already engaging in this type of work, developing a secure sense of self would mean that they would be able to do this work in a way that was less detrimental to themselves. For instance, Sarah Ray spoke about this when I prompted her to reflect on what she believed the future would hold for her and how she viewed her identities:

> I think some people might be more loud in their resistance of those things, like racism and heterosexism. At least for me individually, I think when I do resist those things, I think that's what it's like . . . I care, and this is how I'm showing that I care in a way. It's like I don't care about what you think, but I do care because I want to fight against that, fight against those ideas, those beliefs that you have about me.

For Sarah Ray, a secure sense of self would entail an outright resistance of oppressive behaviors and actions. Thus, from her point of view, this sense of self would represent the opposite of not caring. It will be a high degree of care that will cause her to push back on manifestations of marginalization since she "acknowledge[s] the negative outcomes" that have long been associated with structures tied to her intersecting identities.

Oliver echoed Sarah Ray's sentiments, underscoring the wishes he had connected to his identity exploration. Throughout our interviews together, Oliver frequently mentioned that he saw himself as a "passive person." He would bring up instances in which he did not speak up when he encountered a racial microaggression or when peers would render his queer identity invisible. For this reason, it hit me even more so when he shared the following in our final interview together:

> My goal is to change the way that that my identities are viewed. Because if I say I don't care what they think of me, that means those mentalities, those offensive behaviors and mentalities are still there. They don't change, you know? That would just look like dealing with those comments and that oppression by just letting be. Which I said, is kind of where I'm at now, but it's not where I want to be. I want to be at the point where I want to address those things and hopefully, even change them.

Not seeing himself to be at the point necessary to engage in this kind of resistance, Oliver believed that he would one day achieve a sense of self where he would change the minds and actions of those who had put him down. Like Oliver, Alejo mentioned, "I also think you need to, or at least I feel like I need to not stand for or let, or be complacent of how people are going to treat me." Both Oliver and Alejo thus could imagine a future where they would resist the internalization of negative influences, but also be active in combating these forces.

Ezekiel also commented on how he could see himself eventually engaging in behaviors that would educate those around him. At first, he mentioned that his idea of a secure sense of self would result in "resilience," and the "stamina of being able to endure the societal oppressions that occur," comments that resemble the first group of participants. However, as we continued to discuss these goals of his, Ezekiel then arrived at a new place of clarity:

> If you have a secure sense of self, you don't have to be an educator, but in my ideal world, you would . . . because who else is going to do it? The people aren't going to educate themselves, which is what I've learned through my experiences here. No one's going to go through the effort of educating themselves.

Beyond simply having the ability to control his internal mechanisms, Ezekiel asserted that the newfound resilience that would accompany his secure sense of self would allow him to play the role of an educator. Though his institution had shown him how pervasive whiteness and heteronormativity was in society, he believed that these experiences would catalyze him to transform those who create these conditions.

What is important to note is that these participants wanted to challenge oppressive behaviors not simply for themselves, but for Queer People of Color around them. For example, Dash further reflected on her experiences on the Ultimate Frisbee team at her institution for they conveyed to her what impact developing a secure sense of self would have for others. Namely, now in her sixth year at her HWI, she had been humbled at fellow team members thanking her for being open as a queer Asian American woman. As she remarked, "I now know that me embracing my race and my identity and my sexuality helps others to embrace them as well and encourages others to be confident in who they are as well." For participants like Dash, being secure in who they were would represent a form of resistance in and of itself, which in turn would positively impact Queer People of Color in their communities. Ness communicated a similar point as they thought back on their years at their large public HWI. Because they expended a substantial amount of labor to find opportunities on and off campus to explore their pansexual, Asian American, and non-binary identities, they hoped that others would not have to do the same moving forward. They noted,

> I want to be able to put explanation and power behind the labels that I choose, not just for personal, self-fulfilling purposes, but I also want to be able to eventually contribute to the greater movement for liberation of my people.

For people like Dash and Ness, the relationship they had with their identities had a far-reaching effect. If they continued to find the power and pride behind what it meant to be a Queer Person of Color, they could more easily help other students do the same despite the presence of oppressive systems.

Reflections on Identity

Throughout this chapter, participants shared their ultimate goal for exploring their identities. As highlighted in the literature on identity exploration (Kroger & Marcia, 2011), this process was not an end in itself, but rather, a task that these students were undergoing in service of their overall identity development. Though these Queer Students of Color could only imagine what their futures had in store for them, the comments they provided offer insight into the potential connections between identities, an idealized sense of self, and meaning making.

Specifically, participants stated that their identity exploration would lead them to a place where they could develop this "secure sense of self." In their view, this secure sense of self would mean that they could resist the internalization of systemic and oppressive influences. Returning to the discussion of "sense of self" first introduced in Chapter One, these Queer Students of Color believed that their identities would be less constituted by the people around them and instead be defined internally. In essence, they drew the same distinction mirrored in the literature on identity; whereas sense of self represents an internal construct, identity is inherently formed in relationship to others (Côté & Levine, 2002). Yet, from an intersectional lens, participants had hoped that they could reach a point where they were in control of their view of self, rather than letting societal norms tied to systems like whiteness and heteronormativity shape their perspective.

Though not put in these words, what these conversations showed me is Queer Students of Color actively desired more complex forms of meaning making (Kegan, 1982, 1994) that would allow them to obtain this sense of self. Because they had experienced numerous instances of marginalization at their HWI and beyond, they searched for a place of cognitive complexity that would allow them to push back against these structures – both for themselves and others. Consequently, their wishes mirrored the perspective held by Barber, King, and Baxter Magolda (2013) who asserted that meaning making can develop when people experience situations that create the demand for an internal voice. For these Queer College Students of Color, it seemed as though the manifestations of interlocking structures of oppression could represent a significant contextual factor that demands this internal meaning-making capability. These stories hence contribute to the body of scholarship showcasing the connections that exist between oppressive systems and meaning making (e.g., Abes, 2012;

Hernández, 2012; Torres, 2009). Though research suggests that marginalization can hinder the development of meaning making (Abes, 2012), these stories reveal that Queer People of Color seek out ways to change their realities and those of others.

Conclusion

In hearing the hopes that these Queer Students of Color shared for their future, I encountered bittersweet feelings. On the one hand, I was proud of the ways they thought about what was to come, noticing their desires for more complex meaning making in order to resist the oppressive influences they encountered thus far. On the other hand, I was upset at the fact that the environments they had navigated demanded a more internal voice. On campuses that are built on legacies of racism and heterosexism, I am not naïve to think that professionals can completely eradicate these manifestations of power. However, what would HWIs look like if individuals with dominant identities were as committed to pushing back against systemic oppression as these Queer Students of Color were? This question is a valuable one to keep in mind as readers move on to read the implications of this research, especially as it relates to the responsibilities of faculty, staff, and the institution as a whole

Part 3

Embracing the Intersections

8 Implications for Intersectional Theorizing in Higher Education

Having the ability to collect and write up the stories of these Queer Students of Color was a task that I did not take lightly. As I note throughout this book, I learned a lot from these individuals as they shared their points of joy and moments of hurt with me in our interviews. In their words, I heard thought-provoking lessons that I hope reach faculty and staff working at HWIs. As someone who teaches at an HWI, I ruminated on how I could implement the recommendations that these individuals provided, suggestions that they asserted could make higher education institutions more affirming and equitable for Queer People of Color. Nevertheless, this project not only helped push the way I think about my interactions and advocacy on campus, but it also challenged me to reflect on the theorizing that I engaged in as a researcher.

As someone passionate about the role that theory plays in shaping practice at higher education institutions, this chapter dives deep into the reflections that emerged as a product of conducting this research. Namely, I revisit the central debates surrounding identity, intersectionality, and queer studies that I introduce in Chapter One of this text. In doing so, I assert that intersectionality as a field of study continues to evolve and grow since Crenshaw (1989, 1991) first introduced the term into the academy. As Nash (2019) acknowledged, the stretching of intersectionality's use should not be met solely with defensiveness, but rather, theorists must consider what is gained when the framework is challenged and opened up. For instance, I articulate how my usage of intersectionality sheds a light on the potential that is unlocked when college student development theorists adopt critical and poststructural perspectives, a characteristic of the third wave (Abes et al., 2019; Jones & Stewart, 2016). I then comment on the relationship between intersectional theorizing and queer studies, considering what was gained and lost in my foregrounding of intersectionality as a framework. I end the chapter with where I hope intersectional identity research on Queer Students of Color in higher education will go in the future.

Pushing the Study of Identity in Higher Education

The perspectives of Queer Students of Color showcased throughout the preceding chapters illustrate the power that intersectionality has to push forward the study of identity in higher education. In mobilizing this framework to interrogate their experiences navigating HWIs, I challenge the assertion that some have made stating that intersectionality is insufficient to understand the lived realities of people in society (Staunæs, 2003). In fact, I argue that research on topics of college student development are in dire need of power-based lenses like intersectionality in order to better attend to today's demographics of college students and to implicate the role that institutions play – for better or for worse – in their experiences. Abes (2016) made a similar call when she noted that "the student affairs profession must evolve such that critical and poststructural perspectives, which critique and deconstruct systems of oppression, take hold in student development literature" (p. 9). To illustrate the necessity for critical and poststructural work in higher education identity research, I describe how this project explicitly named the influences institutional practices, policies, and structures had on identity for Queer Students of Color. I then discuss how intersectionality assists the field of higher education and student affairs in reimagining student development theory constructs such as identity.

The Relationship Between Structures and Identity

One of the main reasons that intersectional theorizing is necessary in education involves its focus on how structures of inequality function in society to disenfranchise minoritized groups (Barnett & Felten, 2016; Bhopal & Preston, 2012; Byrd et al., 2019; Davis et al., 2015; Mitchell et al., 2014, 2019). In fact, since its inception, intersectionality has been about "the ways things work" (Cho et al., 2013, p. 923), showcasing how interlocking systems of oppression shape the lives of those with multiple minoritized identities. This is evident in its history as a way to capture how society oppressed Black women and Women of Color through racist and sexist structures (Hancock, 2016). Because of this attention to issues of power, theorists in higher education and student affairs have argued for intersectionality's deployment in research on student development and identity (Jones & Abes, 2013; Jones & Stewart, 2016; Torres et al., 2009; Wijeyesinghe, 2019; Wijeyesinghe & Jones, 2014).

This text shows what results from the pairing of intersectional theorizing's focus on macro-level structures and student development's micro-level perspectives on identity. Rather than seeing the two lenses as oppositional (Staunæs, 2003), the participants' narratives seek to reinforce May's (2015) belief that researchers who use intersectionality can mobilize the framework to embrace a both/and approach. Namely, it was as a result of the participants' view of their own experiences that I was clued into how structures at their HWIs served to oppress them. Therefore, their insights functioned as an entryway to understand how systems of power and oppression minoritized them as Queer People of Color, especially as they posed significant questions about their identities. Those interested in employing an intersectional lens in their own research can hence utilize this as an example of a project that actualized the potential of the framework to interrogate matters of identity.

Ultimately, the stories that participants shared about how they navigated their intersectional identities at HWIs suggest that an intersectional lens is critical to reimagining educational environments with equity at the center. Because one of the tasks of student development theorists has long been to understand how postsecondary settings either "encourage or inhibit growth" (Knefelkamp et al., 1978, p. x), this project underscores the need to answer this inquiry from a power-based lens. Specifically, participants' narratives revealed that postsecondary institutions are complex influences on their identities. Although attending their HWIs gave them access to experiences that prompted reflection around their race, sexuality, and other identities, these Queer Students of Color also articulated how their exploration was limited due to oppressive interactions and structures at these colleges and universities. Drawing upon intersectionality's critical legal origins (Crenshaw, 1989, 1991), for instance, this study illustrated how structures at HWIs like funding and issues of representation played a vital role in informing identity for Queer Students of Color. Thus, if higher education professionals want to better construct environments for minoritized individuals as they ask important questions about identity, they must progressively embrace third wave lenses like intersectionality (Jones & Stewart, 2016) in order to implicate the oppressive influences that the institution itself creates.

Reimagining Identity Exploration in Student Development Theory

In addition to reconciling the relationship between structures of oppression and identity, I also find it imperative to examine how intersectional theorizing reimagines the very constructs that were at the heart of this investigation, such as identity exploration. When I set out to expand upon the work of James Marcia (1966, 1994), I anticipated that the result would suggest that some of his ideas would still stand the test of time while also believing that his formative scholarship would be incomplete to describe the experiences of Queer Students of Color. Both turned out to be true in key ways.

Marcia's (1966, 1994) foundational research conceptualized identity exploration as a process that people underwent as they examined meaningful alternatives. Though he thought about identity as involving one's occupation, religious affiliation, and political beliefs, scholars including myself have extended this to include one's social identities. In using an intersectional framework in this investigation, I came to understand that the inner workings of identity exploration shift when systems of power are foregrounded. Notably, as the stories of the Queer Students of Color revealed, it is impossible to think about matters of identity exploration without considering how structures of oppression play a role in this process.

The presence of oppressive systems meant that these individuals not only evaluated new ways of thinking about their social identities, but that they also had to contend with the existing messages they had adopted from dominant groups. As asserted in Chapter Six of the book, identity exploration for Queer People of Color depended as much on unlearning as much as it did on learning. Because they carried the trauma caused by interlocking structures of domination, these students needed to resist and move away from the oppressive lessons they had been taught relative to their race, sexuality, and other identities. Each participant had eventually hoped to reach a place where they no longer internalized these influences, the "secure sense of self" documented in Chapter Seven. In these perspectives, it becomes clear that notions of identity, identity exploration, and a sense of self must be tied to the presence of structural oppression in order to accurately capture the realities that Queer Students of Color face at HWIs in contemporary times.

The Potential of Queer Studies in Intersectional Theorizing

As I first began imagining the research project that would lead to this very text, I thought deeply and carefully about the specific lens I would apply to the study. For the purposes of this project, this framework became that of intersectionality, a field of study that I had become familiar with throughout my doctoral studies. Although intersectional theorizing could certainly apply to this student development project, I needed to reconcile what it means to employ intersectionality when I would also call into question issues of queerness through my work. This was particularly important given the fact that queerness could represent an identity, practice, or politic (Burford & Allen, 2019). As mentioned in Chapter One of this text, I entered into my research viewing queerness as an identity, using it as a term to describe those who identified as sexually minoritized people. I also ruminated on what it meant to see queerness as a practice and a politic, especially in relationship to my mobilization of intersectionality. However, in having the opportunity to revisit the stories of these 20 Queer Students of Color through this book, I wanted to conclude by revisiting how my own intersectional theorizing would look different if I explicilty engaged other queer frameworks in conjunction with this lens. By doing so, I affirm that queer studies and intersectional theorizing can learn from one another (Bilge, 2012; Christensen, 2018; Collins & Bilge, 2016; Duong, 2012; Olive, 2015; Rahman, 2010).

In another work, a colleague and I thought critically about the strengths that intersectionality offers the study of Queer and Trans People of Color in higher education (Duran & Jackson, 2019). However, we also argued that intersectionality is by far not the only framework that scholars can leverage to understand how structures of oppression create the conditions that Queer and Trans Individuals of Color navigate on campuses. In fact, higher education researchers have increasingly used Queer of Color Critique (Ferguson, 2004) and Quare Theory (Johnson, 2001) as frameworks to engage in these types of projects. What would it look like to pair intersectionality with Queer of Color Critique or with Quare Theory? I offer a couple examples next.

For instance, Queer of Color Critique emerged in the academy to investigate the interconnections between race, sexuality, gender, and class (Ferguson, 2004). Namely, Ferguson (2004) advanced this analytical tool in order to showcase how Queer People of Color are disenfranchised through political and economic means in the United States. A materialist argument is central to Queer of Color Critique, as scholars use the framework to challenge the system of liberal capitalism that regulates the realities of Queer People of Color. Additionally, Queer of Color Critique positions Queer People of Color as agentic in the face of these oppressive structures. In reflecting back on the data I collected using an intersectional framework, I might have thought differently about the ways that HWIs disenfranchised Queer Students of Color from a Queer of Color Critique standpoint. Of note, I did not substantially take up a materialist analysis in my mobilization of intersectionality, yet this is a central project of Queer of Color Critique. Therefore, I posit that future researchers can take up Queer of Color Critique's attention to political economy in conjunction with intersectionality.

Another way that intersectionality can learn from queer studies results when the framework is paired with Quare Theory (Johnson, 2001). Quare theory intervened into the queer theory canon that had long attended to white identities and was undergirded by whiteness. Furthermore, quare theorists use the concept of performance theory, as opposed to performativity (Butler, 1990), in order to acknowledge that Queer People of Color recognize how societal discourses shape their identities and act in intentional ways to subvert these norms. Thus, Quare Theory has a great deal of potential as it relates to Queer Students of Color and their identities in higher education. Instead of simply articulating how structures of oppression shaped these individuals' view of these identities, a Quare Theory perspective would also attend to the agency that Queer People of Color perform in response to these systemic influences. Consequently, intersectional research in higher education would benefit from Quare Theory's interrogation of how individuals resist dominant norms tied to identities in subversive manners. Moreover, Quare Theory would have challenged me to destabilize what I meant by identities, as well as the advantages or limitations to conceptualizing queer as an identity. In addition to examining how intersectionality can learn from other queer studies frameworks, I assert there are several lines of inquiry that would amplify the perspectives on identity highlighted in this book.

Recommendations for Future Intersectional Research on Identity

In reflecting upon my dissertation research and the potential of intersectional theorizing in higher education, I encourage scholars to build upon this work through future scholarship. One way that individuals can contribute to intersectionality studies in higher education is by investigating the concept of identity development specifically, as opposed to identity exploration. Specifically, identity exploration represents a task that that many people undergo in their overall developmental journeys (Kroger & Marcia, 2011). As a result, there is still so much more to learn about how Queer Students of Color relate to their intersecting identities over larger periods of time, including before and after their experiences in college. For example, in Chapter Seven of this book, I highlighted the hopes that Queer Students of Color had for their futures moving forward. Yet, from this study alone, I cannot make any assertions whether these individuals attained this goals and how they did so, keeping in mind the role of structural oppression. For this reason, I encourage researchers to employ longitudinal research designs in order to more accurately get at matters of identity development for Queer Students of Color as contextualized by systems of power. Importantly, this scholarship should employ critical and poststructural lenses in order to document how Queer People of Color perceive the relationship between systemic oppression and their multiple minoritized identities over time.

Apart from needing longitudinal intersectional research on Queer Students of Color and their identities, I also suggest that subsequent scholarship uses institutional types other than HWIs as the contexts of interest. Though I selected HWIs for this project because of their historical legacies of racism (Museus et al., 2015; Wilder, 2013) and heterosexism (Graves, 2009, 2018; Nash & Silverman, 2015), I acknowledge that Queer Students of Color may experience identity exploration differentially if they attended other institutions (e.g., HBCUs and TCUs). Scholarship on HBCUs and Queer People of Color, for instance, continues to rise (Mobley & Johnson, 2015; Mobley & Hall, 2020; Patton & Simmons, 2008), but this body of literature has not explicitly dealt with processes such as identity exploration or development. Therefore, intersectional research on these topics could reveal unique perspectives on how heterosexism and other forms of oppression manifest on campuses founded to serve Communities of Color, together with showing how these environments may shape Queer Students of Colors' identities.

Finally, in my initial sampling, I operationalized queer as an identity to represent those who were sexually minoritized. And still I contend that more literature is needed that depicts the realities that Transgender People of Color face as they explore and navigate their intersectional identities at sites such as HWIs. Gender inevitably emerged as another salient identity in this project, as shown in Chapter Five, with participants who also identified as trans commenting on how this intersected with their race and sexuality. Yet, future projects could more explicitly attend to Trans Students of Color, further investigating how trans oppression plays a role in identity exploration. This recommendation is especially timely given the continued lack of research on Transgender People of Color in higher education and student affairs (see Garvey et al., 2019; Jourian, 2017; Nicolazzo, 2016 for exceptions). Centering the voices of Transgender People of Color at higher education institutions would serve as a catalyst for the implementation of equitable practices that center those most minoritized in society and on college campuses.

Conclusion

As an analytical framework intended to elucidate how systems of power overlap, intersectionality continues to grab the attention of scholars and practitioners striving to create more equitable conditions for minoritized people in educational spaces. However, due to its rise in popularity, several scholars have expressed their worries that people do not substantially honor the framework in their application (Bilge, 2013; Collins, 2015; Davis, 2008). In this chapter, I reflect on this point of caution, especially as I used intersectionality in ways that stretched the analytic's potential. In doing so, I echo the work of Jennifer Nash (2019) who believed that intersectional theorists must be open to reevaluating its reach. Reflecting upon my own use of the framework when studying the lives of Queer Students of Color, I assert that higher education researchers and practitioners can further actualize the power of intersectionality. It is only when we as a field engage deeply on the expansive landscape of intersectional-like thought that we can carve out our own interventions moving forward.

9 Implications for Historically White Institutions

Beyond offering implications for intersectional theorizing, I also find it important to highlight how those working at HWIs can address the systems of power that shape how Queer Students of Color explore their identities. In doing so, I seek to actualize one of intersectionality's core theoretical interventions: the advancement of social justice and social change (Dill & Zambrana, 2009). As scholars have highlighted, it is not enough to simply invoke intersectionality as a framework, but instead, researchers must also leverage intersectional theorizing to advocate for the deconstruction of structural inequalities (Collins, 2009b; Duran & Jones, 2019b; Moradi & Grzanka, 2017). Doing so honors intersectionality's history in which Women of Color, and particularly Black women, argued for the recognition and redress of the effects created by multiple axes of oppression (Crenshaw, 1989, 1991; Hancock, 2016).

To generate these implications, I wanted to honor the epistemic standpoint that the participants in this study held, for as Nash (2008) contended, those with multiple minoritized identities have the knowledge necessary to reimagine a more equitable world. In order to do so, I engaged with the Queer Students of Color about what they hoped would be different at the HWIs they attended. This part of our conversation allowed me to be imagine alongside the participants what HWIs would look like if they started from a place of centering Queer People of Color. These students spoke about specific aspects they wanted to see addressed by the faculty, student affairs staff, and on an institutional level.

In this chapter, I focus on the recommendations that Queer College Students of Color had for HWIs themselves. I offer these implications not as a way to anthropomorphize institutions as living, breathing organizations, but instead to think structurally about how HWIs further the minoritization of Queer People of Color. I acknowledge that institutions themselves do not create these conditions, but that those in power are enact policies, practices, and procedures that oppress those with multiple minoritized identities. Thus, while this chapter focuses on the structural issues present at HWIs and how participants wanted to see them addressed, the following chapter provides recommendations for individuals working on college campuses to effect systematic changes. As John Doe shared in our final interview together, "The problem at these institutions is culture," meaning that in order to shift cultural norms, it requires a reorientation on both the macro- and micro-level. It is hence imperative that readers engage both this chapter and the following one in order to understand the individual actions they can take to support Queer Students of Color in their identity exploration and what changes need to happen on an institutional level.

Attending to Representation at Historically White Institutions

As mentioned throughout the text, it is not the composition of racial/ethnic diversity itself that determines which colleges and universities people can consider *HWIs*, though undeniably the two are linked. Instead, it is the historical legacies of whiteness and white supremacy that undergird these institutions that define their status as historically white (Smith et al., 2007). Additionally, because all forms of oppression are interconnected, it is thus unsurprising that the ways that whiteness operates also leads to environments that marginalize other groups like queer individuals (Graves, 2018). And still, who students see as they walk to class, live in their residence halls, or commute to campus all have an influence on how they see their identities. Therefore, one of the first recommendations that the Queer Students of Color offered in our conversations had to do with who was represented on their campuses.

Of note, the participants in the study disclosed that they would want to have increased representation of those who are queer, People of Color, and Queer People of Color at their HWIs. When I asked Parker, for example, what he would want to be different at his public HWI in the Midwest, he took a pause, thought, and then said, "I would want to see less white people." We then both laughed in unison, while at the same recognizing the truth behind this simple statement. Indeed, Parker's words ring true with perspectives present in the existing scholarship in higher education and student affairs; that is, Queer Individuals of Color are not highly visible at HWIs, as well as at colleges and universities broadly (Abustan, 2017; Aguilar & Johnson, 2017; Duran, 2019d; Goode-Cross & Tager, 2011; Strayhorn, 2012b; Strayhorn et al., 2010; Vaccaro & Mena, 2011).

A major question follows: why is the representation of Queer People of Color crucial for students attending higher education institutions, and specifically, HWIs? On one hand, campus climate scholars have long drawn connections between compositional diversity at colleges and universities and how students perceive their environments in terms of their affirmation of disenfranchised groups (Harper & Hurtado, 2007; Hurtado, Alvarez, Guillermo-Wann, Cuellar, & Arellano, 2012). On the other hand, the stories of the participants' showcase that there is a strong connection between accessing communities with other Queer People of Color and how they navigate issues of identities at HWIs. Therefore, a relationship exists between the composition of one's institution and how these Queer Students of Color view their intersecting identities in developmental terms.

For example, participants like Alejo, Ezekiel, Parker, TJ, Richard, and Rosa commented on how they would feel if they could interact with students, staff, and faculty who identify as Queer People of Color. Richard acknowledged during our time together that "there's not that many" and it would be "nice if there were more." TJ also recognized this point when she shared with me: "As for the institution, I would tell them to make a concentrated effort to actually recruit diverse people . . . so we can get different kinds of people here." The sheer presence of those who are queer, People of Color, and Queer People of Color generates the possibilities that students will be able to understand how others have navigated critical challenges in their lives. As Rosa communicated, "I think that certainly helps exploration when you can go to someone older than you or maybe someone who has a little bit more experience in the world in general that could maybe help you with that." Being able to process through experiences of minoritization or having the opportunity to share joy with other Queer People of Color proves to be a vital part of identity exploration for these students.

Ezekiel went as far as to name where he would want to see a concerted effort at representation when he shared:

> I think I would just put more, what is it, I think I would just put more people in positions of power that have marginalized identities, but that also have a background in social justice because you do have those tokenized people that just, they play the gay card, they play the Black card, the Latino card, but they reinforce the culture.

In this statement, Ezekiel acknowledges that institutional agents cannot simply bring those with minoritized individuals to campus but they must also recruit those with a critical and liberatory orientation. Recruiting Queer Faculty and Staff of Color who have this knowledge and dedication requires significant effort, especially at institutions that have legacies of resisting change to oppressive cultures and practices. Thus, these individuals should also have the ability to access leadership positions where they can contribute positively to the shifting culture of an institution.

Finally, as I have highlighted in other work (Duran, 2019c) using the knowledge provided by Stewart (2017), it is not enough to consider increased representation of Queer People of Color on campus. This focus on simply attending to composition abdicates HWIs from addressing the very real structures of inequalities on which these colleges and universities are based upon in the first place. Therefore, it would behoove individuals working at HWIs to also ask, as Stewart posited, "What conditions have we created that maintain certain groups as the perpetual majority here?" (para. 10). In answering this inquiry, institutional agents will have to think more deeply about how they retain Queer Individuals of Color at their HWIs. To do so, they can consider questions such as:

- In what ways do we reinforce racism, heterosexism, and other forms of oppression through our structures, policies, and practices?
- How are these contemporary manifestations of minoritization tied to historical legacies of oppression at HWIs?
- How do our performance-evaluation strategies value the work that Queer People of Color do in their service to students, colleagues, the institution, and groups outside of our HWI?
- What types of mentorship opportunities do we create for Queer Students, Staff, and Faculty of Color?
- How do we provide Queer Students, Staff, and Faculty of Color the opportunity to practice leadership? What structural barriers exist to allow these groups to do so?
- How are spaces across campus hostile toward Queer Students, Staff, and Faculty of Color? What moves can we take to address this hostility?

Although not exhaustive by any means, these questions become a starting point toward taking the steps to retain Queer People of Color, an aim that is vital for Queer College Students of Color exploring their identities at HWIs. Connected to this mission of recruiting and retaining Queer Individuals of Color, the participants in this study also advocated for a revisiting of funding structures at HWIs.

Revisiting Funding Practices at Institutions

Highlighted in Chapter 3, one of the ways that HWIs influenced how Queer Students of Color explored their identities involved how they observed funding working at their institution. For many, seeing that resources dedicated to Queer People of Color were drastically underfunded and continued to experience budget cuts translated to how they viewed themselves. As shared by numerous participants, if the HWI they were attending did not adequately provide capital toward services for minoritized individuals, this practice informed how they understood their identities as being less than others. With this in mind, it is imperative that individuals at HWIs advocate for increased funding for initiatives centering Queer Individuals of Color.

Queer Students of Color in this study like Carmen, Oliver, Richard, and Ness all mentioned to me that they had hoped that the institutions they attended would allocate more finances to campus services dedicated to minoritized individuals. Inevitably, funding represents one manner in which institutions reify structures of oppression, with dominant groups receiving more human and financial capital than those with minoritized identities. For Carmen, it was giving "more funding to places like that, like the rainbow resource center," the office for queer and trans communities. For Richard, it was the ask to give more money to the student organizations that serve minoritized individuals:

> Give us more funding to do stuff because you can only do so much with weekly meetings. There's conferences and stuff we always wanted to go to, people we want to bring, to like talk about experiences and such. It's just give us more money; we could do more things. That's the biggest thing I can think of.

Though identity resource centers and identity-based student organizations were not without fault themselves, students often turned to these places to seek counsel, create community, and obtain valuable resources that would allow them to navigate their HWIs. Hence, these are a few services that institutional agents at HWIs can dedicate their financial capital to in order to assist Queer Students of Color in the exploration of their identities.

Ness poignantly communicated this point when they stated in their third interview:

> If they will provide the monetary support for spaces that those marginalized communities need . . . then people who have marginalized identities will see that they are valued in those senses as well, which will in turn help them explore their identity more.

Drawing the connection between funding, validation, and identity exploration, Ness' quote captures the necessity to move toward better financial support for Queer Students of Color. Of note, research on offices like LGBTQ Centers (Tillapaugh & Catalano, 2019) and Black Cultural Centers (Harris & Patton, 2017) have consistently underscored the lack of funding and resources dedicated to these spaces, which in turn limits their ability to advocate for multiple minoritized communities. Though those in the field of higher education and student affairs recognize the value of such offices (Patton, 2010), a need still exists to adequately offer assistance to these student life functions. In the case of the Queer Students of Color in this study, attention to these types of centers, as well as the student organizations founded for minoritized groups, would allow them to better explore matters of identity, especially when surrounded by a history of whiteness, heterosexism, and more.

Enacting the Potential of Educational Opportunities

In addition to increased representation and funding, participants spoke about the need for education about minoritized communities targeted at students, staff, and faculty. The reason why I elected to place this recommendation in this chapter focused on structural changes, rather the following one that is explicitly about suggestions that individuals can take up, is that the Queer Students of Color in this study stated that trainings should be ingrained into the institutional fiber. Rather than students, staff, and faculty having the option to opt into educational opportunities, participants hoped that there were mandatory opportunities for people to reflect on their forms of unconscious bias and how they can unlearn harmful behaviors, as well as beliefs.

Students like Alejo, Dash, Ezekiel, Max, Oliver, and TJ each brought up this desire for required training when I asked them to think about how HWIs could positively influence the exploration of their intersecting identities. In offering this implication, these participants regularly acknowledged that these kinds of professional development are already present on campuses, but that the individuals who access these opportunities are those who do not necessarily need this knowledge. In other words, those who evade taking part in educational programs are oftentimes the people who need this chance for reflection and information-gathering the most. For instance, Alejo and I spoke a great deal about what these types of trainings would mean for Queer Students of Color at HWIs. When talking about this, Alejo commented:

> I think a lot of people at [my institution] are participating in trainings, but professors don't have to do that. They're not required to, but they can if they want to. Of course, I think that certain programs like that should be a requirement to make sure that they're hiring faculty that are here to educate and help all type of students and not have preferences of who it should be, who they will teach and who they won't teach, and so I think making that kind of a mandated thing.

In this statement, Alejo implicates faculty members as having the ability to opt out of conversations around supporting minoritized identities, which inevitably means that they also may lack the know-how on how to do this work in the classroom. Thus, participants wanted to see actors such as faculty, as well as staff and students, having to engage with a baseline level of training that would provide them foundational knowledge on how to create welcoming environments within their own spheres of influence. Even more so, Ezekiel contended that senior-level administrators (e.g., provosts, vice presidents, presidents, and members of the board of trustees) should also undergo this type of education: "I would also just make sure that all the high, like senior level administrators and the entire senior level administration. I would put them through the same diversity thing that the staff would have to go through." Doing so would ensure that all positions at the institution comprehend the challenges present at HWIs for Queer Students of Color.

Even more specifically, some participants mentioned that these trainings should have people consider how overlapping systems of oppression impact the lives of those with multiple minoritized identities. One example of this came through in my final interview with Oliver. Having encountered dissonance when he struggled to find courses and spaces on campus that embraced his multiple minoritized identities, Oliver shared the following recommendation to campus professionals:

> I think, for the staff and faculty there should be a required training on . . . This seems very unlikely, but a required training on specifically different days and segments focused on certain racial and ethnic groups, certain queer groups, and then, both. Because I feel like it sounds like, oh, as long as they learn about one and the other, you're fine with those who are both. But it doesn't feel that way. So, I feel like there needs to be more of a focus on that first and then to . . . learn about queer students of color and what we experience or may experience.

In his comments, Oliver gets at the necessity to consider within-group differences that exist within particular populations and echoes formative arguments advanced by Crenshaw (1989, 1991) in her initial work on intersectionality. Namely, it is insufficient to provide trainings on queer individuals and then on People of Color, only to expect faculty and staff to understand how they should know how to support those who hold both minoritized identities. Instead, those designing diversity trainings should be mindful of how Queer People of Color encounter interlocking structures of domination and this uniquely affects their lived realities.

In uplifting this recommendation offered by participants, I also want to acknowledge that the research about diversity trainings on topics such as sexuality (Woodford, Kolb, Durocher-Radeka, & Javier, 2014) and topics of racial diversity (Kulick & Roberson, 2008) in academic settings is mixed. For example, scholarship on diversity courses for college students shows that the amount of classes that individuals take influences people's perceptions toward diversity (Bowman, 2010), which translates to the ways that people conceptualize the effects of diversity education. Consequently, it is imperative that should institutional agents at HWIs mandate these trainings that they consult the current research about how to do so in a meaningful and intentional manner. Additionally, as

Patton, Sánchez, Mac, and Stewart (2019) noted, more scholarship is needed about this topic (especially studies conducted from a critical perspective), meaning that scholar-practitioners present at institutions could help design trainings about Queer People of Color while researching the impacts that they have on participants.

Bringing Intention to Institutional Values of Diversity and Equity

One final implication that the Queer Students of Color generated in our final interviews together concerned the explicit disconnection between the espoused institutional value of diversity and what they in fact saw transpiring on campus. Throughout our interviews together, many students in the study articulated how they selected to attend a particular HWI under the assumption that they would thrive on campus based on the messaging perpetuated by the institution. However, when they arrived, these Queer College Students of Color immediately noticed that the institutional language of diversity diverged from what they observed as it relates to practices, policies, and procedures.

Participants including Alejo, Dash, gentle-breeze, Rose E., and Sarah Ray touched upon these sentiments during our conversations. In our time together, Rose E. expressed the ways that she found communities on and off campus where she could explore who she was as a Black bisexual femme. However, she often felt that she had to stumble throughout her time at the HWI to find these groups. She also came across instances when she felt institutional agents did the opposite of what she would consider as affirming of her intersecting identities. Thus, in her final interview with me, Rose E. stated the following:

> So I think the institution needs to understand that they have to be more direct, more clear about what they want students to know what it means when it comes to inclusivity and making sure that it's not just inclusivity for white people so they feel comfortable.

As we concluded our third interview, Rose E. provided this reflection to point to the fact that though the institutional messaging involved valuing diversity, the ways people on campus enacted this was for the comfort of those with dominant identities. Because diversity holds a multiplicity of meanings (Marvasti & McKinney, 2011), HWIs need to be more direct with what they mean by this term. Furthermore, from an intersectional lens, HWIs must move away from simply placing a value on diversity to embracing a centering of equity (see Stewart, 2017), meaning that they restructure practices to not simply include minoritized populations but to fight for their liberation.

Rosa hit upon this topic when she pushed back against the very policies created to protect minoritized individuals. In the concluding moments of her interview, Rosa spoke about the non-discrimination policies that existed at her institution: "They're like, 'Yeah, we don't discriminate against people,' but there's not really much to do if clubs or other things actively do that." Hearing comments such as these made me think about how Nicolazzo (2017) described non-discrimination policies are in themselves incomplete as they often function in symbolic ways. In other words, non-discrimination policies do very little to in fact alter the conditions in which people live. Moreover, harkening back to Crenshaw's (1989, 1991) foundational work on intersectionality reminds me that law and policies have often erased the lives of people who hold multiple minoritized identities by obscuring their unique experiences of marginalization. Consequently, if HWIs want to affirm and center Queer Collegians of Color, they must move beyond surface-level policies to display this commitment.

Conclusion

As highlighted throughout this chapter, HWIs require a change in culture to better support Queer Students of Color enrolling at these colleges and universities. These shifts necessitate a revisiting of practices, policies, and procedures done on both an institutional, as well as an individual level. From an institutional perspective, participants in this study implicated the role of representation (and retention) of those with multiple minoritized identities, the funding practices present at HWIs, requiring trainings and education, and how language around diversity is enacted. These comments reinforce that students with minoritized identities have a unique perspective necessary in order to imagine equitable educational environments. As a result, it is imperative that those at HWIs listen to these recommendations in order to produce a campus where Queer People of Color can explore their intersecting identities and where racism, heterosexism, as well as other forms of oppression are mitigated. As covered in the subsequent chapter, these institutional moves must be paired with individual commitments to addressing intersecting structures of domination at HWIs.

10 Implications for Professionals

Staff and faculty are uniquely positioned to contribute to the identity exploration of Queer Students of Color enrolled at HWIs. Seen throughout the participants' narratives, for every individual working on campus who perpetuated racist, heterosexist, and other oppressive behaviors, there was a person that gave their time and energy to assist participants in formative moments. Whether it was a director of a cultural center providing counsel to a student when they were questioning what it meant to hold multiple minoritized identities or a faculty member who seamlessly integrated attention to underserved communities in their lessons, these people were integral for Queer People of Color embracing their intersecting identities on campus.

As a result, when speaking with students in the third interview, I found it necessary to not only ask them what structural changes they would want implemented at HWIs, but also how they hoped faculty and staff would alter their oppressive behaviors. The conversations that ensued covered topics such as reimaging how instructors across disciplines construct their curricula, how student affairs practitioners create programming that honors within-group differences, and how counseling professionals offer identity-conscious services. This chapter then concludes with the most common recommendation spoken across participants: wanting individuals on campus to truly listen to their needs and care for them in a way that resists the overlapping forms of oppression that Queer People of Color encounter in society, as well as on campus. In listening to the participants' quotes, I encourage readers to engage in a process of critical self-reflection where they consider how they perpetuate oppressive behaviors and how these narratives can guide their practice moving forward.

Integrating Attention to Minoritized Identities in Coursework

To begin, academic settings served as one of the salient collegiate experiences that allowed Queer People of Color to explore their identities if they observed themselves represented in lessons or read material that spoke to their realities. However, many students discussed how they failed to see attention to their minoritized identities in coursework. Consequently, these Queer Students of Color felt erased and overlooked in the classroom, echoing the body of scholarship that showcases how faculty can posit queer individuals and People of Color as other through their pedagogical practices (e.g., Basile & Lopez, 2015; Gurin, Dey, Hurtado, & Gurin, 2002; Linley & Nguyen, 2015). Carmen, gentle-breeze, Max, Ness, Oliver, and TJ all stated in their final interview that faculty should address oppressed communities, and specifically those with multiple minoritized identities, in their lessons and curricula. gentle-breeze captured this implication when she stated the following: "One thing that I think is good, just that anyone can do is, with your material, just have literature and things and examples that are coming from queer voices and People of Color." In doing so, instructors create the room for Queer People of Color to ask vital questions about identity. Importantly, they argued that these recommendations applied to courses whose subject matter explicitly involved issues of social identities, groups, and inequalities, as well as those that frequently overlook social identities altogether and particularly, STEM disciplines.

Classes Focused on Social Identities, Groups, and Inequalities

Numerous Queer Students of Color represented in this study could point to a class where an educator failed to paint a picture of the complexities that exist within a social group, presenting queer communities or People of Color as monolithic. Yet, in order to support individuals exploring their intersecting identities, instructors must be ready to reveal show how social stratification is magnified for those who hold multiple minoritized identities. As highlighted in their excerpts throughout this book, Ness was a student who often sought out academic opportunities to learn about what it meant to be a pansexual Asian American non-binary person in society. Because they rarely found such chances, Ness believed that it would be beneficial for educators to be mindful of identity intersections in their teaching: "I guess for classes that do offer queer . . . that are centered around maybe queer topics or centered around racial topics, that they should make room for [other groups] . . . classes about race should make room for queer perspectives." As we conversed in the final interview, Ness emphasized how valuable it would have been for their exploration if they had faculty who were attentive to these issues.

Oliver also had similar experiences to Ness, oftentimes feeling left out in his classes focused on Latinx issues. Thus, when I asked him to reflect on potential implications for faculty and staff, he identified these instances as potential areas of improvement. In particular, Oliver mentioned the following:

> A lot of times I've noticed within specific gender, sexuality courses or specific cultural and ethnic classes . . . I feel like if they included more of each other, like how the history of. . . . Say, if I'm in Latino History class, which I'm in right now, if we learned more about the queer Latinos who were influencers that would be not only eye-opening for me as someone who identifies as that but for those who may not to just see that, have that exposure. Whereas, if I were in a queer-oriented classroom, if you focus more on what the Queer People of Color did, then again, that would create more exposure to myself and those who may not share those identities.

In this statement, Oliver communicated a number of important points. The first being that educators who attend to within-group differences can positively shape the lives of students who may not only identify with one minoritized group but multiple. The second is that Oliver also maintained that this practice would serve to educate those with more dominant identities on the structural issues that people with numerous minoritized identities face.

With Ness and Oliver's comments in mind, it would behoove faculty who teach classes on topics of culture and social groups to offer more complex perspectives on minoritized communities. This shift in education requires instructors to critically analyze every aspect of their teaching. For instance, faculty in charge of these types of courses can engage in syllabus audits, in which they assess how many of the readings they assign are written by or about those who hold multiple minoritized identities. Moreover, these instructors can similarly examine whether they relegate those with multiple minoritized identities to a particular week in the semester (i.e., a week on Black queer and trans identities in a queer studies course) or if they integrate an intersectional analysis throughout their course. Doing this work requires instructors to address how oppression is interconnected and how heterosexism manifests differently for those whose bodies are also regulated by anti-Black racism and trans oppression, for example. Beyond these courses that have a particular focus on social identities and groups, however, participants also spoke about STEM disciplines specifically as fields that needs an intervention as it relates to intersectional systems and identity.

Attending to Identity in STEM Disciplines

A number of Queer Students of Color in this study commented on the identity-neutral ways that instructors in STEM disciplines approached their teaching. Albeit not surprising given the literature on the exclusionary attitudes reported by Students of Color (McCoy, Luedke, & Winkle-Wagner, 2017) and queer individuals (Miller, Vaccaro, Kimball, & Forester, 2020), participants stressed that these oppressive climates must receive attention in order to better the lives of Queer People of Color. For instance, though not in a STEM major herself, gentle-breeze went on to comment in her final interview on how she perceived STEM course instructors to erase all matters of identity. Specifically, gentle-breeze stated,

> 'Cause I have friends who are on different science or engineering tracks that are of Color and then some of them identify as queers, but yeah, there's still gonna be issues there. Even if your teacher doesn't think that these [identities] matter in their materials, you assign problem sets that are not . . . there's just a lack of understanding or representation or room for expression.

Because a person's social identities will inevitably shape how they engage with course material or how they show up in the classroom, the participants underscored the necessity for STEM faculty to attend to identities in their teaching. By implementing practices that address identities, instructors validate Queer Students of Color, in addition to potentially mitigating the oppressive interactions that college students may have in their classrooms.

On one hand, participants encouraged faculty in STEM disciplines to resist framing disciplinary knowledge as applicable to all populations. Namely, Queer Students of Color recognized that certain disciplines perpetuate information about social groups without attending to minoritized populations or the systems of power shaping their realties. TJ communicated this reality when she shared:

> I would tell faculty to be cognizant of the fact that not everyone fits in a certain majority identity, so you can . . . I guess you cannot completely ignore a certain group's experiences while trying to teach something. I would tell psych faculty specifically, to remember that psychology is very Westernized and there's a very limited sample that people pull from, and that that doesn't necessarily mean that it extends to the entire population, because I think that sometimes gets lost in the weeds. Especially with intro psych courses.

As a psychology major, TJ recognized the ways that scientific disciplines have long marginalized people through their methods. Thus, she recommended that instructors make an intentional effort to acknowledge these histories in order to show Queer People of Color that they are mindful of these limitations and the application to their lives.

Carmen similarly asked that educators attend to minoritized communities through the examples that they offer in class to teach material. Also referencing their experiences in psychology courses, Carmen mentioned:

> Then also, expand on curriculum, like what you're learning in class. Don't just do hetero-couples, or don't just do white people. I remember, in some of my classes, in the PowerPoints it's always pictures of white people and can you at least add one Person of Color? Just be more mindful of what you're doing because for a lot of professors and faculty, they don't think about it so they think that we don't think about it either, but a lot of us do.

Underscored by Carmen, the classroom environment significantly informed how participants thought about their social identities. Consequently, if instructors want to create affirming environments for Queer People of Color at HWIs, they need to pay attention to how they are integrating these communities into their lessons by normalizing their presence.

Finally, participants also encouraged instructors in these classes to comprehend that their identities have an effect on how students engage with the material and interact with one another. For instance, Max spoke about their experiences in a health-related major in our final interview together. They noted that students' social identities impact how they engage in class and how they think about their performance, echoing the scholarship on phenomena like stereotype threat (Steele, 2010). They shared: "And then faculty, acknowledge that identity plays a role in your class, regardless of what your class. It could be a stats class or a bio class, but acknowledge that it totally influences how students interact with each other." Vital to note is that STEM courses have the potential to further oppressive systems like racism, heterosexism, and others if faculty enter with the assumption that social identities do not play a role in the learning process for students. As a result, instructors should evaluate their teaching approaches and consult existing research to examine how they can better construct classroom environments that account for students' holistic selves. For educators interested in continuing to learn about how they can use intersectionality to guide their teaching, I would encourage them to reference the body of literature on this very topic (e.g., Case, 2017; Jones & Wijeysinghe, 2011; Pliner, Iuzzini, & Banks, 2011). Beyond curricular spaces, however, participants pointed to the necessity to attend to multiple minoritized identities in events, programs, and initiatives on campus.

Attending to Multiple Minoritized Identities in Student Affairs

In their remarks, Queer Students of Color called for student affairs programming and initiatives developed with an intersectional lens in mind. Though the field of higher education and student affairs has since its inception been committed to the education and support of the holistic student (Jones & Abes, 2013; Patton et al., 2016; Rodgers, 1990), more work is needed to generate student engagement opportunities that are intersectional at their very core, especially for Queer Students of Color (Duran, 2019d; Evans & Wallace, 2019; Johnson & Javier, 2017). Hence, it is vital for those who work in student affairs to account for the needs of Queer People of Color.

One of the most striking comments that I heard in my time with these participants involved Avery's reflection on how there was a singular week where it felt like it could be its authentically holistic self. This particular week was when the LGBTQ Center and the Diversity Affairs office on campus collaborated on programming with each other. This experience then came back again when Avery and I had our final interview together. After posing the question to Avery asking for its insights on implications, Avery shared how it hoped that these types of offices on campus would work with one another more intentionally throughout the year. In particular, it stated, "You have students that are exploring and they're trying to figure themselves out, and how can they when it seems like you keep these two resource centers so separate from one another?" The question that Avery offered serves as an important reminder for readers who work in identity centers such as these. In Avery's remarks, it communicated what is often found in the literature: that identity centers frequently default to the majority within these spaces intended for minoritized communities. For instance, scholars have highlighted the whiteness of LGBTQ Centers (Mitchell & Means, 2014) and how other cultural centers (e.g., Black Cultural Centers) may have limited resources to program with within-group differences in mind (Harris & Patton, 2017).

What then can be done to reimagine student affairs programming at HWIs focused on identities? First, a baseline recommendation involves that staff in charge of these initiatives should make intentional efforts to collaborate across offices, particularly if there are other identity-based services available on campus. Being able to work across identity resources saves capital, in addition to utilizing the expertise of professionals at the institution. Second, student affairs practitioners should critically reflect on what types of messages are communicated if they confine conversations around intersectional oppression and within-group differences to a particular week or month in the year. Rather than engaging in this practice, which inherently puts individuals with multiple minoritized identities on the margins, professionals should make an intentional effort to foreground discussions of intersectional topics throughout. By starting from a place that is intersectionally minded in nature, it does not isolate those with majority identities in these spaces (e.g., white queer students in LGBTQ centers). Rather, it centers the needs of Queer Students of Color while giving others the space to reflect on their areas of privilege within a particular minoritized community. What this requires educators to do is analyze what they mean when they produce resources for a specific social group. Does the category of student services for racially minoritized students, for example, also include queer and trans people, those who have disabilities, are from low-income backgrounds? If professionals cannot answer these kinds of questions in the affirmative, then this signals intersectional erasure and failure.

Importantly, these recommendations apply beyond identity-specific services on college campuses and at HWIs. In fact, professionals who work in other offices at institutions should also use this as an opportunity to think critically about how they allow for topics of identity and intersectional oppression in their events, programs, and initiatives. In order to hold space for Queer Students of Color to explore their intersecting identities in the face of oppressive systems at HWIs, it is the responsibility of student affairs educators to reflect on how they play a role in affirming or erasing these individuals' realities.

Providing Identity-Considerate Counseling Services

Another implication that the Queer Students of Color provided involved the nature of counseling services on college campuses. In listening to the stories that they offered, it was undoubtedly clear that an affective dimension of identity exploration exists, as shown in Chapter Six of this book. In their narratives, participants touched upon the very real and difficult emotions that they had to process when unlearning the harmful messages perpetuated in dominant society. Feelings of hurt, shame, and trauma all manifested for these Queer College Students of Color as they inevitably gave way to the potential for pride and confidence. It was thus not surprising to me that Queer Students of Color wanted more support as they explored who they were at their HWIs.

Carmen was one participant who spoke explicitly about their mental health issues throughout our time together. Identifying as mentally ill, this part of their story came back up again when I asked them for what they hoped would change as a result of them sharing their experiences. Alongside other recommendations, Carmen named the following:

> But then, also give counseling resources for people that need it based on identity work and things like that. I would like to see that.

> Or even . . . because I feel that my past experiences with counseling, like within the counseling center, they didn't really explore, or dig deep into like, "How are you making sense with coming out?" Because when I came out for the first time, I remember my counselor was like, "Are you sure?" Like no, you don't say that. . . . And train people, too.

Carmen's own experiences with counseling largely revolved around their academic issues with their therapist not considering how their ability to complete schoolwork would inherently be connected to their identities.

In a time when the topic of mental health on college campuses continues to be a major priority in the United States (Oswalt, Lederer, Chesnut-Steich, Day, Halbritter, & Ortiz, 2020), and when scholars communicate that Queer People of Color report minority stress due to systems of racism and heterosexism (Cyrus, 2017; Datta, Bialer, & McIntosh, 2017), it is of crucial importance that counseling centers provide the necessary assistance for Queer Students of Color exploring matters of identity. This priority would require counselors to be well-versed in understanding the unique mental health challenges that people with multiple minoritized identities face as a result of systemic oppression. Therefore, it would be beneficial for such professionals to seek out training guided by intersectional theorizing so that they may have the knowledge necessary to comprehend these complex realities. Moreover, connected to recommendations provided in Chapter Nine, those working in these centers should advocate for the hiring of Queer People of Color who may be more well-versed in the issues that these students encounter at HWIs. Finally, counselors should consider creating groups specific to queer students who hold multiple minoritized identities to have a space to process through their experiences doing so in college. Though I acknowledge that more research on the interconnections between mental health, intersectional oppression, and identity exploration is needed to inform these practices, I believe that the participants' words can start these important conversations at HWIs.

Offering Care and Support to Queer People of Color

In the final interviews I held with the participants, they each generated concrete implications that would without a doubt improve the conditions that Queer Individuals of Color have at HWIs. However, the final suggestion that the majority of these Queer Students of Color gave was less concrete, but perhaps the most vital. In spending hours with each of the individuals represented in this research, it was clear to me that they had a large amount of hope for the faculty and practitioners who work at HWIs.

They truly believed that faculty and staff alike could make changes that mitigated the presence of oppressive systems and that would create more welcoming environments for those exploring their identities. Their ask of higher education professionals and the one I present now to the readers is that they simply listen, care, and provide support to Queer People of Color. The participants hoped that faculty and staff would inquire about how they could be better advocates for Queer Students of Color and that they would do so constantly. To emphasize this point, I offer four quotes from participants that showcase their wishes.

Parker: *Showing their unconditional care, 'cause you know, being a teacher, and a professor, shouldn't be nearly about grades, and study, but it should also be about growth as a person, and you know, if they could recognize that, which they won't like, soon, but I feel like, it would steer everyone in the right direction of, you know, acceptance, and helping everyone find themselves, and you know, when you're less stressed about that, you can do better in school too, and you can have a more successful future by, you know, not only doing well in school, but having these great relationships, with other people, and yourself.*

Rosa: *For staff and faculty, I would say be receptive, be ready to receive information before you're gonna just start talking. 'Cause sometimes people just shit out their mouth and they just say whatever and it's not helpful. So, listening first, receiving information, trying to be empathetic. 'Cause I know everyone can't understand everything, but going in with the mindset of trying to come from where your student's coming from or where people might be coming from. Being broad and as inclusive as possible, I know some marginalized groups get forgotten about, but being receptive to everything and trying to show that they're putting their best effort into being inclusive, and I think someone's best effort usually shows that a lot of people who have identities like being queer, being a certain race, it'll make it easier for a student to approach a faculty or staff member about things pertaining to that.*

Max: *To my institution, I'd probably say something like stop expecting our labor. Actually, think about how you can support us. . . . Actually try to pay attention to us. And recognize that it's not the same, the way that we experience dress and try to navigate campus is very different from Bethany, from Brighton, Michigan with a bunch of money. We think about other things that weigh on us and affect our stress levels, like don't expect us to perform the same academically. Stop tokenizing us. And just listen.*

Wren: *Maybe I would say . . . I don't know, like try to implement more things that would require actual listening. And like, I'm trying to think of ways to do it, but I'm stumped on ways to frame it to where it can be like something that could produce viable change versus trying to beg for change. I would say really implement things that you can find maximum yield in, that will require listening, that will be big on actual time and space to understand. And like, listen to the community, really. Like, listen to them. Listen to them in a way where you can find it's not this side is what I agree with. If you're not really trying to find balance, then it's always going to be problems. You need to find balance and just a full understanding. Yeah, that's what I'm saying.*

Communicated through these four quotes, these Queer Students of Color assert that one of the major ways that campus staff and faculty can address issues involves having an open channel for feedback, in addition to actively seeking it. Hence, I would encourage educators reading this text to take a pause and consider how they have taken the intentional step to search for knowledge on how to support minoritized communities. Readers must continue to be self-critical of their own perpetuation of oppression and how they can better listen to the stories of Queer People of Color, both in this book but also on their campuses. To engage in the structural change needed to dismantle historical and contemporary legacies of oppression at HWIs requires this willingness to listen, learn, and advocate.

Conclusion

In crafting this chapter and the one that preceded it, I wanted the participants' words to be at the forefront of readers' minds. The reason being that during the time we spent together, I learned a great deal from these students about how to continue to fight toward equity at HWIs. Therefore, I knew that others would benefit profoundly from their knowledge and insights. It is not going to be easy to push back against the ways that racism, heterosexism, and other forms of oppression are ingrained in the fiber of HWIs. However, the work requires professionals to start from a genuine desire to want to positively impact the lives of Queer Students of Color on their campuses. With this type of dedication at heart and the participants' stories in mind, I assert that we as a field can collectively work toward crafting institutional environments that allow for Queer People of Color to explore their identities surrounded by affirming individuals, relationships, and spaces.

Epilogue

> I had my first ever dissertation interview with Ezekiel this morning. During our time together, he offered many thoughts about how he feels stifled by his institution and the town where it is located. At one point, he mentioned that he has grown all he can: "I have no urge to try and explore anything, because I feel like I've hit the furthest place I can go in exploration. . . ." He shared instances where others have seen him as a threat to their white heteronormative lifestyle, leading him to hold a sense of fear as he navigates his historically white institution. My heart dropped when I heard this. . . . Ezekiel later went on to say that despite these feelings, he tries to advocate for those who are like him. In fact, he said the greatest lesson that he's learned is that he is not the only one who has gone through these struggles. Hence, he wants to create a better environment for other QPOC who will follow him. . . . I wonder what other participants will say. Will this be consistent? Will they experience the same stifling around their identities by these higher education institutions? Will they want to fight for others despite the oppressive spaces and behaviors they encountered?
>
> – An excerpt from a memo I wrote in my reflection journal on August 13, 2018

To end this book, I found it fitting to return to the beginning. In this instance of the just-quoted reflection, I acknowledged how Ezekiel felt targeted by those at his HWI and the negative influence these experiences had on his identity exploration. In particular, he shared that he had done all the exploration he could do, wanting to escape elsewhere to further understand who he was. Returning to Knefelkamp et al.'s (1978) call for theoretical knowledge that answers "what factors in the particular environment of a college/university can either encourage *or* inhibit growth" (p. x, emphasis added), it was clear to me from this initial interview (of which 55 more interviews would occur with the other 19 participants) that HWIs were environments that needed to be further interrogated from an intersectional perspective. If Ezekiel stated that he encountered racism and heteronormativity that in turn limited his ability to explore his identities, surely this was an issue that others faced as well.

What followed was an experience unlike any other. In the interviews with the 20 participants, these Queer Collegians of Color shared how the HWIs they attended greatly informed how they viewed their identities and the sense of self they constructed. Returning to John Doe's short, yet poignant quote (i.e., "I am who I am because of the institution I attend"), I recognized the ways that HWIs engaged in forms of intersectional erasure and violence. Specifically, how faculty and staff created their classroom environments, programming structures, and institutional policies rendered Queer Communities of Color invisible, leading to feelings of being unwanted and not cared for within their collegiate environments. Importantly, these realities occurred in their home lives, surrounding cities and towns, as well as in the sociopolitical discourse.

Throughout, I was reminded of Kimberlé Crenshaw's (1989, 1991) foundational work where she argued that Black women had experienced this form of intersectional erasure in the law and in identity movements because people failed to use a frame that acknowledged how systems like sexism and racism constituted one another. In a similar way, institutional agents at the colleges and universities represented in this study (re)produced this same way of thinking by ignoring the compounding effects of structures like racism and heterosexism – an intersectional failure that in turn, obscured the realities and needs of Queer People of Color on campus. Equally concerning were the narratives that participants shared where they were hypervisible on and off campus, feeling targeted due to oppressive attitudes and behaviors. I saw in action how historical legacies of racism (Museus et al., 2015; Wilder, 2013) and heterosexism (Graves, 2009, 2018; Nash & Silverman, 2015) present at HWIs continue to intersect to this day, informing how Queer Individuals of Color explore their identities. Thus, in the same fashion that scholars have long conceptualized identity as a product of how one sees themselves in relation to others, it is impossible to separate conversations of identity from structures of power and oppression.

However, what also captured my attention were the ways that these Queer College Students of Color learned new ways of viewing their identities, unlearning the negative messages they had previously internalized about their race, sexuality, and more. Whether it was being in community with other Queer People of Color or seeing themselves represented in readings, curricula, or media, these students began to embrace who they were in the face of systemic oppression. The bonds that these students formed with their contemporary and historical Queer Communities of Color proved to be important catalysts that helped them adopt positive understandings of and sentiments connected to their intersecting identities. It was these relationships that sparked some of the participants' interests to continue to fight the manifestations of racism, heterosexism, and other forms of oppression at their institutions and beyond.

It is with the hopes of the 20 Queer Students of Color in mind that I would like to offer a select group of questions that this project prompted for me as a way of concluding this text:

- What would HWIs (in addition to other institutional types) look like if we centered Queer Students of Color?
- How would Queer Students of Color feel if they saw themselves represented in student affairs programming, classroom spaces, and on campus?
- How do higher education professionals work with the surrounding communities to get Queer Students of Color connected to meaningful groups and organizations? How do practitioners help address the oppressive instances Queer Students of Color have off campus?
- How do staff and faculty contribute to the breakdown of systems like racism, heterosexism, trans oppression, anti-Blackness, and others – keeping in mind how they are positioned in structures of power and oppression based on their own identities?
- How do staff and faculty help Queer Students of Color to actualize their hopes at and beyond HWIs?

These questions are a few of many that crossed my mind as I was interviewing the 20 Queer Students of Color who entrusted me with their stories. Specifically, they did so with the wish that their participation in this study would mobilize higher education professionals to better create conditions for Queer People of Color who attend college. Although the recommendations that these participants generated in Chapters Nine and Ten are a starting point, it is going to take a genuine commitment to doing the self-work required to advocate for institutional changes that will lead to shifts at HWIs. It is only when staff and faculty embrace this responsibility to address overlapping systems of oppression present at HWIs that colleges and universities will become sites where Queer Students of Color can fully explore *and* embrace their intersections.

Methodological Appendix

For those interested in the research process that led to the data presented in this text, I wanted to include a brief appendix providing key details about the study design I employed. Although this appendix does not offer an exhaustive description of the project (see Duran, 2019a for a more complete look at the research design), I hope that it spurs thinking and imagining within those who want to contribute to this body of scholarship. As mentioned throughout this book, the field of higher education and student affairs would benefit from more engagement with third wave college student development theorizing (Abes et al., 2019; Jones & Stewart, 2016). The following sections thus show my attempt to contribute meaningfully to this third wave as I sought to actualize the framework of intersectionality (Crenshaw, 1989, 1991) at every point in the research process.

An Epistemological Blending: Constructivist and Critical Perspectives

One of the most crucial decisions I made at the onset of the project concerned the epistemological foundation that I would set to inform the rest of the research. Regarded as "the theory of knowledge imbedded in the theoretical perspective and thereby in the methodology" (Crotty, 1998, p. 3), a study's epistemology functions as the lens that a scholar uses to construct their research question, to decide the methods that they will employ, and how they will interpret the data collected. With this in mind, I had to reflect thoroughly on how my epistemological framing would center the knowledge held by participants with multiply minoritized identities while at the same time, interrogating the overlapping systems of power and oppression that shape their realities.

Revisiting Abes' (2009) formative work on the use of theoretical borderlands in student development theorizing led me on the path toward developing an epistemological base that would allow me to honor the stories of Queer Students of Color in this study and that simultaneously permitted me to critique structures like racism, heterosexism, and more. In particular, Abes argued that "all theoretical perspectives that guide research are incomplete" (p. 141), meaning that it may be necessary for researchers to blend multiple theoretical perspectives and epistemologies to generate a more complex understanding of data. Drawing upon Gloria Anzaldúa's (1987) conceptualization of the borderlands, this approach pushes researchers to consider the implications of bringing together divergent traditions in favor of a richer analysis that accounts for systems of power, privilege, and oppression. To make meaning of the participants' multiple minoritized identities in the context of my own research, I employed a process similar to Abes' by using both constructivism and critical theory in conjunction with one another in this study.

To begin, one of the epistemological traditions that I mobilized in this project was constructivism. Constructivism asserts that knowledge is a product of a social construction and it challenges researchers to understand how people make meaning of phenomena based on contextual influences and social interactions (Charmaz, 2000, 2011, 2014; Denzin & Lincoln, 2000; Guba & Lincoln, 1998; Lincoln & Guba, 1985). As Crotty (1998) named it, constructivism encapsulates "the view that all knowledge, and therefore all meaningful reality as such, is contingent upon human practices, being constructed in and out of interaction between human beings and their world, and developed and transmitted within an essentially social context" (p. 42). Of note, constructivist researchers also acknowledge that their own lenses will inform how they interpret data in a project (Charmaz, 2014; Mertens, 2015). If participants themselves engage in meaning making based on their environments so do the researchers. A majority of qualitative research on college student identity stems from a constructivist epistemological stance (Duran & Jones, 2019b), as researchers seek to understand how participants construct their perceptions of who they are in society. Consequently, I believed that constructivism lent itself well to the study of identity exploration for Queer Students of Color at HWIs. However, constructivism itself felt incomplete as I strove to engage in an analysis that would implicate larger structures of power (e.g., racism, heterosexism) that influenced how Queer Students of Color explored who they were.

Critical theory (Denzin, 2015, 2017; Kincheloe & McLaren, 2002; Lincoln & Denzin, 2000) hence proved to be the missing piece that would allow me to also foreground a power-based analysis in this study. Namely, critical scholars enter research in with the aim to analyze "competing power interests between groups and individuals within a society – identifying who gains and who loses in specific situations" (Kincheloe & McLaren, 2002, p. 90). Recognizing that systems of power play a central role in influencing how reality and knowledge are constructed, critical schools of thought helped me name how participants' meaning making was always situated within cultural, political, and social realities. Like constructivism, critical qualitative researchers also acknowledge the necessity to engage in a reflexive inquiry process, meaning that I had to reflect on how my forms of privilege and marginalization influenced my approach to this project. Critical theory ultimately provided the epistemological assumptions necessary to critique how racism, heterosexism, and other forms of oppression manifested in matters of identity for Queer College Students of Color.

Importantly, by employing constructivism and critical theory together, I adhered to May's (2015) reading of intersectionality as a framework that embraces the both/and. Intersectional scholars purport that individuals can mobilize the framework to center the knowledge that minoritized populations hold (akin to constructivism) in order to recognize how structures of oppression function in society (like critical theory) (Collins & Bilge, 2016; Nash, 2008; May, 2015). Therefore, I could adhere to participants' perspectives on their identity exploration, while at the same, being guided by their meaning making to comprehend how overlapping systems of power functioned in this process. This reading of intersectionality hence served as a reasoning for why a theoretical borderlands approach (Abes, 2009) benefitted the framing of this research project.

Methodological Approach: Constructivist Grounded Theory

As mentioned in the introduction to this text, I adopted constructivist grounded theory as a methodology (Charmaz, 2014), leading to the stories presented in the preceding chapters. For those unfamiliar with grounded theory methodology broadly, this research approach allows scholars to create a theory inductively from data collected in the hopes of developing a "theoretical explanation about the why and how something happens" (Corbin & Strauss, 2015, p. 15). Grounded theorists oftentimes seek to understand social processes and in the case of this project, the process of interest was that of identity exploration. In other words, how does identity exploration occur for Queer Students of Color at HWIs? Although early traditions of grounded theory strove for goals of objectivity (see Glaser, 1992, 1998; Glaser & Strauss, 1967) and would argue that there is one answer to the question that proceeds this statement, future researchers like Kathy Charmaz (2014) wanted to "highlight the flexibility of the method and resist mechanical applications of it" (p. 13). It is in this view of grounded theory that I used to guide the research project.

Notably, constructivist grounded theories do not believe in laying claims to objectivity, instead arguing that the researcher plays a vital role in collecting, analyzing, and interpreting data (Charmaz, 2000, 2002, 2008a, 2008b, 2014). In addition to elaborating on the influence that the researcher has on the analytical procedure, constructivist grounded theory scholars elevate the importance of examining how contexts and social situations influence the process of interest at the heart of a study. Because of its rejection of objectivity, this tradition of grounded theory brings to light "the usually invisible and inchoate social features of a situation . . . all the key elements in the situation and their interrelations; the social worlds and arenas in which the phenomena of interest are embedded" (Clarke, 2003, p. 572). Much like constructivism as an epistemology interrogates how meaning is constituted within one's environment, constructivist grounded theory examines this as it relates to the social process under investigation. Pertinent to the study I undertook, Charmaz (2011, 2014, 2017) argued that constructivist grounded theory can be used to advance social justice aims. Thus, constructivist grounded theory was also an appropriate methodological tradition to pair with the critical theory epistemology undergirding this research.

Study Purpose and Participant Recruitment

Using constructivist grounded theory as a methodology, I set out to understand the process of identity exploration for Queer College Students of Color at HWIs. Specifically, the research questions that guided this study that led to this book included the following: (a) How do Queer Students of Color explore their identities during their time at HWIs?; (b) How do collegiate experiences play a role in the process of identity exploration for Queer Students of Color at HWIs?; (c) How do systems of power influence the process of identity exploration for Queer Students of Color at HWIs?; and (d) How do Queer Students of Color at HWIs make meaning of their identities during the process of identity exploration? To answer these questions, I used numerous forms of data collection that aligned with the epistemological and methodological decisions I have discussed.

In order to answer the research questions, I knew I needed to develop meaningful sampling criteria (Jones, Torres, & Arminio, 2014). After much thought, I created the criteria that participants needed to: (a) be an undergraduate student who was 18–25 years of age; (b) identify as Students of Color, including individuals who identify as multiracial or biracial; (c) identify under the umbrella term of queer. This included, but was not limited to, people who identify as gay, lesbian, bisexual, pansexual, polysexual, demisexual, and asexual; (d) feel comfortable talking about how they have explored their identities as a Queer Person of Color in college; (e) have attended their current institution for at least 2 years; (f) must represent a diverse range of sexualities, races/ethnicities, genders, social classes, ability, and faith identities; and (g) must come from a variety of institutional types and backgrounds (e.g., size, public versus private, and institutional resources). By selecting people who fit this profile, I would acquire a sample that would get at the beautiful diversity that exists within Queer Communities of Color while at the same time, having a group of individuals that were bound enough in the ways that they would experience the process of identity exploration similarly.

For instance, I identified that participants must have been undergraduate students who were 18–25 years of age. The assumptions that I entered in with when generating this criterion is that undergraduate students would have very different perspectives on identity than those who had already completed one higher education degree and gone on to another. Moreover, the decision to search for those who were 18–25 years of age was predicated on the belief that these individuals would be encountering similar developmental journeys, which Arnett (2000, 2010, 2011) would term as the beginning of a stage named emerging adulthood. Additionally, I put in place the criterion describing that participants must have attended their current institution for at least two years. I had hoped that by spending at least this period at their HWI would mean that these individuals could speak meaningfully to the policies, practices, and interactions they had at the institution.

One of the main points of consideration I wrestled with was who exactly I would include to represent a category as large as Queer People of Color. I recognized that the ways that individuals would experience interlocking systems of oppression would differ based on where they were positioned alongside structures like racism, anti-Blackness, heterosexism, trans oppression, and more. For this reason, I sought to diversify the sample as much as possible as it relates to people's races, sexualities, and other social identities (e.g., gender, ability, un/documented status). In doing so, I believed that this approach would attend to intersectionality's focus on within-group differences that exist in populations (Dill & Zambrana, 2009) like Queer Students of Color. However, as highlighted below in the *Limitations and Future Opportunities* section, I contend that researchers should continue to add nuance to the study of identity by exploring specific racial and sexuality groups (e.g., queer Latinx individuals). On a similar note, I also wanted to ensure that the individuals whom I interviewed for the research project would provide insight into how institutional characteristics could inform their identity exploration process. For this reason, I paid attention to where potential participants' institutions were located in the country, how many students were enrolled, and what types of resources were available on campus for those with minoritized identifies. After a process of maximum variation sampling (Mertens, 2015), trying out different configurations of people that would compose the sample, I selected 20 participants who were located all across the country and represented a wide range of social identities.

Data Collection Methods

Once I had identified the participants, the fulfilling part of collecting data began. In accordance with constructivist grounded theory's mission to have data that showcases "participants' views, feelings, intentions, and actions as well as the contexts and structures of their lives" (Charmaz, 2014, p. 23), I provided a number of opportunities for the Queer Students of Color in the study to reflect on their intersecting identities and the power systems that shaped them. To begin, intensive interviewing is one method widely used in constructivist grounded theory research. In fact, Charmaz shared that the relationship between intensive interviewing and the methodology itself is that they are both "open-ended yet directed, shaped yet emergent, and paced yet unrestricted" (p. 85). Specifically, I drafted interview protocols that would provide structure to the conversations that I would have with the participants while allowing the discussions to go in the direction in which these individuals led me. Because I strove for a rich understanding of their experiences, I elected to have three interviews with each participant. Yet, both E and Mirella Blackwell needed to discontinue their engagement with the research after the first interview. Additionally, I acknowledged that people process through their thoughts differently and may benefit from a concerted time to reflect on their own rather than in an interview with a researcher. For this reason, I had participants write a series of reflection journals in between the first and second interview.

After choosing the methods themselves, I needed to make the decision on what would be covered in each of these data collection opportunities. How would one interview be different than the next, for example? Next, I outline the structure.

- Interview #1: To align with my epistemological foundations, I constructed the first interview protocol to focus mainly on the perceptions that students had about their identities and how they engaged in this process of exploration. Doing so, in my mind, honored the constructivist epistemological base of the project.
- Reflection Journal: In the reflection journal, I then had them reflect on how their HWI had influenced them in this process of identity

exploration, posing questions about how they felt privileged or disadvantaged on campus. Furthermore, the questions included in the reflection journal had them identify some of the practices, policies, and structures that shaped their realities as Queer People of Color.

- Interview #2: The journal thus set the stage for the more critically-leaning second interview where the conversations centered explicitly on the role of power, privilege, and oppression in their identity exploration. Therefore, while I still honored the participants' meaning making as true, the second interview foregrounded issues of systemic inequalities in a greater fashion.
- Interview #3: Following the second interview, I started to see major theoretical categories emerging in my analytical process. This meant that the third interview was my opportunity to further refine any points where I was still unclear in the hopes of reaching a phenomenon known as theoretical saturation (see Charmaz, 2014) and to engage in a member-checking procedure (further elaborated on in a subsequent section).

Analytical Process

Grounded theory research has a number of defining characteristics that distinguish the methodology, including the use of a constant comparative approach, theoretical sampling, and theoretical saturation (Hood, 2007). Another major feature of grounded theory studies is that data collection and analysis happen concurrently with the former informing the latter throughout and vice-versa (Charmaz, 2014). Though I once again invite readers to reference the dissertation that emerged from this project (Duran, 2019a) to understand the totality of my analytical process, I will highlight a few key decisions that I made to analyze the data from the intensive interviews and reflection journals.

On the Constant Comparative Approach and Coding

To start, I employed several rounds of coding, which Charmaz (2014) described as a way of "naming segments of data with a label that simultaneously categorizes, summarizes, and accounts for each piece of data" (p. 111). Specifically, after each round of data collection, I utilized initial, focused, and theoretical coding. To participate in initial coding, I analyzed the participants' narratives line by line, giving a name to what I saw happening in the data. Of note, I analyzed the data line by line twice, first through a constructivist lens followed by another reading from a more critical standpoint. Following this initial coding, I moved to focused coding which is where grounded theorists attempt to identify which concepts have the most "analytical power" (Charmaz, 2014, p. 140). I set out to accomplish this task by following the principles of the constant comparative approach, for as Charmaz (2014) noted, "Assessing your initial codes involves comparing them with data and distinguishing those codes that have greater analytic power. . . . Comparing codes with codes heightens your sense of the direction your analysis is going and clarifies the theoretical centrality of certain ideas" (p. 140). Though I followed the constant comparative approach throughout the project, it was particularly helpful in moving from initial coding to focused coding. Similar to Abes' (2009) research, I gave the same analytic weight to both my constructivist codes, as well as those that came about from my critical reading. In seeing where the two both diverged and converged, I started to notice patterns present across the participants' stories. After focused coding, I moved to a theoretical coding procedure.

Theoretical coding allowed me to make sense of the participants' experiences by using sensitizing concepts from existing literature. Though theoretical coding is not intended to disrupt the inductive nature that undergirds constructivist grounded theory (Charmaz, 2014), it does provide researchers the opportunity to analyze the relationships they notice in their data from the perspective of extant knowledge in one's discipline. For this study, I developed coding families that related to how scholars have discussed matters of sexuality, racial identity, intersectional theorizing, and multiple identities. In comparing these coding families to the focused codes I created, I began to identify notable theoretical categories that explained the social process of identity exploration for Queer Students of Color. Theoretical coding also challenged me to consider whether or not I was reaching theoretical saturation, a point in grounded theory research where the researcher assesses that they have honed in on theoretical categories that depict why and how the process of interest occurs (Charmaz, 2014). To reflect on whether or not I had attained what I believed to be theoretical saturation, I engaged in other defining traits of grounded theory research: memoing and diagramming.

On Memoing and Diagramming

In the Epilogue of this book, I opened with an excerpt from one of the many memos that I wrote throughout this research project. For constructivist grounded theorists, memo writing and diagramming are important keys to open up their thinking about what is occurring in the data. I often lived by the words of Charmaz (2014) when engaging in memo writing: "when you write memos, you stop and analyze your ideas about the codes in any – and every – way that occurs to you during the moment" (p. 162). Memo writing allowed me to reflect on how I was bringing my own assumptions to the data, how the stories participants were sharing were relating to one another, and how this collectively contributed to my understanding of identity exploration for Queer Students of Color at HWIs. Because of the gravity of this task, I wrote three different types of memos throughout the project (i.e., operational, coding, and analytical; Birks, Chapman, & Francis, 2008) and would also write entries whenever I had a thought that entered my mind.

In addition to writing these memos, I also diagrammed, a practice that was intensified toward the end of my data collection. Diagramming is especially beneficial to grounded theory researchers because it pushes scholars to view data from a visual point of view. Diagramming was helpful to me as I wrote analytical memos, because it helped me hone in on the ways that the theoretical categories I was noticing related to one another. Furthermore, I had the assistance of a peer debriefer who was instrumental to offering feedback on the diagrams I created. Her insight, in addition to that of my dissertation committee, led me to develop the model based on theoretical categories that were salient in the participants' data. Throughout the study, including the analytical process, I attended to several measures of trustworthiness.

Trustworthiness Criteria

Trustworthiness has long been a staple of academic research, as scholars attempt to show that the ways they arrived to their findings were dependable and that the findings have an impact for other contexts (Maxwell, 1992). In this study, I attended to common strategies to ensure trustworthiness including credibility, transferability, confirmability, and dependability (see Guba & Lincoln, 1989; Jones et al., 2014; Morrow, 2005).

Credibility

For instance, credibility signifies that researchers are in the "field" for a significant amount of time and that they may use other individuals to verify their analytical insights (Jones et al., 2014, p. 36). One of the ways that I addressed confirmability was by having a peer debriefer that I could turn to affirm what I was noticing in the data or provide an entirely new and different perspective. I solicited the assistance of someone who identified differently than I do (as a white bisexual woman), which meant that she was both an insider and outsider to the communities present in this study. Additionally, the third interview I conducted with participants served as a chance for me to engage in a process known as member-checking, another way to show credibility. Prior to this final interview with each participant, I created a rough list of theoretical categories and any questions I had about these specific to the individual.

In the third interview, I asked them to offer their thoughts on whether these themes spoke to their experiences and if they did not, the reasons why that was the case. Most participants shared that the themes captured their experiences, but a few discussed some minute ways that they conceived of their lived realities differently, which was beneficial to hear as I neared the end of data collection.

Transferability

Next, I sought out to adhere to transferability, an aim that scholars achieve so that readers can translate findings to their own environments (Morrow, 2005), by offering thick description of the participants' experiences. Rather than offer short excerpts or limited interpretation of their stories, I included long quotes in addition to including vital pieces of knowledge concerning their contexts so that readers can imagine how these experiences translate to their campuses. Furthermore, having different types of institutions represented in the study allows those reading participants' narratives to determine how they align or do not align with the places they are located.

Confirmability and Dependability

For confirmability (i.e., showing the connections between data and one's analysis) and dependability (i.e., making evident the steps taken in a research process), I leaned upon the various memos I wrote. Namely, the operational memos I wrote challenged me to think heavily about the study design decisions, whereas the coding and analytical memos showcased how my analysis stemmed from the data itself. Ultimately, I made all of these decisions to ensure that my research was sound and that I was honoring the participants' contributions. However, I also recognize that any research project has limitations and consequently, opens the door for future scholarship.

Study Considerations and Future Opportunities

As I sit here and reflect on the boundaries and limitations of the study at the heart of this text, I am excited at what these mean for research to follow. For instance, as I noted earlier, my intention was to develop a theory that could speak to the experiences of people who fall within the large category of Queer People of Color. I recognize that in doing so, I also can unintentionally flatten the nuances that people face along different axes of oppression (e.g., racism, anti-Blackness, settler colonialism, trans oppression). The participants' stories did reveal these differences (as seen in Chapter Five's discussion of the various privileged and oppressed identities shaping these students' identity exploration), but future research centering specific samples of identity groups would build upon this work (e.g., investigating the experiences of queer Asian/Asian American students at HWIs).

Similarly, a boundary of this study is that I focused initially on issues of sexuality and racial identity, which may have precluded participants from foregrounding other salient identities. I intended to reveal the within-group dynamics that are integral to intersectional theorizing (Cole, 2008; Crenshaw, 1991; Dill & Zambrana, 2009; Hancock, 2007b, 2016; McCall, 2005) through my sampling considerations and the questions that I posed of students. Still, in seeking to learn about how Queer Students of Color explored their race, sexuality, *and* other identities, I may have reduced the complexities of their experiences to one where they chose to focus narrowly on two axes of oppression (e.g., racism and heterosexism). I took intentional steps to allow for participants to comment on their salient identities broadly in order to avoid rendering my intersectional theorizing to a place where only two forms of oppression were at the forefront, a caution of scholars like May (2015). I know that this is a tension that intersectional researchers will continue to wrestle with, so I mention it to motivate others to think about this consideration alongside myself.

Finally, another limitation of this study troubled me greatly due to intersectional theorizing's commitment to social justice (Collins, 2000/2009a; Crenshaw, 1989, 1991; Dill & Zambrana, 2009; Hancock, 2007b, 2015, 2016). Intersectional scholars assert that individuals should use the framework in order to effect change on the structural level (Hancock, 2007a). Though I no doubt believe that the academic outcomes of this research project, including this book, can have a positive impact on how staff and faculty at HWIs create better conditions for Queer People of Color, I found myself wishing that I could provide targeted recommendations to the institutions present in the study. Yet, doing so may have compromised the identities of participants. Thus, I recommend future researchers to weigh heavily how they can attend to the social justice goals that are vital in studies using intersectionality.

Final Reflections

In showing vulnerability concerning these limitations, I am in fact disclosing the hopes and dreams that I have for this body of research. Detailed throughout the book, I have committed my personal and professional aspirations to uplifting the lives and needs of Queer People of Color in higher education. This motivation led me to undergo this study, an experience that I will forever hold near to my heart. I encourage those reading this text to reflect similarly on their drives and passions for Queer Communities of Color. This final section of this methodological appendix is an invitation for work that highlights Queer Students of Color, that pushes back on the systems of oppression that disenfranchise this community, and that envisions radically new possibilities at HWIs and higher education as a whole.

References

Abes, E. S. (2009). Theoretical borderlands: Using multiple theoretical perspectives to challenge inequitable power structures in student development theory. *Journal of College Student Development*, *50*(2), 141–156.

Abes, E. S. (2012). Constructivist and intersectional interpretations of a lesbian college student's multiple social identities. *The Journal of Higher Education*, *83*(2), 186–216.

Abes, E. S. (2016). Situating paradigms in student development theory. In E. S. Abes (Ed.), *Critical perspectives on student development theory*, New Directions for Student Services no. 154 (pp. 9–16). San Francisco, CA: Jossey-Bass.

Abes, E. S., & Jones, S. R. (2004). Meaning-making capacity and the dynamics of lesbian college students' multiple dimensions of identity. *Journal of College Student Development*, *45*(6), 612–632.

Abes, E. S., Jones, S. R., & McEwen, M. K. (2007). Reconceptualizing the model of multiple dimensions of identity: The role of meaning-making capacity in the construction of multiple identities. *Journal of College Student Development*, *48*(1), 1–22.

Abes, E. S., Jones, S. R., & Stewart, D-L. (Eds.). (2019). *Rethinking college student development using critical frameworks*. Sterling, VA: Stylus.

Abustan, P. (2017). Collectively feeling: Honoring the emotional experiences of queer and transgender student of color activists. In J. M. Johnson & G. C. Javier (Eds.), *Queer people of color in higher education* (pp. 31–56). Charlotte, NC: Information Age Publishing.

Aguilar, D., & Johnson, J. M. (2017). Queer faculty and staff of color: Experiences and expectations. In J. M. Johnson & G. Javier (Eds.), *Queer people of color in higher education* (pp. 57–72). Charlotte, NC: Information Age Publishing.

Anzaldúa, G. (1987). *Borderlands/la frontera: The new mestiza*. San Francisco, CA: Aunt Lude Books.

Arnett, J. J. (2000). Emerging adulthood: A theory of development from the late teens through the twenties. *American Psychologist*, *55*(5), 469–480.

Arnett, J. J. (2010). *Emerging adulthood: The winding road from the late teens through the twenties* (2nd ed.). New York, NY: Oxford University Press.

Arnett, J. J. (2011). Emerging adulthood(s): The cultural psychology of a new life stage. In L. A. Jensen (Ed.), *Bridging cultural and developmental approaches to psychology: New syntheses in theory, research, and policy* (pp. 255–275). New York, NY: Oxford University Press.

Barber, J. P., King, P. M., & Baxter Magolda, M. B. (2013). Long strides on the journey toward self-authorship: Substantial developmental shifts in college students' meaning making. *The Journal of Higher Education*, *84*(6), 866–896.

Barnett, B., & Felten, P. (Eds.). (2016). *Intersectionality in action: A guide for faculty and campus leaders for creating inclusive classrooms and institutions*. Sterling, VA: Stylus.

Basile, V., & Lopez, E. (2015). And still I see no changes: Enduring views of students of color in science and mathematics education policy reports. *Science Education*, *99*(3), 519–548.

Baxter Magolda, M. B. (1999a). *Creating contexts for learning and self-authorship: Constructive-developmental pedagogy*. Nashville, TN: Vanderbilt University Press.

Baxter Magolda, M. B. (1999b). The evolution of epistemology: Refining contextual knowing at twentysomething. *Journal of College Student Development*, *40*(4), 333–334.

Baxter Magolda, M. B. (2001). *Making their own way: Narratives for transforming higher education to promote self-development*. Sterling, VA: Stylus.

Baxter Magolda, M. B. (2009). The activity of meaning making: A holistic perspective on college student development. *Journal of College Student Development*, *50*(6), 621–639.

Beal, F. M. (1970). Double jeopardy: To be Black and female. In T. Cade (Ed.), *The Black woman: An anthology* (pp. 90–100). New York, NY: Signet. (Original work published in 1969).

Bhopal, K., & Preston, J. (2012). *Intersectionality and "race" in education*. New York, NY: Routledge.

Bilge, S. (2012). Developing queer solidarities: A plea for queer intersectionality. In M. Smith & F. Jaffer (Eds.), *Beyond the queer alphabet: Conversations in gender, sexuality and intersectionality* (pp. 19–23). Edmonton, AB: University of Alberta.

Bilge, S. (2013). Intersectionality undone. *Du Bois Review*, *10*(2), 405–424.

Birks, M., Chapman, Y., & Francis, K. (2008). Memoing in qualitative research: Probing data and processes. *Journal of Research in Nursing*, *13*(1), 68–75.

Blockett, R. A. (2017). 'I think it's very much placed on us': Black queer men laboring to forge community at a predominantly white and (hetero)cisnormative research institution. *International Journal of Qualitative Studies in Education*, *30*(8), 800–816.

Bowman, N. A. (2010). Disequilibrium and resolution: The nonlinear effects of diversity courses on well-being and orientations toward diversity. *The Review of Higher Education*, *33*(4), 543–568.

BrckaLorenz, A., Duran, A., Fassett, K., & Palmer, D. (2019). The within-group differences in LGBQ+ college students' belongingness, institutional commitment, and outness. *Journal of Diversity in Higher Education*. Advance online publication. https://doi.org/10.1037/dhe0000135

Burford, J., & Allen, L. (2019). Starting with queer: An enigmatic concept for higher education research and practice. In E. F. Henderson & Z. Nicolazzo (Eds.), *Starting with gender in international higher education research: Conceptual debates and methodological considerations* (pp. 126–143). New York, NY: Routledge.

Butler, J. (1990). *Gender trouble: Feminism and the subversion of identity*. New York, NY: Routledge.

Byrd, W. C., Brunn-Bevel, R. J., & Ovink, S. M. (Eds.). (2019). *Intersectionality and higher education: Identity and inequality on college campuses*. New Brunswick, NJ: Rutgers University Press.

Carastathis, A. (2013). Basements and intersections. *Hypatia*, *28*(4), 698–715.

Carbado, D. W. (2013). Colorblind intersectionality. *Signs: Journal of Women in Culture and Society*, *38*(4), 811–845.

Carter, B. A. (2013). "Nothing better or worse than being Black, gay, and in the band": A qualitative examination of gay undergraduates participating in historically Black college or university marching bands. *Journal of Research in Music Education*, *61*(1), 26–43.

Case, K. A. (Ed.). (2017). *Intersectional pedagogy: Complicating identity and social justice*. New York, NY: Routledge.

Chan, C. D., Erby, A. N., & Ford, D. J. (2017). Intersectionality in practice: Moving a social justice paradigm to action in higher education. In J. M. Johnson & G. C. Javier (Eds.), *Queer people of color in higher education* (pp. 9–29). Charlotte, NC: Information Age Publishing.

Chan, J. (2017). "Am I masculine enough?": Queer Filipino college men and masculinity. *Journal of Student Affairs Research and Practice*, *54*(1), 82–94.

Charmaz, K. (2000). Grounded theory: Objectivist and constructivist methods. In N. K. Denzin & Y. S. Lincoln (Eds.), *Handbook of qualitative research* (2nd ed., pp. 509–535). Thousand Oaks, CA: Sage.

Charmaz, K. (2002). Grounded theory: Methodology and theory construction. In N. J. Smelser & P. B. Baltes (Eds.), *International encyclopedia of the social and behavioral sciences* (pp. 6396–6399). Amsterdam, NL: Pergamon.

Charmaz, K. (2008a). Constructionism and the grounded theory. In J. A. Holstein & J. F. Gubrium (Eds.), *Handbook of constructionist research* (pp. 397–412). New York, NY: The Guilford Press.

Charmaz, K. (2008b). The legacy of Anselm Strauss for constructivist grounded theory. In N. K. Denzin (Ed.), *Studies in symbolic interaction* (Vol. 32, pp. 127–141). Bingley, UK: Emerald Group.

Charmaz, K. (2011). Grounded theory methods in social justice research. In N. K. Denzin & Y. S Lincoln (Eds.), *The Sage handbook of qualitative research* (4th ed., pp. 359–380). Thousand Oaks, CA: Sage.

Charmaz, K. (2014). *Constructing grounded theory* (2nd ed.). Thousand Oaks, CA: Sage.

Charmaz, K. (2017). The power of constructivist grounded theory for critical inquiry. *Qualitative Inquiry*, *23*(1), 34–45.

Christensen, J. F. (2018). Queer organising and performativity: Towards a norm-critical conceptualisation of organisational intersectionality. *Ephemera: Theory & Politics in Organization*, *18*(1), 103–130.

Cho, S. (2013). Post-intersectionality: The curious reception of intersectionality in legal scholarship. *Du Bois Review*, *10*(2), 385–404.

Cho, S., Crenshaw, K. W., & McCall, L. (2013). Toward a field of intersectionality studies: Theory, applications, and praxis. *Signs: Journal of Women in Culture and Society*, *38*(4), 785–810.

Clarke, A. E. (2003). Situational analyses: Grounded theory mapping after the postmodern turn. *Symbolic Interaction*, *26*(4), 553–576.

Clarke, C. (1983). The failure to transform. In B. Smith (Ed.), *Home girls: A Black feminist anthology* (pp. 197–208). New Brunswick, NJ: Rutgers University Press.

Cole, E. R. (2008). Coalitions as a model for intersectionality: From practice to theory. *Sex Roles*, *59*(5–6), 443–453.

Cole, E. R. (2009). Intersectionality and research in psychology. *American Psychologist*, *64*(3), 170–180.

Collins, P. H. (2009a). *Black feminist thought: Knowledge, consciousness and the politics of empowerment*. New York, NY: Routledge (Original work published 2000).

Collins, P. H. (2009b). Foreword. In B. T. Dill & R. E. Zambrana (Eds.), *Emerging intersections: Race, class, and gender in theory, policy, and practice* (pp. vii–xiii). New Brunswick, NJ: Rutgers University Press.

Collins, P. H. (2015). Intersectionality's definitional dilemmas. *Annual Review of Sociology*, *41*(1), 1–20.

Collins, P. H., & Bilge, S. (2016). *Intersectionality*. Boston, MA: Polity Press.

Combahee River Collective. (1983). The Combahee River collective statement. In B. Smith (Ed.), *Home girls: A Black feminist anthology* (pp. 264–275). New Brunswick, NJ: Rutgers University Press (Original work published in 1977).

Corbin, J., & Strauss, A. (2015). *Basics of qualitative research: Techniques and procedures for developing grounded theory* (4th ed.). Thousand Oaks, CA: Sage.

Côté, J. E., & Levine, C. (1987). A formulation of Erikson's theory of ego identity formation. *Developmental Review*, *7*(4), 273–325.

Côté, J. E., & Levine, C. (2002). *Identity formation, agency, and culture: A social psychological synthesis*. Mahwah, NJ: Lawrence Erlbaum Associates, Inc.

Crenshaw, K. (1989). Demarginalizing the intersection of race and sex: A Black feminist critique of antidiscrimination doctrine, feminist theory, and antiracist politics. *University of Chicago Legal Forum*, *8*(1), 139–167.

Crenshaw, K. (1991). Mapping the margins: Intersectionality, identity politics, and violence against women of color. *Stanford Law Review*, *43*(6), 1241–1299.

Cross, W. E., Jr., & Fhagen-Smith, P. (2001). Patterns in African American identity development: A life span perspective. In C. L. Wijeyesinghe & B. W. Jackson, III (Eds.), *New perspectives on racial identity development: A theoretical and practical anthology* (pp. 243–270). New York, NY: New York University Press.

Crotty, M. (1998). *The foundations of social research: Meaning and perspective in the research process*. Thousand Oaks, CA: Sage.

Cyrus, K. (2017). Multiple minorities as multiply marginalized: Applying the minority stress theory to LGBTQ people of color. *Journal of Gay & Lesbian Mental Health*, *21*(3), 194–202.

Datta, V., Bialer, P. A., & McIntosh, C. A. (2017). Queerly invisible: LGBTQ people of color and mental health. *Journal of Gay & Lesbian Mental Health*, *21*(3), 191–193.

Davis, D. J., Brunn-Bevel, R. J., & Olive, J. L. (Eds.). (2015). *Intersectionality in educational research*. Sterling, VA: Stylus.

Davis, K. (2008). Intersectionality as buzzword: A sociology of science perspective on what makes a feminist theory successful. *Feminist Theory*, *9*(1), 67–85.

Denzin, N. K. (2015). What is critical qualitative inquiry? In G. Cannella, M. Pérez, & P. Pasque (Eds.), *Critical qualitative inquiry: Foundations and futures* (pp. 31–50). Walnut Creek, CA: Left Coast Press.

Denzin, N. K. (2017). Critical qualitative inquiry. *Qualitative Inquiry*, *23*(1), 8–16.

Denzin, N. K., & Lincoln, Y. S. (2000). The discipline and practice of qualitative research. In N. K. Denzin & Y. S. Lincoln (Eds.), *Handbook of qualitative research* (2nd ed., pp. 1–28). Thousand Oaks, CA: Sage.

Dhamoon, R. K. (2011). Considerations on mainstreaming intersectionality. *Political Research Quarterly*, *64*(1), 230–243.

Dill, B. T., & Zambrana, R. E. (2009). Critical thinking about inequality: An emerging lens. In B. T. Dill & R. E. Zambrana (Eds.), *Emerging intersections: Race, class, and gender in theory, policy, and practice* (pp. 1–21). New Brunswick, NJ: Rutgers University Press.

Dillon, F. R., Worthington, R. L., & Moradi, B. (2011). Sexual identity as a universal process. In S. J. Schwartz, K. Luyckx, & V. L. Vignoles (Eds.), *Handbook of identity theory and research* (pp. 649–670). New York, NY: Springer.

Duong, K. (2012). What does queer theory teach us about intersectionality? *Politics and Gender*, *8*(3), 370–386.

Duran, A. (2019a). *An intersectional grounded theory study examining identity exploration for queer collegians of color at historically white institutions* (Unpublished doctoral dissertation), The Ohio State University, Columbus.

Duran, A. (2019b). A photovoice phenomenological study exploring campus belonging for queer students of color. *Journal of Student Affairs Research and Practice*, *56*(2), 153–167.

Duran, A. (2019c). Outsiders in a niche group: Using intersectionality to examine resilience for queer students of color. Advance online publication. https://doi.org/10.1037/dhe0000144

Duran, A. (2019d). Queer *and* of color: A systematic literature review on queer students of color in higher education. *Journal of Diversity in Higher Education*, *12*(4), 390–400.

Duran, A., Blockett, R. A., & Nicolazzo, Z. (2020). An interdisciplinary return to queer and trans* studies in higher education: Implications for research and practice. In L. W. Perna (Ed.), *Higher education: Handbook of theory and research* (Vol. 35, pp. 1–64). New York, NY: Springer.

Duran, A., & Jackson, R. (2019). Thinking theoretically with and beyond intersectionality: Frameworks to center QTPOC experiences. In D. Mitchell Jr., J. Marie, & T. Steele (Eds.), *Intersectionality and higher education: Theory, research, and practice* (2nd ed., pp. 41–50). New York, NY: Peter Lang.

Duran, A., & Jones, S. R. (2019a). Context and contextualizing student development using critical theory. In E. S. Abes, S. R. Jones, & D-L. Stewart (Eds.), *Rethinking college student development theory using critical frameworks* (pp. 171–186). Sterling, VA: Stylus.

Duran, A., & Jones, S. R. (2019b). Using intersectionality in qualitative research on college student identity development: Considerations, tensions, and possibilities. *Journal of College Student Development*, *60*(4), 455–471.

Duran, A., & Pérez, D., II. (2017). Queering *la familia*: A phenomenological study reconceptualizing familial capital for queer Latino men. *Journal of College Student Development*, *58*(8), 1149–1165.

Duran, A., & Pérez, D., II. (2019). The multiple roles of chosen familia: Exploring the interconnections of queer Latino men's community cultural wealth. *International Journal of Qualitative Studies in Education*, *32*(1), 67–84.

Erikson, E. H. (1963). *Youth: Change and challenge*. New York, NY: Doubleday.

Erikson, E. H. (1964). *Insight and responsibility*. New York, NY: W. W. Norton.

Erikson, E. H. (1968). *Identity: Youth and crises*. New York, NY: W. W. Norton.

Erikson, E. H. (1994). *Identity and the life cycle*. New York, NY: W. W. Norton.

Evans, M. E., & Wallace, J. K. (2019). No longer cast aside: A critical approach to serving queer and trans students of color in higher education. In D. Mitchell Jr., J. Marie, & T. Steele (Eds.), *Intersectionality & higher education: Theory, research, & praxis* (2nd ed.). New York, NY: Peter Lang.

Ferguson, R. A. (2004). *Aberrations in Black: Toward a queer of color critique*. Minneapolis, MN: University of Minnesota Press.

Fotopoulou, A. (2012). Intersectionality queer studies and hybridity: Methodological frameworks for social research. *Journal of International Women's Studies*, *13*(2), 19–32.

Gallegos, P. I., & Ferdman, B. M. (2012). Latina and Latino ethnoracial identity orientations: A dynamic and developmental perspective. In C. L. Wijeyesinghe & B. W. Jackson III (Eds.), *New perspectives on racial identity development: Integrating emerging frameworks* (2nd ed., pp. 51–80). New York, NY: New York University Press.

García, A. (Ed.). (1997). *Chicana feminist thought: The basic historical writings*. New York, NY: Routledge.

Garcia, C. E., & Duran, A. (2020). "In my letters, but I was still by myself": Highlighting the experiences of queer men of color in culturally-based fraternities. *Journal of Diversity in Higher Education*. Advance online publication. https://doi.org/10.1037/dhe0000167

Garvey, J. C., Mobley, S. D., Jr., Summerville, K. S., & Moore, G. T. (2019). Queer and trans* students of color: Navigating identity disclosure and college contexts. *The Journal of Higher Education*, *90*(1), 150–178.

Gedalof, I. (2013). Sameness and difference in government equality talk. *Ethnic and Racial Studies*, *36*(1), 117–135.

Glaser, B. G. (1992). *Basics of grounded theory analysis*. Mill Valley, CA: Sociology Press.

Glaser, B. G. (1998). *Doing grounded theory: Issues and discussions*. Mill Valley, CA: Sociology Press.

Glaser, B. G., & Strauss, A. L. (1967). *The discovery of grounded theory: Strategies for qualitative research*. Chicago, IL: Aldine.

Goode-Cross, D. T. (2009). *"It's just about staying focused": How African American gay and bisexual men persist at a predominantly white institution* (Doctoral dissertation). Retrieved from https://mospace.umsystem.edu/

Goode-Cross, D. T., & Good, G. E. (2008). African American men who have sex with men: Creating safe spaces through relationships. *Psychology of Men & Masculinity*, *9*(4), 221–234.

Goode-Cross, D. T., & Good, G. E. (2009). Managing multiple-minority identities: African American men who have sex with men at predominantly white universities. *Journal of Diversity in Higher Education*, *2*(2), 103–112.

Goode-Cross, D. T., & Tager, D. (2011). Negotiating multiple identities: How African-American gay and bisexual men persist at a predominantly white institution. *Journal of Homosexuality*, *58*(9), 1235–1254.

Goodman, D. J. (2014). The tapestry model: Exploring social identities, privilege, and oppression from an intersectional perspective. In D. Mitchell, C. Y. Simmons, & L. A. Greyerbiehl (Eds.), *Intersectionality and higher education: Theory, research, and praxis* (pp. 99–108). New York, NY: Peter Lang.

Graves, K. (2009). *And they were wonderful teachers: Florida's purge of gay and lesbian teachers*. Champaign, IL: University of Illinois Press.

Graves, K. (2018). The history of lesbian, gay, bisexual, transgender, queer issues in higher education. In M. B. Paulsen (Ed.), *Higher education: Handbook of theory and research* (Vol. 33, pp. 127–173). New York, NY: Springer.

Gresham, S. L. (2009). Negotiating cultural contexts: An exploratory investigation of Black gay male strategy employment. *Journal of GLBT Family Studies*, *5*(3), 247–267.

Guba, E. G., & Lincoln, Y. S. (1989). *Fourth generation evaluation*. Thousand Oaks, CA: Sage.

Guba, E. G., & Lincoln, Y. S. (1998). Competing paradigms in qualitative research. In N. K. Denzin & Y. S. Lincoln (Eds.), *The landscape of qualitative research: Theories and issues* (pp. 195–220). Thousand Oaks, CA: Sage.

Gurin, P., Dey, E. L., Hurtado, S., & Gurin, G. (2002). Diversity and higher education: Theory and impact on student outcomes. *Harvard Educational Review*, *72*(3), 330–366.

Hancock, A.-M. (2007a). Intersectionality as a normative and empirical paradigm. *Politics & Gender*, *3*(2), 41–45.

Hancock, A.-M. (2007b). When multiplication doesn't equal quick addition: Examining intersectionality as a research paradigm. *Perspectives on Politics*, *5*(1), 63–79.

Hancock, A.-M. (2015). Intersectionality's will toward social transformation. *New Political Science*, *37*(4), 620–627.

Hancock, A.-M. (2016). *Intersectionality: An intellectual history*. New York, NY: Oxford University Press.

Harper, S. R., & Hurtado, S. (2007). Nine themes in campus racial climates and implications for institutional transformation. In S. R. Harper & L. D. Patton (Eds.), *Responding to the realities of race on campus*, New Directions for Student Services no. 120 (pp. 7–24). San Francisco, CA: Jossey-Bass.

Harper, S. R., Wardell, C. C., & McGuire, K. M. (2011). Man of multiple identities: Complex individuality and identity intersectionality among college men. In J. A. Laker & T. Davis (Eds.), *Masculinities in higher education: Theoretical and practical considerations* (pp. 81–96). New York, NY: Routledge.

Harris, A. (1989). Race and essentialism in feminist legal theory. *Stanford Law Review*, *42*(3), 581–616.

Harris, W. G. (2003). African American homosexual males on predominantly white college and university campuses. *Journal of African American Studies*, *7*(1), 47–56.

Harris, J. C., & Patton, L. D. (2017). The challenges and triumphs in addressing students' intersectional identities for Black culture centers. *Journal of Diversity in Higher Education*, *10*(4), 334–349.

Harris, J. C., & Patton, L. D. (2019). Un/doing intersectionality through higher education research. *The Journal of Higher Education*, *90*(3), 347–372.

Hernández, E. (2012). The journey toward developing political consciousness through activism for Mexican American women. *Journal of College Student Development*, *53*(5), 680–702.

Higgins, J. (2015). *Working at the intersections: Examining the first-year experiences of queer men of color in higher education* (Doctoral dissertation). Retrieved from http://pqdtopen.proquest.com/

Holloman, D. B., & Strayhorn, T. L. (2010). Challenges and support of Black gay men at predominantly white campuses. In T. L Strayhorn & M. C. Terrell (Eds.), *The evolving challenges of Black college students: New insight for practice and research* (pp. 85–104). Sterling, VA: Stylus.

Hood, J. (2007). Orthodoxy versus power: The defining traits of grounded theory. In A. Bryant & K. Charmaz (Eds.), *Handbook of grounded theory* (pp. 151–164). Thousand Oaks, CA: Sage.

hooks, b. (2000). *All about love: New visions*. New York, NY: William Morrow and Company, Inc.

Horse, P. G. (2012). Twenty first century Native American consciousness: A thematic model of Indian identity. In C. L. Wijeyesinghe & B. W. Jackson III (Eds.), *New perspectives on racial identity development: Integrating emerging frameworks* (2nd ed., pp. 108–120). New York, NY: New York University Press.

Hughes, K. L. (2015). *The experiences queer college women of color have of friendship* (Doctoral dissertation). Retrieved from http://athenaeum.libs.uga.edu/

Hurtado, S., Alvarez, C. L., Guillermo-Wann, C., Cuellar, M., & Arellano, L. (2012). A model for diverse learning environments: The scholarship on creating and assessing conditions for student success. In J. C. Smart & M. B. Paulsen (Eds.), *Higher education: Handbook of theory and research* (Vol. 27, pp. 41–121). New York, NY: Springer.

Hutchinson, D. L. (1997). Out yet unseen: A racial critique of gay and lesbian legal theory and political discourse. *Connecticut Law Review*, *29*(2), 561–645.

Hutchinson, D. L. (2001). Identity crisis: Intersectionality, multidimensionality, and the development of an adequate theory of subordination. *Michigan Journal of Race and Law*, *6*, 285–317.

Johnson, E. P. (2001). "Quare" studies, or (almost) everything I know about queer studies I learned from my grandmother. *Text and Performance Quarterly*, *21*(1), 1–25.

Johnson, J. M., & Javier, G. C. (Eds.). (2017). *Queer people of color in higher education*. Charlotte, NC: Information Age Publishing.

Jones, S. R. (1997). Voices of identity and difference: A qualitative exploration of the multiple dimensions of identity development in women college students. *Journal of College Student Development*, *38*(4), 376–386.

Jones, S. R., & Abes, E. S. (2013). *Identity development of college students: Advancing frameworks for multiple dimensions of identity*. San Francisco, CA: Jossey-Bass.

Jones, S. R., & McEwen, M. K. (2000). A conceptual model of multiple dimensions of identity. *Journal of College Student Development*, *41*(4), 405–414.

Jones, S. R., & Stewart, D-L. (2016). Evolution of student development theory. In E. S. Abes (Ed.), *Critical perspectives on student development theory*, New Directions for Student Services no. 154 (pp. 17–28). San Francisco, CA: Jossey-Bass.

Jones, S. R., Torres, V., & Arminio, J. (2014). *Negotiating the complexities of qualitative research in higher education: Fundamental elements and issues* (2nd ed.). New York, NY: Routledge.

Jones, S. R., & Wijeyesinghe, C. L. (2011). The promises and challenges of teaching from an intersectional perspective: Core components and applied strategies. In M. L. Ouellett (Ed.), *An integrative analysis approach to diversity in the college classroom*, New Directions for Teaching & Learning no. 125 (pp. 11–20). San Francisco, CA: Jossey-Bass.

Jourian, T. J. (2017). "Fun and carefree like my polka dot bowtie": Disidentifications of Trans*masculine Students of Color. In J. M. Johnson & G. C. Javier (Eds.), *Queer people of color in higher education* (pp. 123–144). Charlotte, NC: Information Age Publishing.

Kegan, R. (1982). *The evolving self: Problem and process in human development*. Cambridge, MA: Harvard University Press.

Kegan, R. (1994). *In over our heads: The mental demands of modern life*. Cambridge, MA: Harvard University Press.

Kendall, F. E., & Wijeyesinghe, C. L. (2017). Advancing social justice work at the intersections of multiple privileged identities. In C. L. Wijeyesinghe (Ed.), *Enacting intersectionality in student affairs*, New Directions for Student Services no. 157 (pp. 91–100). San Francisco, CA: Jossey-Bass.

Kim, J. (2012). Asian American racial identity development theory. In C. L. Wijeyesinghe & B. W. Jackson III (Eds.), *New perspectives on racial identity development: Integrating emerging frameworks* (2nd ed., pp. 138–160). New York, NY: New York University Press.

Kincheloe, J. L., & McLaren, P. (2002). Rethinking critical theory and qualitative research. In Y. Zou & E. T. Trueba (Eds.), *Ethnography and schools: Qualitative approaches to the study of education* (pp. 87–138). Lanham, MD: Rowman & Littlefield Publishers.

King, A. R. (2011). Environmental influences on the development of female college students who identify as multiracial/ biracial-bisexual/pansexual. *Journal of College Student Development*, *52*(4), 440–455.

Knefelkamp, L. L., Widick, C., & Parker, C. A. (Eds.). (1978). *Applying new developmental findings*, New Directions for Student Services no. 4. San Francisco, CA: Jossey-Bass.

Kroger, J., & Marcia, J. E. (2011). The identity statuses: Origins, meanings, and interpretations. In S. J. Schwartz, K. Luyckx, & V. L. Vignoles (Eds.), *Handbook of identity theory and research* (pp. 31–53). New York, NY: Springer.

Kulick, C. T., & Roberson, L. (2008). Common goals and golden opportunities: Evaluations of diversity education in academic and organizational settings. *Academy of Management Learning & Education*, *7*(3), 309–331.

Kwan, P. (1997). Jeffrey Dahmer and the cosynthesis of categories. *Hastings Law Journal*, *48*(6), 1257–1292.

Kwan, P. (2000). Complicity and complexity: Cosynthesis and praxis. *DePaul Law Review*, *49*(3), 673–692.

Lange, A. C., Duran, A., & Jackson, R. (2019). The state of LGBT and queer research in higher education revisited: Current academic houses and future possibilities. *Journal of College Student Development*, *60*(5), 511–526.

Lee, R., & Ahtone, T. (2020, March 30). Land-grab universities. *High Country News*. Retrieved from www.hcn.org/issues/52.4/indigenous-affairs-education-land-grab-universities

Lewis, G. (2013). Unsafe travel: Experiencing intersectionality and feminist displacements. *Signs: Journal of Women in Culture and Society, 38*(4), 869–892.

Lincoln, Y. S., & Denzin, N. K. (2000). The seventh movement: Out of the past. In N. K. Denzin & Y. S. Lincoln (Eds.), *Handbook of qualitative research* (2nd ed., pp. 1047–1065). Thousand Oaks, CA: Sage.

Lincoln, Y. S., & Guba, E. G. (1985). *Naturalistic inquiry*. Thousand Oaks, CA: Sage.

Linley, J. L., & Nguyen, D. J. (2015). LGBTQ experiences in curricular contexts. In D-L. Stewart, K. A. Renn, & G. Blue Brazelton (Eds.), *Gender and sexual diversity in U.S. higher education: Contexts and opportunities for LGBTQ college students*, New Directions for Student Services no. 152 (pp. 41–53). San Francisco, CA: Jossey-Bass.

Lorde, A. (1982). *ZAMI: A new spelling of my name*. Freedom, CA: Crossing Press.

Marcia, J. E. (1966). Development and validation of ego-identity status. *Journal of Personality and Social Psychology, 3*(5), 551–558.

Marcia, J. E. (1994). Ego identity and object relations. In J. Masling & R. F. Bornstein (Eds.), *Empirical perspectives on object relations theory* (pp. 59–103). Washington, DC: American Psychological Association.

Marvasti, A. B., & McKinney, K. D. (2011). Does diversity mean assimilation? *Critical Sociology, 37*(5), 631–650.

Matsuda, M. (1987). Looking to the bottom: Critical legal studies and reparations. *Harvard Civil Rights-Civil Liberties Law Review, 22*(3), 323–399.

Matsuda, M. (1992). When the first quail calls: Multiple consciousness as jurisprudential method. *Women's Rights Law Reporter, 14*(2–3), 297–300.

Maxwell, J. A. (1992). Understanding and validity in qualitative research. *Harvard Educational Review, 62*(3), 279–300.

May, V. M. (2015). *Pursuing intersectionality, unsettling dominant imaginaries*. New York, NY: Routledge.

McCall, L. (2005). The complexity of intersectionality. *Signs: Journal of Women in Culture & Society, 30*(3), 1771–1800.

McCoy, D. L., Luedke, C. L., & Winkle-Wagner, R. (2017). Encouraged or weeded out: Perspectives of students of color in the STEM disciplines on faculty interactions. *Journal of College Student Development, 58*(5), 657–673.

Means, D. R. (2017). "Quaring" spirituality: The spiritual counterstories and spaces of Black gay and bisexual male college students. *Journal of College Student Development, 58*(2), 229–246.

Means, D. R., & Jaeger, A. J. (2013). Black in the rainbow: "Quaring" the Black gay male student experience at historically Black universities. *Journal of African American Males in Education, 4*(2), 124–140.

Means, D. R., & Jaeger, A. J. (2015). Spiritual borderlands: A Black gay male college student's spiritual journey. *Journal of Student Affairs Research and Practice, 52*(1), 11–23.

Means, D. R., & Jaeger, A. J. (2016). "Keep pressing on": Spiritual epistemology and its role in the collegiate lives of Black gay and bisexual men. *Journal of College and Character, 17*(1), 23–39.

Mertens, D. M. (2015). *Research and evaluation in education and psychology* (4th ed.). Thousand Oaks, CA: Sage.

Miller, R. A., & Vaccaro, A. (2016). Queer student leaders of color: Leadership as authentic, collaborative, culturally competent. *Journal of Student Affairs Research and Practice*, *53*(1), 39–50.

Miller, R. A., Vaccaro, A., Kimball, E. W., & Forester, R. (2020). "It's dude culture": Students with minoritized identities of sexuality and/or gender navigating STEM majors. *Journal of Diversity in Higher Education*. Advance online publication. https://doi.org/10.1037/dhe0000171

Min-Ha, T. T. (1989). *Women, native, other: Writing post-coloniality and feminism*. Bloomington, IN: Indiana University Press.

Mitchell, D., Jr., Marie, J., & Steele, T. (Eds.). (2019). *Intersectionality & higher education: Theory, research, and praxis* (2nd ed.). New York, NY: Peter Lang.

Mitchell, D., Jr., & Means, D. R. (2014). "Quadruple consciousness": A literature review and new theoretical consideration for understanding the experiences of Black gay and bisexual college men at predominantly white institutions. *Journal of African American Males in Education*, *5*(1), 23–25.

Mitchell, D., Jr., Simmons, C. Y., & Greyerbiehl, L. A. (Eds.). (2014). *Intersectionality & higher education: Theory, research, and praxis*. New York, NY: Peter Lang.

Mobley, S. D., Jr., & Johnson, J. M. (2015). The role of HBCUs in addressing the unique needs of LGBT students. In R. T. Palmer, C. R. Shorette II., & M. Gasman (Eds.), *Exploring diversity at historically Black colleges and universities: Implications for policy and practice*, New Directions for Student Services no. 170 (pp. 79–89). San Francisco, CA: Jossey-Bass.

Mobley, S. D., Jr., & Hall, L. (2020). (Re)defining queer and trans* student retention and "success" at historically Black colleges and universities. *Journal of College Student Retention: Research, Theory, & Practice, 21*(4), 497–519.

Moradi, B., & Grzanka, P. R. (2017). Using intersectionality responsibly: Toward critical epistemology, structural analysis, and social justice activism. *Journal of Counseling Psychology*, *64*(5), 500–513.

Moraga, C. L., & Anzaldúa, G. E. (1983). *This bridge called my back: Writings by radical Women of Color* (2nd ed.). New York, NY: Kitchen Table/Women of Color Press.

Morrow, S. L. (2005). Quality and trustworthiness in qualitative research in counseling psychology. *Journal of Counseling Psychology*, *52*(2), 250–259.

Museus, S. D., Ledesma, M. C., & Parker, T. L. (2015). Racism and racial equity in higher education. *ASHE Higher Education Report*, *42*(1), 1–112.

Mutua, A. D. (2013). Multidimensionality is to masculinities what intersectionality is to feminism. *Nevada Law Journal*, *13*(2), 341–367.

Narui, M. (2011a). *A Foucauldian analysis of Asian/Americans gay, lesbian, and bisexual students' process of disclosing their sexual orientation and its impact on identity construction* (Doctoral dissertation). Retrieved from https://etd.ohiolink.edu/

Narui, M. (2011b). Understanding Asian/American gay, lesbian, and bisexual experiences from a poststructural perspective. *Journal of Homosexuality*, *58*(9), 1211–1234.

Nash, J. C. (2008). Re-thinking intersectionality. *Feminist Review*, *89*(1), 1–15.

Nash, J. C. (2019). *Black feminism reimagined: After intersectionality*. Durham, NC: Duke University Press.

Nash, M. A., & Silverman, J. A. R. (2015). "An indelible mark": Gay purges in higher education in the 1940s. *History of Education Quarterly*, *55*(4), 441–459.

Nicolazzo, Z. (2016). "It's a hard line to walk": Black non-binary trans* collegians' perspectives on passing, realness, and trans*-normativity. *International Journal of Qualitative Studies in Education*, *29*(9), 1173–1188.

Nicolazzo, Z. (2017). *Trans* in college: Transgender students' strategies for navigating campus life and the institutional politics of inclusion*. Sterling, VA: Stylus.

Núñez, A.-M. (2014a). Advancing an intersectionality framework in higher education: Power and Latino postsecondary opportunity. In M. B. Paulsen (Ed.), *Higher education: Handbook of theory and research* (Vol. 29, pp. 33–92). New York, NY: Springer.

Núñez, A.-M. (2014b). Employing multilevel intersectionality in educational research: Latino identities, contexts, and college access. *Educational Research*, *43*(2), 85–92.

Olive, J. L. (2015). Queering the intersectional lens: A conceptual model for the use of queer theory in intersectional research. In D. J. Davis, R. J. Brunn-Bevel, & J. L. Olive (Eds.), *Intersectionality in educational research* (pp. 19–30). Sterling, VA: Stylus.

Oswalt, S. B., Lederer, A. M., Chesnut-Steich, K., Day, C., Halbritter, A., & Ortiz, D. (2020). Trends in college students' mental health diagnoses and utilization of services, 2009–2015. *Journal of American College Health*, *68*(1), 41–51.

Patton, L. D. (Ed.). (2010). *Culture centers in higher education: Perspectives on identity, theory, and practice*. Sterling, VA: Stylus.

Patton, L. D., Renn, K. A., Guido, F. M., & Quaye, S. J. (2016). *Student development in college: Theory, research, and practice* (3rd ed.). San Francisco, CA: Jossey-Bass.

Patton, L. D., Sánchez, B., Mac, J., & Stewart, D-L. (2019). An inconvenient truth about "progress": An analysis of the promises and perils of research on campus diversity initiatives. *The Review of Higher Education*, *42*(5), 173–198.

Patton, L. D., & Simmons, S. L. (2008). Exploring complexities of multiple identities of lesbians in a Black college environment. *The Negro Educational Review*, *59*(3–4), 197–215.

Perez, R. J. (2019). Paradigmatic perspectives and self-authorship: Implications for theory, research, and praxis. *Journal of College Student Development*, *60*(1), 70–84.

Phinney, J. S. (1993). A three-stage model of ethnic identity development in adolescence. In M. E. Bernal & G. P. Knight (Eds.), *Ethnic identity: Formation and transmission among Hispanics and other minorities* (pp. 61–79). Albany, NY: State University of New York Press.

Pliner, S. M., Iuzzini, J., & Banks, C. A. (2011). Using an intersectional approach to deepen collaborative learning. In M. L. Ouellett (Ed.), *An integrative analysis approach to diversity in the college classroom*, New Directions for Teaching & Learning no. 125 (pp. 43–51). San Francisco, CA: Jossey-Bass.

Poynter, K. J., & Washington, J. (2005). Multiple identities: Creating community on campus for LGBT students. In R. L. Sanlo (Ed.), *Gender identity and sexual orientation: Research, policy, and personal*, New Directions for Student Services no. 111 (pp. 41–47). San Francisco, CA: Jossey-Bass.

Quaye, S. J., Harper, S. R., & Pendakur, S. L. (Eds.). (2019). *Student engagement in higher education: Theoretical perspectives and practical approaches for diverse populations* (3rd ed.). New York, NY: Routledge.

Rahman, M. (2010). Queer as intersectionality: Theorizing gay Muslim identities. *Sociology*, *44*(5), 944–961.

Rankin, S. R., Garvey, J. C., & Duran, A. (2019). A retrospective of LGBT issues on U.S. college campuses: 1990–2020. *International Sociology Journal*, *34*(4), 435–454.

Reason, R. D., & Kimball, E. W. (2012). A new theory-to-practice model for student affairs: Integrating scholarship, context, and reflection. *Journal of Student Affairs Research and Practice*, *49*(4), 359–376.

Renn, K. A. (2003). Understanding the identities of mixed-race college students through a developmental ecology lens. *Journal of College Student Development*, *44*(3), 383–403.

Renn, K. A. (2004). *Mixed race students in college: The ecology of race, identity, and community on campus*. Albany, NY: State University of New York Press.

Renn, K. A. (2010). LGBT and queer research in higher education: The state and status of the field. *Educational Researcher*, *39*(2), 132–141.

Renn, K. A., & Reason, R. D. (2012). *College students in the U.S.: Characteristics, experiences, and outcomes*. San Francisco, CA: Jossey-Bass.

Revilla, A. T. (2010). Raza womyn – making it safe to be queer: Student organizations as retention tools in higher education. *Black Women, Gender & Families*, *4*(1), 37–61.

Reynolds, A. L., & Pope, R. L. (1991). The complexities of diversity: Exploring multiple oppressions. *Journal of Counseling and Development*, *70*(1), 174–180.

Rodgers, R. F. (1990). Recent theories and research underlying student development. In D. Creamer & Associates (Eds.), *College student development: Theory and practice for the 1990s* (pp. 27–79). Alexandria, VA: American College Personnel Association.

Rogers, M., & Lott, P. (1997). Backlash, the matrix of domination, and log cabin republicans. *Sociological Quarterly*, *38*(3), 497–512.

Smith, W. A., Allen, W. R., & Danley, L. L. (2007). "Assume the position . . . you fit the description": Psychosocial experiences and racial battle fatigue among African American male college students. *American Behavioral Scientist*, *51*(4), 551–578.

Staunæs, D. (2003). Where have all the subjects gone: Bringing together the concepts of intersectionality and subjugation. *NORA – Nordic Journal of Feminist and Gender Research*, *11*(2), 101–110.

Steele, C. M. (2010). *Whistling Vivaldi: How stereotypes affect us and what we can do*. New York, NY: W. W. Norton & Company.

Stewart, D-L. (2009). Perceptions of multiple identities among Black college students. *Journal of College Student Development*, *50*(3), 253–270.

Stewart, D-L. (2017). Language of appeasement. *Inside Higher Ed*. Retrieved from www.insidehighered.com/views/2017/03/30/ colleges-need-language-shift-not-one-you-think-essay

Strayhorn, T. L. (2012a). Coming out, fitting in: Interrogating the social experiences of Black gay male undergraduates at predominantly white institutions. In T. E. Dancy II & M. C. Brown (Eds.), *African American males and education: Researching the convergence of race and identity* (pp. 151–170). Charlotte, NC: Information Age Publishing.

Strayhorn, T. L. (2012b). Sense of belonging and gay students. In T. L. Strayhorn (Ed.), *College students' sense of belonging: A key to educational success for all students* (pp. 39–49). Routledge.

Strayhorn, T. L. (2013). And their own received them not: Black gay male undergraduates' experiences with white racism, Black homophobia. In T. E. Dancy, M. C. Brown II, & J. E. Davis (Eds.), *Educating African American males: Contexts for consideration, possibilities for practice* (pp. 105–120). New York, NY: Peter Lang.

Strayhorn, T. L. (2014). Beyond the model minority myth: Interrogating the lived experiences of Korean American gay men in college. *Journal of College Student Development*, *55*(6), 586–594.

Strayhorn, T. L., Blakewood, A. M., & DeVita, J. M. (2008). Factors affecting the college choice of African American gay male undergraduates: Implications for retention. *The NASAP Journal*, *11*(1), 88–108.

Strayhorn, T. L., Blakewood, A. M., & DeVita, J. M. (2010). Triple threat: Challenges and supports of Black gay men at predominantly white campuses. In T. L. Strayhorn & M. C. Terrell (Eds.), *The evolving challenges of Black college students: New insights for practice and research* (pp. 85–103). Sterling, VA: Stylus.

Strayhorn, T. L., & Mullins, T. G. (2012). Investigating Black gay male undergraduates' experiences in campus residence halls. *The Journal of College and University Student Housing*, *39*(1), 140–161.

Strayhorn, T. L., & Tillman-Kelly, D. L. (2013). Queering masculinity: Manhood and Black gay men in college. *Spectrum: A Journal on Black Men*, *1*(2), 83–110.

Squire, D. D., & Mobley, S. D. (2015). Negotiating race and sexual orientation in the college choice process of Black gay males. *The Urban Review*, *47*(3), 466–491.

Syed, M., Walker, L. H. M., Lee, R. M., Umaña-Taylor, A. J., Zamboanga, B. L., Schwartz, S. J., . . . Huynh, Q.-L. (2013). A two-factor model of ethnic identity exploration: Implications for identity coherence and well-being. *Cultural Diversity and Ethnic Minority Psychology*, *19*(2), 143–154.

Tajfel, H. (1978). *Differentiation between social groups: Studies in the social psychology of intergroup relations*. London, UK: Academic Press.

Tajfel, H. (Ed.). (1982). *Social identity and intergroup relations*. Cambridge, UK: Cambridge University Press.

Tajfel, H., & Turner, J. C. (1979). An integrative theory of inter-group conflict. In W. G. Austin & S. Worchel (Eds.), *The social psychology of inter-group relations* (pp. 33–47). Monterey, CA: Brooks/Cole.

Tillapaugh, D., & Catalano, D. C. J. (2019). Structural challenges affecting the experiences of public university LGBT services graduate assistants. *Journal of Diversity in Higher Education*, *12*(2), 126–135.

Tillapaugh, D., & Nicolazzo, Z. (2014). Backward thinking: Exploring the relationship among intersectionality, epistemology, and research design. In D. Mitchell Jr., C. Y. Simmons, & L. A. Greyerbiehl (Eds.), *Intersectionality &*

higher education: Theory, research, and praxis (pp. 111–122). New York, NY: Peter Lang.

Torres, V. (2009). The developmental dimensions of recognizing racist thoughts. *Journal of College Student Development*, *50*(5), 504–520.

Torres, V., & Hernandez, E. (2007). The influence of ethnic identity development on self-authorship: A longitudinal study of Latino/a college students. *Journal of College Student Development*, *48*(5), 558–573.

Torres, V., Jones, S. R., & Renn, K. A. (2009). Identity development theories in student affairs: Origins, current status, and new approaches. *Journal of College Student Development*, *50*(6), 577–596.

Torres, V., Jones, S. R., & Renn, K. A. (2019). Student affairs as a low-consensus field and the evolution of student development theory as foundational knowledge. *Journal of College Student Development*, *60*(6), 645–658.

Umaña-Taylor, A. J., Kornienko, O., Bayless, S. D., & Updegraff, K. A. (2018). A universal intervention program increases ethnic-racial identity exploration and resolution to predict adolescent psychosocial functioning one year later. *Journal of Youth and Adolescence*, *47*(1), 1–15.

Vaccaro, A., & Mena, J. A. (2011). It's not burnout, it's more: Queer college activists of color and mental health. *Journal of Gay & Lesbian Mental Health*, *15*(4), 339–367.

Vaccaro, A., & Miller, R. A. (2017). Experiences of Queer Student Leaders of Color: Expanding leadership paradigms in higher education. In J. M. Johnson & G. C. Javier (Eds.), *Queer People of Color in higher education* (pp. 195–210). Charlotte, NC: Information Age Publishing.

Valdes, F. (1995). Sex and race in queer legal culture: Ruminations on identities and inter-connectivities. In R. Delgado & J. Stefancic (Eds.), *Critical race theory: The cutting edge* (pp. 334–339). Philadelphia, PA: Temple University Press.

Valdes, F. (1997). Queer margins, queer ethics: A call to account for race and ethnicity in the law, theory, and politics of "sexual orientation." *Hutchinson Law Journal*, *48*(6), 1293–1341.

Vega, G. P. (2016). *Latina lesbian students: Understanding their experiences and perceived sexual identity development at a Hispanic-serving institution* (Doctoral dissertation). Retrieved from http://digitalcommons.fiu.edu/

Washington, J., & Wall, V. A. (2010). African American gay men: Another challenge for the academy. In S. R. Harper & F. Harris III (Eds.), *College men and masculinities: Theory, practice, and implications for practice* (pp. 136–147). San Francisco, CA: Jossey-Bass.

Whitehead, K. A., Ainsworth, A. T., Wittig, M. A., & Gadino, B. (2009). Implications of ethnic identity exploration and ethnic identity affirmation and belonging for intergroup attitudes among adolescents. *Journal of Research on Adolescence*, *19*(1), 123–135.

Wilder, C. S. (2013). *Ebony & ivy: Race, slavery, and the troubled history of America's universities*. New York, NY: Bloomsbury Press.

Wijeyesinghe, C. L. (2012). The intersectional model of multiracial identity: Integrating multiracial identity theories and intersectional perspectives on social identities. In C. L. Wijeyesinghe & B. W. Jackson III (Eds.), *New perspectives on racial identity development: Integrating emerging frameworks* (2nd ed., pp. 81–107). New York, NY: New York University Press.

Wijeyesinghe, C. L. (2019). Intersectionality and student development: Centering power in the process. In E. S. Abes, S. R. Jones, & D-L. Stewart (Eds.), *Rethinking college student development using critical frameworks*. Sterling, VA: Stylus.

Wijeyesinghe, C. L., & Jones, S. R. (2014). Intersectionality, identity, and systems of power and inequality. In D. Mitchell, C. Y. Simmons, & L. A. Greyerbiehl (Eds.), *Intersectionality and higher education: Theory, research, and praxis* (pp. 9–19). New York, NY: Peter Lang.

Woodford, M. R., Kolb, C. L., Durocher-Radeka, G., & Javier, G. (2014). Lesbian, gay, bisexual, and transgender ally training programs on campus: Current variations and future directions. *Journal of College Student Development*, *55*(3), 317–322.

Worthington, R. L., Navarro, R. L., Savoy, H. B., & Hampton, D. (2008). Development, reliability, and validity of the measure of sexual identity exploration and commitment (MoSIEC). *Developmental Psychology*, *44*(1), 22–33.

Index

Page numbers in *italics* indicate figures; page numbers in **bold** indicate tables.

Abes, Elisa 18
ability identity and 81
academic scholarship, Queer People of Color 29–30
activism: Queer Students of Color 22; Women of Color 19, 20–21
African American identity 7; research on gay and bisexual 31; Wren and 7, 45
Alejandro (Alejo) (participant): demographic information **38**; educational opportunities 130; faith and 80; identity centers on campus 64; institutional funding for minorities 49; institutional values 132; learning identities 90; local contexts of HWIs 52; off-campus experience 72; representation at HWIs 127; romantic relationships 68; sense of self 109, 110
All About Love (hooks) 109
analytical process 153–155; comparative approach and coding 153–154; memoing and diagramming 154–155; *see also* study design
anti-Black racism 7, 32, 46, 54, 107, 136
Anzaldúa, Gloria 97, 104, 148
Asian/American identity 8, 49, 157: Dash and 106, 111; gay, lesbian and bisexual students 32; Ness and 60–61, 66, 71, 78, 98, 111, 135; Richard and 96; sexuality in 55
Avery Demán (participant): demographic information **38**; faith and 80; identity centers on campus 64; interpersonal interactions 57–58; learning connections 101; programming and curricula 51; romantic relationships 68–69; *see*king connections 94; student affairs 139

Baxter Magolda, Marcia 18
Black women, intersection of racism and sexism 19
Brophy College Preparatory 3, 4

capitalism 46, 121
Carmen (participant) 8; ability and identity 81; assimilatory norms 93; counseling services 140–141; coursework focus on identities 135; curricular experience 63; demographic information **38**; faith and 80; funding practices at HWIs 128–129; gender identity 79–80; identity centers on campus 64–65; identity pattern 77; institutional funding for minorities 49–50; interpersonal interactions 57–58; learning identities 90–91; *see*king connections 94; sociopolitical climate 54; STEM disciplines 138; story of 74–76; undocumented status 82; unlearning beliefs of being only one 100
Cisgender Men of Color 37
college student(s): development of 14–18; intersecting identities 17; meaning making and its connection to identities 17–18; perspectives on identity exploration and the self 14–15; social identity exploration and development 16–17

colonialism: perception of 46; post- 62–63, 69; settler 5, 90, 156
Combahee River Collective 7
confirmability 156
constructivism 148–150; *see also* study design
Cooper, Anna Julia 20
counseling services, providing identity-considerate 140–141
coursework: focus on social identities groups and inequalities 135–136; identity in STEM disciplines 136–138; integrating attention to minoritized identities 134–138; *see also* historically white institutions (HWIs)
credibility, criteria 155–156
Crenshaw, Kimberlé 19, 55, 117, 145; intersectional theorizing and 19–20
critical theory 148–149; *see also* study design
curricula: co-curricular activities 64–67; experiences of Queer Students of Color 62–64; identity centers on campus 64–65; student organizations 65–67

Dash (participant): demographic information **38**; educational opportunities 130; faith and 80; goals for self 106–107; institutional values 132; learning healing and pride 98–99; local contexts of HWIs 52–53; off-campus experience 71; programming and curricula 51; sense of self 111–112; student organizations 66
dependability 156
development theory 14; *see also* college student(s)
diversity, institutional values 132–133
Diversity Affairs office 51, 139
DREAMer status 54, 82–83

E (participant) 37; curricular experience 62–63; demographic information **38**; discontinuation of 152; identity centers on campus 64; romantic relationships 68–69; study abroad participation 70
education *see* higher education
ego identity, Erikson's notion of 15
equity, institutional values 132–133
Erikson, Erik 14, 15
Ezekiel (participant): campus climate 48; cultural dynamics and norms 55; demographic information **38**; educational opportunities 130; identity exploration 144; identity patterns 76; institutional funding for minorities 49; learning identities 90; local contexts of HWIs 52; off-campus experience 71; representation at HWIs 127; sense of self 109, 111; unlearning stereotypes 88

faith, identity and 80–81
feminists, Women of Color 20–21
fluidity 89–92

gender identity: intersecting 78–80; Queer Students of Color and 36
gentle-breeze (participant): ability and identity 81; coursework focus on identities 135; demographic information **38**; institutional values 132; learning identities 90; seeking connections 95; sense of self 109
Grindr (app) 56, 81

higher education 117; formative support networks for Queer Students of Color 33–35; future intersectional research on identity 122–123; identity exploration in student development theory 119–120; potential of queer studies in intersectional theorizing 120–122; pushing study of identity in 118–120; relationship between structures and identity 118–119
Hispanic-Serving Institutions 29
Historically Black Colleges and Universities (HBCUs) 6, 29, 123
historically white institutions (HWIs) 2; campus climate for Queer People of Color 47–49; definition of 5; enacting educational opportunities 130–132; funding and recruitment for minoritized populations 49–50; identity centers on campus 64–65; identity-considerate counseling services in 140–141; integrating minoritized identities in coursework 134–138; intentional values of diversity and equity 132–133; interpersonal interactions of Queer Students of Color on

56–58; intersectional erasure in programming and curricula 50–52; intersectionality interventions 21–22; minoritized identities in student affairs 139–140; offering care and support to Queer People of Color 141–143; oppressive experiences for Queer Students of Color at 30–32; oppressive experiences in siloed identity groups 31–32; Queer College Students of Color and 2–3, 5–6; representation at 126–128; resisting funding practices at 128–132; as sites of investigation 5–6; sociopolitical climate of 53–54; student organizations on 65–67; *see also* coursework
hooks, bell 63, 97, 105, 109

identity: concept 13; Erikson's stages of development 14; exploration and development 16–17; future intersectional research on 122–123; intersecting 17; intersectionality as framework to 6–7; Marcia and exploration of 15; meaning making and its connection to 17–18; perspectives on identity exploration self and 14–15; questions of 1; reflections of intersectionality on 58; reflections on 72–73; *see also* college student(s)
identity exploration: adopting new behaviors 94–96; challenging assimilatory norms 92–94; development and 16–17; intersectional model of *40*; learning connections 100–102; learning healing and pride 97–99; learning systemic oppression fluidity and language 89–92; notion of 15; reflections on 102–103, 112–113; role of actions 92–96; role of connection 99–102; role of emotions 96–99; role of thoughts 87–92, 89–92; *see*king connections 94–96; unlearning beliefs of being only one 99–100; unlearning self-hate shame and trauma 96–97; unlearning stereotypes and oppressive messages 87–89
intersectional identities 6–7, 83–84; ability and 81; faith and 80–81; gender and 78–80; patterns tied to race and sexuality 76–78; potential of queer studies in higher education 120–122; role of other identities 78–83; socioeconomic status and 83; undocumented status and 82–83
intersectional influences: cultural dynamics and norms 55–56; historically white institutions (HWIs) 47–52; identity and 58; interpersonal interactions on campus 56–58; local contexts 52–53; social group membership 55–56; sociopolitical climate 53–54
intersectionality: college student identity and 13; constructing environments for Queer People of Color 7–8; Crenshaw's contributions to theory 19–20; histories of theorizing on 20–21; landscape of scholarship of 18–22; popularity in education 13; queerness as identity and 25–26; queerness as practice and 26–27; relationship with queer studies 24–27; tension between power and identity 23–24; theoretical interventions of 21–22; use in researching identity 23–27
intersectional model of identity exploration, Queer Students of Color *40*

John Doe (participant): culture of institutions 126; demographic information **38**; faith and 80; intersecting identities 47; off-campus experience 72; sense of self 145; social connections 67
Jones, Susan 18

Kahlo, Frida 101
Kegan, Robert 17
Korean American gay college students 34

Levix (participant): campus climate 48–49; demographic information **38**; faith and 80; goals for self 108; learning identities 92; local contexts of HWIs 52; off-campus experience 71; romantic relationships 68–70; *see*king connections 95; socioeconomic status 83; unlearning stereotypes 88–89
LGBT community 31

LGBTQ Center 49, 51; Carmen and 74–75; funding of 129; identity centers on campus 64–65; New York University 4; Richard and 86, 96; student affairs 139–140; student organizations 65; TJ and 99
LGBTQ Centers 32
Lorde, Audre 63, 97

Make American Great Again hats 53–54
Marcia, James 15, 16, 119–120
Max Aguirre (participant) 8; ability and identity 81; assimilatory norms 92–93; coursework focus on identities 135; curricular experience 62; demographic information **39**; demographic information on **39**; educational opportunities 130; faith and 80; HWIs offering care and support 142; identity centers on campus 64; identity exploration 109; institutional funding for minorities 49; learning identities 90, 97–98; self–hate shame and trauma 97; sense of self 109; social connections 68; sociopolitical climate 53; story of 104–106; unlearning stereotypes 87–88
May, Vivian 23
meaning making: concept 13; connection to identities 17–18
methodology *see* study design
Miami University, Student Affairs in Higher Education 4
Mirella Blackwell (participant) 37; demographic information **39**; demographic information on **39**; discontinuation of 152; local contexts of HWIs 52; student organizations 65
Model of Multiple Dimensions of Identity (MMDI) 17

Nash, Jennifer 19, 123
National Coming Out Day 75
Ness (participant): ability and identity 81; assimilatory norms 93–94; coursework focus on identities 135, 136; cultural dynamics and norms 55–56; curricular experience 62; demographic information on **39**; funding practices at HWIs 128–129; gender identity 79; identity pattern 78; institutional funding for minorities 49; learning connections 101–102; learning healing and pride 98; learning identities 90, 112; local contexts of HWIs 52; off-campus experience 71–72; story of 60–61; student organizations 65–66
Ness (vignette) 8
New York University 4

off-campus involvement, Queer Students of Color and 70–72
Ohio State University (OSU) 4–5
Oliver (participant): coursework focus on identities 135, 136; demographic information **39**; educational opportunities 130–131; funding practices at HWIs 128; identity centers on campus 64; institutional funding for minorities 49; interpersonal interactions 56–57; learning healing and pride 99; learning identities 91–92; local contexts of HWIs 52; *see*king connections 94–95; sense of self 109, 110; sociopolitical climate 54; undocumented status 82–83; unlearning beliefs of being only one 100
oppressive messages, unlearning 87–89

Parker (participant): ability and identity 81; campus climate 47–48; cultural dynamics and norms 56; curricular experience 63–64; demographic information **39**; HWIs offering care and support 142; identity centers on campus 64; identity patterns 76; representation at HWIs 126–127; social connections 67–68; socioeconomic status 83; sociopolitical climate 53
participants: demographic information of **38–39**; recruitment of 36–37, 150–152; *see also* study design
Phinney, Jean 16
predominantly white institutions (PWIs) 5, 31, 33, 50, 95
professionals: identity-considerate counseling services 140–141; offering care and support to Queer People of Color 141–143

Quare Theory 27, 121–122
Queer College Students of Color 2; historically white institutions (HWIs) and 2–3, 5–6; *see also* Queer Students of Color
Queer Collegians of Color 87
Queer Communities of Color 32, 68, 158; collegiate environments for 145; diversity 84, 151; gender identity and 36; identity exploration 101; literature on 35–36; religion and 35–36; social connections 77
queerness: intersectionality and, as identity 25–26; intersectionality and, as practice 26–27
Queer of Color Critique 27, 121
Queer People of Color 1, 2; campus climate for 47–49; constructing environments for 7–8; offering care and support to 141–143; providing identity-considerate counseling 140–141; racism and heterosexism 27; resources and representation lacking for 32–33; student development of 27–28
Queer Students of Color 2; academic scholarship on 29–30; curricular experiences of 62–64; gender identity and 36; histories of oppression and 21–22; identity exploration 15; identity exploration for 72–73; intersectionality 19, 24–27; intersectional model of identity exploration *40*; lack of resources and representation for 32–33; meaning making and 18; navigating HWIs 47–52, 58–59; off-campus involvement 70–72; oppressive experiences at HWIs 30–32; oppressive experiences in siloed identity groups 31–32; participant information **38–39**; questions for hopes of 146; racism and religious intolerance 35–36; representation at HWIs 126–128; romantic relationships and 68–70; sense of self 15; social connections 67–68; sociopolitical climate of HWIs 53–54; student affairs programming 139–140; study abroad by 70–72; study of 36–37; support networks in higher education 33–35
queer studies: intersectionality and queerness as identity 25–27; intersectionality and queerness as practice 26–27; intersectionality's relationship with 24–27; potential in higher education 120–122
queer theory 26–27, 121
Queer Women of Color 26, 36, 97–98

race and sexuality, identity patterns of 76–78
Reconceptualized Model of Multiple Dimensions of Identity (RMMDI) 17
relationships: romantic 68–70; social connections 67–68
religion, Queer Students of Color and 35–36
research *see* study design
Richard (participant) 8; assimilatory norms 93; cultural dynamics and norms 55; demographic information **39**; funding practices at HWIs 128–129; identity centers on campus 64; identity pattern 78; institutional funding for minorities 49; learning identities 90; local contexts of HWIs 52; programming and curricula 51; romantic relationships 68; self-hate shame and trauma 96–97; story of 85–86; student organizations 66–67
romantic relationships, Queer Students of Color and 68–70
Rosa (participant): demographic information **39**; HWIs offering care and support 142; institutional values 133; learning connections 100–101; learning identities 91–92; representation at HWIs 127; romantic relationships 68–69
Rose E. (participant): campus climate 48; cultural dynamics and norms 55; demographic information **39**; faith and 80–81; gender studies 89; goals for self 107–108; identity centers on campus 64–65; institutional values 132; learning connections 100–101; local contexts of HWIs 52; off-campus experience 71; romantic relationships 68; self-hate, shame, and trauma 97; study abroad participation 70

Sarah Ray (participant): curricular experience 63; demographic information **39**; faith and 80;

identity pattern 77; institutional values 132; interpersonal interactions 57; romantic relationships 68; sense of self 109–110; study abroad participation 70–71
self: concept of 13; perspectives on identity exploration and 14–15; sense of 15, 112, 120
self, secure sense of: pushing back against systemic oppression 109–112; resisting internalizing systemic influences 106–109
siloed identity groups, oppressive experiences in 31–32
social connections, Queer Students of Color and 67–68
social identity: diversity of 1; exploration 16–17; *see also* identity exploration
social justice 21, 26, 125, 127, 150, 157
socioeconomic status, identity and 83
Sojourner Truth 20
STEM disciplines identity in 135, 136–138
Stewart, Maria 20
student(s) *see* college student(s)
student development theory, identity exploration in 119–120
student organizations, identity-based 34–35
study abroad, Queer Students of Color and 70–72
study design: analytical process 153–155; confirmability and dependability 156; constructivist and critical perspectives of 147–149; constructivist grounded theory 36, 149–150; credibility 155–156; data collection methods 152–153; final reflections on 157–158; future opportunities 156–157; intersectional model of identity exploration *40*; participant information **38–39**; participant recruitment 36–37, 150–152; purpose 150–152; Queer Students of Color 36–37; transferability 156; trustworthiness criteria for 155–156
support networks, formative, for Queer Students of Color 33–35
systemic influences, resisting internalizing 106–109
systemic oppression 89–92; pushing back against 109–112

Tajfel, Henri 16
TJ (participant): coursework focus on identities 135; cultural dynamics and norms 55; demographic information **39**; educational opportunities 130; goals for self 107–108; identity centers on campus 64–65; identity patterns 76–77; representation at HWIs 127; sociopolitical climate 54; STEM disciplines 137; unlearning beliefs of being only one 99–100; unlearning stereotypes 87
transferability 156
Transgender Students of Color 36, 121, 123
Tribal Colleges and Universities (TCUs) 6, 123
Trump, President 53–54
trustworthiness criteria: confirmability 156; credibility 155–156; dependability 156; transferability 156; *see also* study design

undocumented status, identity and 82–83

Women of Color: activism 19, 20–21; feminism 25, 26; intersection of racism and sexism 19–20
Wren (participant) 7–8; demographic information **39**; HWI experience of 45–46; HWIs offering care and support 143; institutional funding for minorities 49–50; learning identities 90; local contexts of HWIs 53; sense of self 109; social connections 68, 95–96; social construction of identities 89–90; socioeconomic status 83; story of 45–47; study abroad participation 70

Made in the USA
Las Vegas, NV
28 October 2024

5f0ea383-b6e8-418d-97dc-9c780aaebacbR01